THE DEBATABLE LAND

Also by Graham Robb

BALZAC

VICTOR HUGO

RIMBAUD

STRANGERS
Homosexual Love in the Nineteenth Century

THE DISCOVERY OF FRANCE

PARISIANS
An Adventure History of Paris

THE ANCIENT PATHS

THE DEBATABLE LAND

The Lost World Between Scotland and England

GRAHAM ROBB

W. W. Norton & Company
Independent Publishers Since 1923
New York   London

For information about permission to reproduce selections from this book, write to
Permissions, W. W. Norton & Company, Inc., 500 Fifth Avenue, New York, NY 10110

For information about special discounts for bulk purchases, please contact
W. W. Norton Special Sales at specialsales@wwnorton.com or 800-233-4830

Manufacturing by Quad Fairfield

ISBN: 978-0-393-28532-1

W. W. Norton & Company, Inc., 500 Fifth Avenue, New York, N.Y. 10110
www.wwnorton.com

W. W. Norton & Company Ltd., 15 Carlisle Street, London W1D 3BS

1 2 3 4 5 6 7 8 9 0

To Gill Coleridge

and in affectionate memory of

Deborah Rogers and David Miller

Contents

List of Illustrations

List of Figures

A Guide to Pronunciation

Annan: stress on first syllable

Arthuret: Arthrut

Berwick: Berrick

Buccleuch: Bucloo (stress on second syllable)

Burgh by Sands: Bruff be Sands

Carlisle: on pronunciations and spellings, see p. 28n.

Fenwick: Fennick

Furness: as 'furnace'

Gaelic (Scottish): gaa-lik

Hawick: Hoik

Haythwaite: Hethet

Hepburn: Hebburn

Hollows: Hollus

Kershope: Kirsop

Kielder: Keelder

knowe (hill): as 'now'

Langholm: Lang'um (silent 'g')

Liddesdale: in three syllables

Lochmaben: Lochmayb'n (stress on second syllable)

Note o' the Gate: 'Note' as 'knot'

pele (tower): peel

Penton: stress on second syllable (as 'Penrith')

reiver: reever

Sanquhar: Sankhar (stress on first syllable)

Scrope: Scroop

Stanegarthside: Stingerside

Stanwix: Stannix

Whithaugh: Whitaff

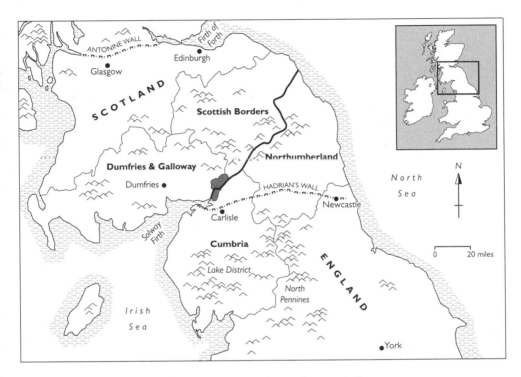

The four Border counties in the early twenty-first century.

PART ONE

1

Hidden Places

Early one evening in the autumn of 2010, my wife Margaret and I stood in front of Carlisle railway station in the far north-west of England with two loaded bicycles and a one-way ticket from Oxford. After twenty-three years in the South, we had decided to move to Scotland. The idea was to live closer to my mother – her son and daughter-in-law becoming every day a more distant memory – and to find a home more conducive to those two inseparable pursuits: writing and cycling. By chance, our search had ended just short of Scotland, at a lonely house on the very edge of England. The title deed showed that we would own a stretch of the national border. If Scotland regained its independence – which seemed a remote prospect – we would be custodians of an international frontier.

During our last months in Oxford, I had read about our future home and discovered that the river which almost surrounds the house had once marked the southern boundary of a region called the Debatable Land. For several centuries, this desolate tract running north-east from the Solway Firth had served as a buffer between the two nations. Within those fifty square miles, by parliamentary decrees issued by both countries in 1537 and 1551, 'all Englishmen and Scottishmen are and shall be free to rob, burn, spoil, slay, murder and destroy, all and every such person and persons, their bodies, property, goods and live-stock . . . without any redress to be made for same'. By all accounts, they availed themselves of the privilege. Under Henry VIII, Elizabeth I, James V and James VI, the Debatable Land had been the bloodiest region in Britain.

Finding out about the area as it exists today had proved surprisingly difficult. The name on the postal address, a collective term for a scattering of small settlements and isolated farms, seemed to refer to a mythical place. It was missing entirely from a book titled *The Hidden Places of Cumbria* (1990); even the long valley in which it lies had remained invisible to the author. When, a few weeks after moving, I mentioned the name of the place to a Carlisle taxi driver, a faraway look appeared in his eyes. 'I've *heard* of it,' he said, as though I was asking to be driven to a place out of legend.

Those days of first contact with the borderlands now seem to belong to a distant past. I had no idea how much there was to be explored and no intention of writing a book about the place in which we had found a home. The history of the area was a threadbare tapestry on which scenes of fruitless chaos in a derelict realm were monotonously depicted. The border itself was little more than a quaint memento of the Anglo-Scottish wars, and there were few signs that it would rise from the enormous burial mound of British history, proclaiming its ancient identity like a sleeping knight to whom life but not memory had been restored.

Then, under the powerful spell of idle curiosity, documents and maps arrived unbidden: the land and its inhabitants seemed to have become aware that someone was taking an interest in them. The story unfolded itself between 2010 and 2016, and the independent territory which used to exist between Scotland and England began to look like a crucial, missing piece in the puzzle of British history.

It was towards the end of that period, when the United Kingdom was entering a new and unpredictable world, that I made the two discoveries described in the last part of this book. One was a second-century atlas of Iron Age and Roman Britain so wonderfully accurate that it could still be used today. The other was the earliest account of a major historical event in Britain from a British point of view. The past, too, then seemed to dissolve and reshape itself, and the existence of those ancient documents would have seemed fantastic were it not for the tangible reality of their revelations.

✻

The country in miniature known as the Debatable Land came to the attention of the outside world in the sixteenth century. Surveyors were sent from London to explore and chart its moors and meadows, its plains and wooded gorges, its bogs and hidden glens. Fifty years later, when most of its population was slaughtered or deported, it became the last part of Great Britain to be conquered and brought under the control of a state.

The Debatable Land – a name it acquired in the last two centuries of its existence – is the oldest detectable territorial division in Great Britain. Its roots lie in an age when neither England nor Scotland nor even the Roman Empire could be imagined. At the height of its notoriety, it preoccupied the monarchs and parliaments of England, Scotland and France. Today, though some of its boundaries survive as sections of the national border, it has vanished from the map and no one knows exactly where and what it was.

This book, which I had never expected to write, now seems almost too slender to encompass that magically expanding realm. From its northernmost point, one thousand feet above sea level, to the great estuary into which all its becks, burns, gills, sikes and waters flow, the Debatable Land measures only thirteen miles. The widest crossing is eight and a half miles, and it can be circumambulated – with difficulty – in two days. There are three ranges of hills, one mountain and, when the tide is in, a mile of coastline. A main artery of the British road system passes through it, yet it is quite possible to spend a long day walking across it without seeing another human being, even in the distance.

In that emptiness, paths stretch far back in time. For several years, I explored every corner of the medieval Debatable Land: I saw in its ruins the remnants of an older civilization, and I knew that this unique survivor of a maligned society had fostered the formation of a United Kingdom. But the mystery of its origins remained intact until those two chance discoveries relaunched the expedition.

These treasures have implications for a much wider world, but the keys to their decipherment and their long-term significance belong to the Debatable Land. The light of the Border fells, which can suddenly illumine a hidden valley when the rest of the landscape is in darkness, gives even the most extraordinary discovery the air of a natural occurrence. Yet it still seems a wonder to have found in the remotest past of the Anglo-Scottish frontier a path which led back to the present.

2

Outpost

Travellers arriving in the 'Border City' of Carlisle on the north-bound train are likely to be taken unawares. One moment, there is a view of scraggly sheep chomping at the foot of a drystone wall as they shelter from the horizontal rain. A moment later, without the warning of any noticeable suburb, the train is pulling into the airy gloom of a Victorian Gothic railway station, and there is just enough time to untether the bicycles and rescue the luggage from the rack.

A hundred years ago, a train was approaching Carlisle Station from the opposite direction. This was the night express from Scotland, due to arrive in London the following morning. In one of the compartments, a newly married couple were staring out at the black night of the borderlands, watching for the first signs of England. The bulk of a great castle rose on the left and the station lights glimmered up ahead. Lowering the window, the bridegroom leaned out to shout his joy, probably hoping to startle any Englishmen who might be standing on the platform. The station roof was in no better repair than when I first saw it in 2010. A steel cable had become detached from the gantries. Its sagging loop snagged the shouting Scotsman, his body slumped onto the floor of the compartment, and a severed head leapt onto the seat, leaving the young bride in a gruesome tête-à-tête with her late husband as the train screamed on towards the dark Cumbrian fells.

No trace of this unhappy incident can be found in any newspaper of the time. The story might have been invented to explain the headless ghost which is occasionally seen in the undercroft of Carlisle Station, built in 1847 on a slum clearance area called 'the Fever Pit'. This sounds like a specimen of North Cumbrian humour served up to tourists who expect to hear tales of cross-border conflict: English patriots exulting at the mishaps of loud-mouthed haggis-eaters, or kilted clansmen wreaking romantic revenge on the stout and stuck-up yeomanry of England.

Anyone who leaves Carlisle Station on a Saturday night when the pubs of Botchergate are disgorging their clientele stands a reasonable chance of witnessing some inter-tribal violence. The border lies just a few miles to the north at Gretna, and Carlisle is the only significant urban centre between Newcastle, sixty miles to the east, and Dumfries, thirty-five miles to the west. But the battles in the streets of Carlisle are rarely between Scots and English. A few extended local families preserve the traditions of feuding Border clans, but the frightened faces pressed up against a taxi driver's window, begging to be rescued from a gathering mob, are more likely to be those of lads from Furness, the coastal part of Cumbria, where they say 'me marrer' instead of 'me mate'. Cumbria's tribal map is as complex as its history. Carlisle itself once belonged to Scotland – as quite a few English people still believe to be the case – which is why the Domesday Book of 1086 contains no mention of Carlisle.

A great many other books contain no mention of Carlisle. It may be the capital (and only) city of the county of Cumbria and the former western command centre of Hadrian's Wall, but with its population of seventy-three thousand, Carlisle is a poor relation to the famous, poet-celebrated Lake District, which has an annual tourist population of sixteen million. After a municipal reassessment of the city's economic potential, a forlorn sign on the station platform now proclaims 'The Border City' to be 'The City of the Lakes', but most tourists from the South will have alighted long before at Oxenholme or Penrith. The standing water in the vicinity of Carlisle consists mainly of brackish ponds, slurry lagoons and, with increasing frequency, floodwater which submerges a large part of the modern city, leaving the medieval districts high and dry, and inducing the long-suffering burghers of Carlisle to rebrand it 'The City of the Lake'.

That evening in 2010, as we stood in front of the station, dazed by the long journey and a sense of the irreparable, Carlisle itself looked like the last place in England. From there, it would be a ride of almost twenty miles to the house, which is why we had booked a room at the County Hotel. It stared at us with its flaking facade from the other side of a car-clogged square, beyond the iron railings of a disaffected public toilet. The bicycles might have been stowed in the removal van, which was travelling overnight, but a bus ran only twice a week – and only to within two miles of the house – and the railway known as the Waverley Line, which once connected Carlisle with Edinburgh, had been closed for forty years. Its closure had transformed an area of a thousand square miles into a vast backwater. One roadless settlement, Riccarton, had been entirely cut off. The only noticeable economic advantage was the depressing effect on house prices.

The sign at the hotel entrance suggested that, in some respects, it was a popular venue: '*Anti-Social Behaviour Will Not Be Tolerated*'. The hotel appeared to have been partially renovated in the 1960s and its prices were correspondingly reasonable. An hour later, we were sitting in a vast bedroom overlooking the spartan 'leisure zone' of Botchergate. In the days when the long journey from London forced businessmen and dignitaries to spend the night in Carlisle, it must have been considered palatial. One of the removal men, a native of North Cumbria, had told us that the small town we would pass through next day on our way to the house was known locally as 'Dodge City'. With its decor of red velours and tasselled armchairs, the room reminded me of a brothel above a Wild West saloon. From the street below came bellowings in an unfamiliar dialect.

After dinner, I went for a stroll and passed between the two squat towers of the nineteenth-century Citadel which replicates the old southern defences of the city. A plaque on the wall commemorated 'the last public execution in Carlisle, 15th March 1862'. An engine driver called Charlton had murdered an old widow at a nearby railway crossing with a pick axe and a hedge slasher and robbed her of the money she had saved up for her funeral. Beyond the Citadel lay the main shopping area: English Street, then Scotch Street. I walked as far as the bridge over the river Eden until I could see the road leading north to the Border fells and Scotland.

A cold wind was blowing from the north. This would mean an extra-early start in the morning. It was not yet ten o'clock and a restaurant was already closing its doors. I reflected that, from now on, this would be our nearest centre of civilization. The shop windows hinted at a lack of disposable income and the city was as dimly lit as it must have been in the age of gas-lamps. The narrow vennels on either side were impenetrable to the eye, but there was no sign of any anti-social behaviour, which was not surprising, since the place was almost deserted.

I turned to go back to the hotel, trying to interpret the feeling of dread as the thrill of adventure. Something in particular made it impossible to forget that we were a long way from the south of England: the few people who passed in the street looked me in the eye and wished me good evening, as though, as far as they were concerned, I already belonged to their world.

✻

At dawn the following morning, we cycled across the Eden and ped-alled up to the ridge on which the Romans had built the fort of Uxellodunum. Green mountains appeared to the north and suddenly I felt an air of childhood holidays. The wind must have changed since the bicycle seemed full of eagerness despite the weight, and I felt only the excitement of going to live – very nearly – in Scotland.

Though we had settled on the place more by accident than design, it seemed appropriate in an anecdotal sort of way. I liked the idea of a 'debatable land' in the middle of Britain which was once neither Scottish nor English. My sister and I are the first in the history of our family to be born in England. I grew up understanding the Scots language but never speaking it except to tease my father. One of my uncles was an Aberdonian farmer who appeared to be able to speak nothing but Buchan (or Doric). Since the dialect was incomprehensible to me, I took it to be a foreign language. In a spirit of compromise but, according to school friends, with typical Scottish wilfulness, I supported the Scottish national football team and, because of my place of birth, Manchester United, whose manager, right half and inside right were all Scots.

Living in England, my parents often had to brush off silly remarks about funny accents, atrocious weather, sporrans, kilts and haggis. At primary school, my sister and I were sometimes corrected for 'mispro-nouncing' certain words, such as 'iron' with an 'r', but once we had lost the accent of home, we almost never experienced anti-Scottish ridi-cule. Instead, our parents made fun of our English accents. I once (only once) referred to my little finger as my 'pinkie', and I tried to keep my

middle name a secret. 'Macdonald' had been a tongue-in-cheek hom-
age to my mother's father, a sports reporter in Glasgow, who had
discovered, in the usual way of genealogical research, that an ancestor
had been present at – and presumably escaped from – the Massacre of
Glencoe in 1692, when the Campbells, in league with the English, had
exterminated the Macdonalds, that tribe of cattle-rustling Highlanders
whose chiefs, nonetheless, had sent their sons to the Sorbonne. But
there was nothing I could do to disguise my surname. The Aberdonian
ancestors had sailed from the Norse Lands, settling on the farms they
had destroyed, which is why the name 'Robbe', with a terminal 'e', is
also found in Normandy. They were, undeniably, robbers or, as they
used to say in the borderlands, 'reivers'.

Thanks to an annual migration, otherwise known as a summer
holiday, I saw a great deal of Scotland. A day after crossing the border,
the Ford Anglia would still be heading north, which proved that
my mother was right to suspect the television weather map of fore-
shortening Scotland. In spite of her endless battle against English
meteorological prejudice, it nearly always rained. Once, probably near
Gretna Green, my father took a photograph of his son and daughter
standing on the national frontier. At that moment, I discovered the
demystificatory magic of borders. One of my legs was English and the
other Scottish, but the vegetation was the same and the rain fell
equally on both sides.

Much later, in France, I sometimes made a point of claiming to be
Scottish. In Paris, at the age of eighteen, I became friends with an
Algerian Highlander, and we decided that one of the reasons we liked
each other was that we had a common heritage of heroic resistance,
even if mine was purely ancestral. Later still, in *la France profonde*,
Scottishness – combined with arriving on a bicycle – practically
guaranteed a warm welcome. To the inevitable question, '*Vous êtes
anglais?*', I used to reply, '*Non, britannique, et ma femme est américaine,*' or,
after learning of Samuel Beckett's answer to the same question,
'*Au contraire.*'

On one occasion, in a remote and unheated hostelry in the Avey-
ron, the question was asked by the proprietress in a faintly sinister
tone. As usual, I declared my Scottish ancestry. '*Ah! Écossais!*' she said
– relieved that I was neither English, Dutch nor Parisian – and called
to her husband: '*Monsieur est écossais!*' Flushed with excitement, she

went on, 'We didn't realize till a few days ago that the English did to you what the Parisians did to us!' I must have looked mystified since she explained, '*Oui! Nous avons vu le film,* Braveheart!' Mel Gibson's biopic of William Wallace, who trounced the English in 1297 before terrorizing and laying waste to Cumbria and Northumberland, must be one of the most brazenly inaccurate and tendentiously nationalistic films of the last fifty years. I heard a voice from within, speaking in a distinct Scottish accent, 'Serves ye right fer tryin' tae cash in oan yir ancestors!'

✤

Following the left-right-right-left itinerary of National Cycle Network Route 7, we cycled out of Carlisle through an urban planner's labyrinth of cul-de-sacs and driveways. At a roundabout on the outer edge of Carlisle, north-bound touring cyclists can often be seen trying to solve what seems to be the Cycle Network's challenge: reach Scotland without ever heading north. As the Solway Plain opened up on all sides, human habitation disappeared and, still on this major artery of the national network, we found ourselves on the narrowest cycle path I have ever seen. It runs on the old track bed of the Waverley Line and is not much wider than the wobble of a wheel. Tall weeds lashed the panniers and rabbits sprang from the brambles. It is easy to picture carts and chariots rattling along the former Roman road a few yards to the east, but it takes a strenuous effort of the imagination to visualize a heavy locomotive pulling a passenger train at fifty miles an hour between the rabbity hedges.

On the main street of Longtown, a local minibus was taking children to school. The name of the place was painted on the side of the bus in two languages: 'Longtown' and 'Langtoon' – the latter being indistinguishably Cumbrian or Scots. Near the end of the long row of low white houses, before the bridge which carries the A7 over the Esk, two thinly dressed men were sunning themselves on the pavement in front of a hardware store: perhaps the chilliness of the morning existed only in the minds of outsiders.

After Longtown, the road climbed gradually until the few arable fields gave way to rough pasture. Hardly a car went by. In the middle distance, there were small farmhouses on hilltops surrounded by enormous barns and cattle sheds like the outbuildings of castle keeps, as though, at night, the farmer withdrew into his fastness, leaving the fields to owls and interlopers. In the Solway Plain, the land had been vague and indecisive. Now, it proclaimed its ancient identities. Just before the summit of the road, where the pasture turned into moorland bog, the view encompassed four hill ranges: the mountains of the Lake District behind, the last buttresses of the North Pennines on the right, the hills of Langholm and Eskdale to the left, and, up ahead, Liddesdale stretching away towards the Cheviots, where the border follows the watershed line.

On a parallel road to the east, a line of white cottages might have been the outpost of a straggling suburb, but there was no settlement beyond. We dropped down into a wood-darkened valley where the road became a track and then wandered off into a field of cows. At a distance of a mile, when the trees are bare, a corner of the house and a chimney can sometimes be glimpsed from a particular spot, but even then, the bewildering topography makes it almost impossible to locate. In 2005, the house had nearly burned to the ground while fire engines from Longtown and Langholm roamed the lanes, searching for a means of access.

At the Bodleian Library, I had discovered a book, published in 1946, in which the wife of a Methodist minister whose *nom de plume* was 'Romany' recounted their first journey out to the border from Carlisle. 'Romany' was an early natural history broadcaster on the BBC. He and his wife had known the house by the river around the time of the First World War when the tenant, Elizabeth Mitchell, sublet two of her rooms to anglers. They had arrived by train on the Waverley Line and set off in search of their lodging:

> Down a steep bank we slid, across a trickle of a stream and up the other side we clambered, until finally we caught sight of a lonely, whitewashed house, almost surrounded by the river. I suppose at one time there must have been some sort of a road down to it, or the house could not have been built, but I never saw any signs of one.

No trace remained of the path through the woods. Instead, a thin track cut into the steep hillside ran alongside a crashing burn. Some branches of the leaning trees had been smashed by the removal van, which we expected to see, at each bend of the track, wedged into the narrowing tunnel of vegetation.

Five months before, on our prospective visit, everything had seemed cosier and less expansive, and the warmth of the owners had dispelled the intimidation. The babbling brook was now a torrent. Almost at once, it plunged into a ravine, leaving the track suspended high above. In its rush to reach the river, it tumbled over crags and rockfalls, some of which had trapped large pieces of rubbish – an old coat bleached by the torrent and, curiously immobile, an object resembling a large plastic football. We reached a part of the bank where the hazel and willow had been toppled by a landslip to reveal the chasm below. Looking down, I realized that the coat was a fleece and the football a distended bladder. The 'rubbish' consisted entirely of dead sheep – the farther downstream, the greater the decomposition, until what had once been a fleece was no larger than a facecloth. They looked like a grisly guard of honour which had died waiting for the new owners to arrive.

The track turned sharply to the right. A sloping, overgrown garden fleetingly reminiscent of an untended Fellows' garden in an Oxford college appeared on the edge of a large meadow. Given its complete invisibility from any other point in the landscape, the existence of the meadow seemed almost miraculous – as did the presence of the removal van in front of the house. But the overwhelming impression was the noise of the river, amplified by an amphitheatre of hanging woodland. An endless downpour of sound filled the whole space. These were the cataracts of the river Liddel, whose name means 'loud dale', and in that world of natural destruction, the birds sang as loudly as they sing in the middle of a city, to be heard above the roar of the traffic.

❋

As we cycled up to the house, one of the removal men was returning from the riverbank with crayfish in a jar and some lugubrious news: 'There's a dead swan in your river!' He pointed to the opposite bank and we saw a large puff-ball the colour of yellowing meringue. It was rotating slowly in a deep pool formed by fallen boulders. The 'swan', I later discovered, was the froth created by a chemical reaction of the peat which the Liddel washes out of the deep bogs or 'mosses' near its source.

Twenty-five miles to the north-east – five miles less as the crow flies – beyond the northern edge of the Kielder Forest, which is the largest wooded area in England, the Liddel rises among the wild fells of the border. Because of its meandering course, it can be hard to tell which country is which. From where we stood in England, Scotland lay to the south. On the borderline itself, halfway across the river, there were little islands each with its own micro-habitat of stunted trees and grasses thrashed by the flood.

While the removal men drank their tea, we joked about smuggling cheap whisky from a future independent Scotland. But I knew that the woods and reedy pastures on the opposite bank had once belonged to neither nation. The Debatable Land was doubly foreign – Scottish now and something quite different in the past. The land across the river looked entirely peaceful. It would serve, I thought, as the undistracting backdrop of a writer's study.

Unwilling to witness the process by which thousands of books slotted into boxes and unloaded in another place liberate themselves from the tyranny of the alphabet, I watched the river's dazzling performance. It danced around the rocks, frothing and cascading happily at the obstacles, sometimes flowing against itself, as if each of its tributaries had retained its own characteristics in the common stream. Something concealed by the overhanging branches moved across the vertical cliff on the Scottish side: it might have been a badger or a fox. Downstream, near a shingle bar, a heron stood watching the water. That evening, after the removal men had driven off, snapping the threads which tied us to Oxford, I walked down some stone steps to a grassy riverside platform barely four feet wide. From beneath the bank, an otter padded up and we stared at each other for a quarter of a minute. It seemed to conduct an assessment of the new inhabitant, saw no danger or nothing of interest, and slithered nonchalantly away.

In the mausoleum-like entrance hall which had been created by an earlier occupant, there was not just a dead swan but a whole mortuary-menagerie of hunted fish, fowl and fur carved out of limestone. The sculpted walls of the mausoleum captured the voice of the river and sent it swirling round the elliptical space. That night, in the bedroom above the hall, I listened to the river's incessant whisper. It seemed to have risen and was singing now in a higher key, accompanied by an occasional rumble and thud.

Four hundred years ago, at the downstream bend, two horsemen employed by the English government reached the end of their nightly watch. When the river was low, the flat slabs known as tombstone limestone served as a ford. Their task was to intercept the cattle-rustling reivers who maintained the entire border region in a perpetual state of anarchy. The reivers drove their stolen herds out of the Debatable Land to stark stone towers which were like the miniature castles of tiny principalities. The upstream watch was kept by four horsemen because, from that point on, there were, and still are, even fewer farms and settlements. All along that quiet stretch of the Liddel, the wild reivers of the borderlands had passed from one country to the next as freely as the otter.

3

Panic Button

The first knock at the door came at half-past ten the next morning. A postman stood there holding a letter. Oddly, there was no sign of a post van. Handing me the letter, he nodded in the direction of the gate and said, with a smile, 'Looks like yer've got a chainsaw job up there . . .'

We walked the three hundred yards up to the gate. A giant birch tree had fallen from the muddy slope and neatly barricaded the lonning.* 'Welcome to North Cumbria!' said the postman before climbing into his van and disappearing in reverse. It was only as I set to work on the knobbly trunk with a bow saw that I was struck by the obvious fact: since the only other means of access was the river, with its powerful currents and slippery stones, we could quite easily be cut off from the outside world, or at least from any assistance requiring a motorized vehicle.

In the months that followed, I came to recognize the site as a typical reiver's lair. It had long views in two directions along the valley and yet was practically invisible. It stood on the brink of a geological fault monopolized by a violent river, and it could be rendered unapproachable with little more labour than it would take to raise a drawbridge.

Twenty years before, army frogmen had stood in the river, watching the house. The Prime Minister was paying a secret visit to one of her closest friends, who had recently completed the limestone carvings for his new entrance hall. Nicholas Ridley, who is remembered

---

* A 'lonning' (Scots, 'loaning') is a lane along which farm animals, especially cattle, are allowed to pass. The word is commonly applied to any farm track.

with affection in the area by people who met him, was at that time one of the most unpopular politicians in Britain. He had helped to introduce the inequitable poll tax, which was first 'tried out' in Scotland in 1989, three years after he had purchased the whitewashed house by the Liddel as a rural retreat.

The Ridleys of Northumberland had been one of the main reiving families, and there seemed to be something of the reivers' devil-may-care attitude in Nick Ridley's handling of delicate political situations. But this was not a mischievous outlaw mocking the high and mighty: Ridley was a Cabinet minister in Her Majesty's Government. His memoirs, which were written at the house and published two years before his death in 1993, show a reckless delight in antagonizing opponents, however impotent they might have been. His comment on Scottish resistance to the poll tax, which dealt a near-fatal blow to the Conservative Party in Scotland and created a surge of support for independence, was typically undiplomatic: 'It is hard to be right with the Scots!'

The fact that Ridley had settled on the border itself was a kind of provocation, as was the title he chose for himself when he was created a life peer: Baron Ridley of Liddesdale. If only in name, he would be lord of that troublesome valley, a greater part of which belongs to Scotland than to England and which would thenceforth be officially associated with one of Margaret Thatcher's most devoted servants. The righteous anger of political enemies was a minor consideration for Baron Ridley of Liddesdale, but the presence in a front room of a red button set in a brass plate and connected – we assumed, no longer – to the nearest police station was a reminder that the United Kingdom had been a nation at war.

Of Thatcher's three closest friends in parliament, two had been murdered by Irish Republican terrorists. Airey Neave was killed by a car bomb outside the House of Commons in 1979. Ian Gow was blown up in his own driveway in Sussex in 1990, two weeks after Ridley's resignation from the Cabinet. Ridley himself was the obvious next target. Irish drug dealers were known to use the old smugglers' route between Galloway and the North Sea, and their vehicles were occasionally seen in the area. Several local people who worked on the house remember having to obtain security clearance before they could paint a wall or install a toilet.

There was a pleasant irony in the thought that an occupant of this border hermitage had been so recently embroiled in the political history of Britain. The border itself was just a detail in the estate agent's description, an obsolete curiosity like the panic button in the front room. It had ceased to exist as a national frontier in 1707 when England and Scotland had become the Kingdom of Great Britain. But perhaps the peace was deceptive. Tremors of indignation at the Westminster government's high-handed treatment of the Scots were still perceptible in Scotland and, in some minds, the border was once again a serious political division.

The river which served as a moat and the ancient woodland which formed the battlements encouraged a longer view. The song of the river had filled the ears of people who lived here long ago. Five hundred years before, there had been anarchy and bloodshed, compared to which the political debate on devolution was a polite conversation. I wondered whether, when the planting season came, the spade would turn up a reiver's skull, a rusted lance or another relic of the Border wars. There was nothing in anything I had read to suggest that the serenity of the land across the river was a faithful image of its past.

✵

As soon as the business of moving in allowed, we began to explore the surrounding area. There were provisions to be bought, the nearest shop was ten miles away, and since public transport was almost non-existent, it was essential to acquaint the bicycles with the topography and terrain. A bicycle seems to have a memory for gradients and surfaces and the ways of the wind: the better it knows them, the more efficient it becomes. It was just as well that we took advantage of the weather, because that autumn, when a warm Gulf Stream wind wafted in from the Solway Firth, proved to be a brief concession before the great freeze.

One day, as we hurtled down a steep hill to cross the Liddel into Scotland, I realized that we had been there before. In 2002, we had been cycling up to Perthshire to visit my mother. A 'Scotland Welcomes You' sign had suddenly appeared at the bottom of a twisting descent. At the foot of the sign was a burnt-out car. It looked like a warning to English visitors not to expect a tourist-friendly Brigadoon and it would have made a nice picture to show my mother, who, as a proud Glaswegian, had always complained about the Scots' undeserved reputation for rowdiness. But the last thing a cyclist wants to do when faced with a climb is lose momentum. I accepted the gift of gravity and shot up the opposite slope. The unphotographed image left a vivid impression and I was glad not to have stopped.

Now, in 2010, even if there had been no sign, it would have been obvious that we were crossing a frontier. On the English side, a man was walking a dog. He saw us approaching and pulled the animal onto the verge. I thanked him as we passed, and he answered, in a clear Cumbrian accent, 'No trouble at all.' Half a mile into Scotland, the same thing happened, but this time the answer was, 'Nae bother!', in an unmistakably Scottish accent.

This was an arresting discovery. In most parts of England, accents mutate as gradually as the terrain, but on either side of the Anglo-Scottish border, despite the sameness of the landscape, the change is abrupt. The distance perceptible to the ear between Canonbie in Scotland and Longtown five miles away in England is equivalent to about a hundred miles in the south. The fact which surprises many Scots as well as English is that this sharp divide in accent has no social equivalent. In shops and pubs, at church, at sheepdog trials and auctions, the Scottishness or Englishness of a person is never a matter for comment, let alone antagonism.

To say that border Scots and English get on well together would be to attach significance to an insignificant trait. Only twice have I heard any pointed reference to the border as a dividing line of adversaries. A farm worker who had helped the previous owners of the house with the garden assured me that the molehills we could see had been created by moles 'from ower there'. Not content with the boggy earth on the Scottish side, the determined creatures had allegedly swum across the Liddel to help themselves to English worms. There was, however, no suggestion that humans 'from ower there' presented a comparable threat.

The other reference was made by one of the firemen who had come to the house five years before. He had stayed on to repair the damage and became a painter and decorator. He now covers, sometimes single-handedly, an area of about two hundred and fifty square miles. After meeting his two sons, I observed that while one of them spoke with a Cumbrian accent like his father, the other sounded entirely Scottish. 'Aye, he does,' he agreed. 'But he's no thistle-muncher!' This picturesque term had been elicited purely by my clumsy observation. The man who was with him at the time was a 'thistle-muncher' himself and cheerfully admitted it.

The borderers' indifference to nationality is not a recent development. During the First World War, a nine-mile-long cordite factory stretched from Longtown in England to Eastriggs in Scotland. Twenty thousand workers were accommodated in the surrounding farms and villages. Pubs and breweries were taken over by the government to prevent drunkenness from interfering with the manufacture of explosives, but there was never any cross-border tension. Longtown owed its nickname, 'Dodge City', partly to its long main street and partly to the unruliness of local lads who found enough to keep them occupied on Saturday nights without resorting to nationalism.

According to the national censuses, the house where we now lived – along with some temporary structure long since vanished – had been a model of Anglo-Scottish cohabitation. In 1841, it was occupied by a Scottish woodman with a Cumbrian wife and daughter. In 1861, a Scottish blacksmith and his family lived alongside a Scottish railway worker and a railway superintendent from Yorkshire with an Irish wife. Ten years later, the resident blacksmith was English, as were the quarryman and his family who shared the house with a Scottish labourer and his family. This struck me as a good example of mobility in the Victorian Age, but it had been typical of the region many centuries before the two enemy nations had become a united kingdom.

4

The True and Ancient Border

Settling in to a new place is always complicated by the perception of time. Immediate concerns compete with a long-familiar past and an unfathomable future, but the new world has its own time scale to which the incomer has to adjust. I wanted to know, not just where the nearest post office was and when the buses ran, but where we were in historical time and space. The border was the boundary line of half our property and I felt that it was as important to find out exactly what it represented and how it had come to be as it was to locate the stopcock and to plumb the mysteries of the heating system.

The answers, of course, might turn out to be trivial and obvious. The accent divide, for instance, is probably quite recent. Local children have the accent of their primary school: pupils at Bewcastle School sound English while pupils at Newcastleton School, six miles away in Scotland, sound Scottish. Before compulsory education to the age of fourteen, there seems to have been very little difference in the speech of Scottish and English borderers. The vernacular of the Border characters of Walter Scott and John Buchan could be voiced just as well by a Cumbrian or a Northumbrian as by a Lowland Scot.

To some urban Scots, the border might stand for a cultural and historical chasm, but to the local population, it is primarily an administrative nuisance. People in need of a hospital who live less than fifteen miles from Carlisle but on the Scottish side of the border are forced to travel twice that distance to Dumfries Infirmary. No modern borderer would think that the national frontier was something worth dying for.

✷

In a place where geological forces can be seen at work every day in the boulder clay which slithers off the slopes and the river which carries it away, historical time contracts. On a local time scale, the national border itself is recent. Before the Romans, there were tribal divisions which I assumed to be untraceable. The Romans then created their own temporary borders as they moved north through Britain. When the Romans departed, the British tribes established or restored their own frontiers.

The muddle of those Dark Age kingdoms is sometimes tidily represented on speculative maps purporting to show the outlines of Bernicia, Deira, Rheged, Strathclyde, Northumbria and Cumbria. While nationalists, regionalists and genealogists in search of historical homelands find such maps evocative and convincing, historians tend to be more philosophical about the gaps in the record. A professor of Medieval History who visited us not long after we moved in was amazed to discover, as he drove up through Cumbria and saw road signs to the gigantic 'Rheged' visitor centre near Penrith, that the location of that unlocatable and perhaps fictitious sixth-century kingdom had been so confidently identified.

None of those shifting borders appear to match the future Anglo-Scottish border: the kingdoms of Northumbria and Cumbria encompassed lands on either side. Assuming that the political boundaries of Dark Age kingdoms reflected cultural or linguistic differences, place names might provide more tangible clues than early medieval poems celebrating the exploits of legendary leaders. But the place names of Liddesdale are the jumbled residue of centuries of invasion and settlement. Within half an hour of home, there are hills which form part of the same small range but whose names are derived from several different languages: Cumbric (an extinct form of Celtic), Old English, Old Norse, Middle English and Scots.

The first sign that any part of the future border was used as a frontier comes from the mid-ninth century: according to later traditions, Kenneth MacAlpin, the Pictish king who is popularly considered to be the first king of Scotland, claimed land as far south as the river Tweed. The Tweed still forms most of the border from Carham to the North Sea – eighteen miles of river, plus a five-mile deviation called the Bounds of Berwick. Scottish possession of lands north of the Tweed was confirmed by the Battle of Carham in 1018. In the west,

Carlisle and the kingdom of Cumbria also came under Scottish rule, which explains why Carlisle belonged to the diocese of Glasgow.

In 1092, William Rufus, son of the Conqueror, made Cumbria an English colony. Although Carlisle changed hands again more than once, the border as it now exists was effectively set. On-the-ground details are lacking until 1245, when a Northumbrian knight called Hugh de Bolbec sent a letter to Henry III of England, describing an apparently futile meeting which had taken place on Friday, 13 October at Reddenburn near Carham on the Tweed.

To resolve a boundary dispute between two estates, the King had ordered the eastern marches to be settled 'as they were in the time of King John and his predecessors'. Six knights were chosen by each side to walk along the line separating England from Scotland. The six English knights confidently traced 'the true and ancient divisions and marches between the two kingdoms', while the six Scottish knights 'dissented and contradicted' at every step.

The first walk having failed to produce agreement, six more knights were appointed by each side, making two parties of twelve ('for greater security', the letter explained) and the process was repeated. The freshly harvested fields of the Tweed Valley now saw twenty-four knights, with their servants and men-at-arms, processing along the border line. Once again, the Scottish knights voiced their unanimous disagreement. The 'true and ancient' boundary was proving elusive. Despite this second failure, doggedness prevailed over diplomacy and another twelve knights were sworn in on either side.

This time, before the forty-eight knights strode forth, the English took the precaution of declaring 'on oath' that the true border ran from the confluence of Reddenburn and Tweed south to Tres Karras and Hoperichelawe (no longer identifiable) and then in a straight line to Witelawe (White Law hill, on the main watershed of the Cheviot Hills).* But as they set off along an increasingly muddy border line, the leaders of the Scottish contingent turned aggressive, 'opposing with force and impeding the perambulation with threats', whereupon the English, perhaps having no further knights to hand in that northern extremity, 'firmly asserted that the places aforementioned were the true and ancient marches and divisions'.

---

* See fig. 1: 'The Anglo-Scottish border and the Marches'.

Hugh de Bolbec sent his report to Henry III, and since the Scots had apparently acted out of pure mischief, the 'ancient' border remained where it had already been for several generations. If either side had cause for complaint, it would have been the English rather than the Scots. Some time between 1018 and 1245, Scotland had acquired a great deal of land south of the Tweed, but the English never tried to push the border back to the north. A similar perambulation took place in 1246. After that, except for local disputes over fishing rights and the occasional English field sown with Scottish wheat, the border appeared to be fixed for all time. The significant exceptions were the Bounds of Berwick-upon-Tweed, which was captured by the English in 1482, and the Debatable Land in the west, the extraordinary nature of which would never be fully recognized by either side, then or since.

✿

This surprisingly persistent border between two rival nations is probably the oldest national land boundary in Europe. Pre-modern borders are sometimes said to have been zones rather than lines, but each frontier has its own peculiarities. Most of the Anglo-Scottish border was defined as precisely as on a modern map. Not until the age of motorways, when tarmac and speed turned physical geography into an esoteric branch of historical investigation, was it described as 'arbitrary'.

It followed streams and rivers, ran over named passes and peaks, and along the main watershed of the Cheviot Hills: the Chevyotte 'mounteyne' (or range), a survey of 1542 explained, 'devydethe England and Scotland by the heighte of yt as the water descendeth and falleth'. This might account for the southward dip of the line after Carham: the southern limits of the Tweed catchment area rather than the Tweed itself were taken as the border. It threaded onto a remarkably consistent diagonal a hundred-mile-long sequence of traditional, perhaps prehistoric meeting or 'trysting' places, where cross-border affairs were discussed (fig. 1). In the few sections where nature became vague, it was marked by field boundaries, dykes, crosses, ancient oaks, standing stones and cairns, and, in one part, by just over a mile of Roman road. As the land dropped down towards the Solway, it continued on the same diagonal by following the Kershope Burn, the Liddel and then the Esk.

The natural logic of the border is, paradoxically, a sign of its bureaucratic origin. In later centuries, colonial committees would draw straight lines on maps and then transfer them to the ground. In the Middle Ages, lacking accurate maps, administrators used the straight lines provided by nature. In theory, no one could quarrel with a river or a watershed line, and, apart from the disputatious knights and a few invasive ploughmen, no one did. The only serious deviation of the line occurred more than six hundred years after the knights' perambulation in what must be the most obscure episode in Anglo-Scottish history.

Contradicting all previous maps and the knights of Henry III, the Ordnance Survey six-inch map of 1859 moved the border half a mile to the east, leaving White Law and the high moors of Yetholm Common well inside Scotland. On the second edition of the map (1896), without any explanation and, it seems, without anyone ever noticing, the border returned to White Law. No doubt this had some-thing to do with the gypsies who camped on Yetholm Common and who owed allegiance to neither nation, but this sudden, brief wavering of the line also suggests that, by then, the meanderings of the border mattered as little to human beings as they did to birds of prey.

Three years after moving to Cumbria, I began to compile a cata-logue of cols and passes and found the borderlands to be one of the most scantily mapped areas of the British Isles. Several of the passes mentioned in sixteenth-century lists of the 'ingates and passages forth of Scotland' have disappeared from the map though not, of course, from the landscape. The physical separation of the two nations was evidently a subject of such indifference that the highest mountain on the border has lost its original name (Windgate Fell) and acquired another (Windy Gyle), which was never the name of a mountain.

One section of the border, however, mattered a great deal to the people who lived along it in the Middle Ages and long before. Near its south-western terminus, it split into two, describing an area known as the Debatable Land. Here, the line became a zone and the border acquired a third dimension. Not only was this bulge of unclaimed territory anomalous, its northern and western boundaries were also a frontier of a different kind: it was impossible to recognize them simply by looking at the landscape.

This relic of a distant age was more minutely described in documents than the rest of the border, and it stretched so far back in time that it was already ancient when the forty-eight knights of England and Scotland nearly came to blows on the banks of the Tweed. These boundaries survived because they remained engraved in the minds of the local people. Yet to the medieval officials who policed the border, the Debatable Land was synonymous with anarchy. Somehow, that enclave of lawlessness overrun by murderous savages with no respect for private property had retained its intricate contours.

Since this was also the boundary of our property and a manageably small area for exploration, I decided to find out all I could about the people who had unexpectedly preserved the integrity of the Debatable Land. I knew that Carlisle had a reputable museum, built on the site of a Roman fort. It seemed a good place to start. After a month on the border, I had made only one brief return trip to the capital of Cumbria, and I was quite ready now to think of it as a city.

For three mornings in a row, there was a hard frost. Since the roads were icy, I decided to try out what remained of public transport. But on the fourth morning, we woke to a brilliant covering of deep snow. Local radio on both sides of the border announced the closure of schools and the cancellation of buses. No tyre tracks would spoil the whiteness which surrounded the house. In a city, the silence after a heavy fall of snow has a softening effect, but in a place which is normally peaceful, it suggests a hesitation of nature, a holding of breath rather than repose. It took a few moments to realize that what gave the silence its air of imminence was the fact that the river, too, had been hushed and that thin sheets of ice were inching out from the opposite bank.

5

'The Sewer of Abandoned Men'

Water pipes usually survive a freeze until the temperature reaches minus six degrees centigrade. That November, the night-time drop in temperature was sudden and extreme. The following morning, the thermometer showed minus sixteen degrees and for the first time in living or even recorded memory, the Liddel froze and the two countries were joined. A band of Scottish sheep, grey against the snow, nuzzled the riverbank in search of grass and seemed to threaten invasion.

The cold did not relent. Even the postmen were unable to reach the house. Every day, we scrunched through the snow for half a mile to reach the road and to see whether any mail had been deposited in the black rubbish bin placed there for the purpose. Sometimes, the only tracks on the road were those of deer and pheasant. That particular stretch is not included on the council's list of highways to be cleared, and so the nearest negotiable route for postmen and anyone else now lay more than a mile to the south.

Our only visitors were a gamekeeper holding a brace of soft, dead pheasants and a man with some squirrel traps which he asked us to place in likely locations, since the border is also a frontline in the war between native red squirrels and imported greys. Both men wanted to make sure that the new people without a car were surviving the Cumbrian winter. We had enough food for an imaginative cook but wine supplies were running perilously low and we were preparing for a Lenten Christmas when news came that the twice-weekly bus from the Scottish village of Newcastleton* was going to attempt the journey to Carlisle.

---

* 'Newcastleton' is the name on maps and road signs; locally, it is known as Copshawholm

The bus stop is purely a matter of convention: there is no shelter and no sign, only a misplaced milestone at a meeting of two roads. From that wind-lashed spot, the view extends across the valley of the Liddel. If the drenching mist has cleared the tops or is reluctant to rise from the river, an occasional vehicle can be seen threading its way along the hillside until it disappears back into the pine forest. A small white rectangle is either the bus bound for Dumfries in the west or the cross-border 127 from Newcastleton.

That morning, in the crystal-clear air, the far side of the valley could be seen as though through a pair of binoculars. A buzzard was soaring over the whiteness, but nothing moved on the road. At last, a white rectangle appeared, then vanished as it plunged into the valley towards a narrow bridge and a gear-stripping climb. Several minutes passed in silence. Then the little bus was rattling over the old railway bridge and accelerating towards the invisible bus stop with no apparent intention of stopping.

A wild-looking man was at the wheel, somewhat out of scale with the diminutive vehicle. He might have been a Celtic charioteer who had been forced to commandeer a child's toy. I saw several faces at the windows as the bus roared past. A few yards up the hill, it juddered to a halt. I walked smartly to the door, half expecting it to drive away. 'Ye thought ah wisnae goan tae stop, didn't ye?' said the charioteer. Half a dozen women were already on the bus. They were smiling, evidently quite happy with the service. Perhaps this was how Scottish bus drivers usually behaved as soon as they crossed the border. I asked for a return to Carlisle, and as the driver stabbed his ticket machine, I heard him say distinctly 'Caer-liol'. Either he was a student of historical etymology or the medieval form of 'Carlisle' was still in use.*

By the time the bus left Longtown, it was carrying a roughly equal number of Scottish and English passengers. The few men sat together at the back, but there was no division between English and Scots. The women exchanged news and gossip and enquired after the health of

---

(the site on which the village was built in 1793) and even more locally as 'the Holm' or 'the Village'.

* The name of the city is pronounced variously Car*lisle*, *Car*lisle, Ca(e)r*li*ol and Caerl. The Latinized Celtic name, Luguvalium, produced 'Luel' or 'Liol'. A '*caer*', in Cumbric or Welsh, was a fort.

mutual acquaintances. Someone's roof had collapsed under the weight of the snow; a farmer had been out since before dawn, rescuing sheep from a snow drift. Some of the passengers talked about the shopping they hoped to do in Carlisle.

The cross-border 127 bus is the ghost of a train. When the Waverley Line was closed in 1969 after more than a hundred years of service, the people of the Borders were promised that transport links would always be maintained. Buses would run – weather and road repairs permitting – on the route of the old North British Railway. As a result, even without snow drifts, floods or subsidence, the journey from Newcastleton is now a dangerous excursion. Forty-four-ton logging trucks race along the winding roads carting timber from the Kielder Forest which should have gone by rail. Sheep and cattle trucks from Wales and the Scottish Lowlands, piloted by weary drivers, sometimes run off the road or collide with other vehicles. Not long after we moved to Cumbria, a 127 bus was crushed by a livestock wagon on the road to Carlisle and a young woman from Newcastleton was killed.

Promises made at the time of the railway closures have no legal force. The government's devil-take-the-hindmost policy expected rural populations to acquire a motor car or to move to a city. No one who rides the 127 bus could doubt its social worth, but a council's finance department, especially when faced with the complexity of a twenty-four-mile bus route which runs through three counties – one English and two Scottish – is incapable of computing the value of a transnational village hall on wheels. Now and then, a Carlisle council official whose car stands outside the council offices in a subsidized car park creates a list of 'savings' by proposing the eradication of various rural bus routes, including the cross-border 127.

*

The rest of the journey passed without major incident, while the driver kept up a running commentary on all the minor incidents which occur when trying to drive at speed through slow-moving traffic. We crested the hill in the shabby-genteel suburb of Stanwix, and there, looking south over Carlisle, I glimpsed what must be, despite some defiantly unimaginative modern buildings, one of the most beautiful views from any English city. Beyond the river Eden at the foot of the Roman vallum, the castle and cathedral rise over a rabble of Victorian and Edwardian brick houses while the snowy mountains of the northern Lake District give the scene the air of a frontier town.

Since moving to Cumbria, I had seen Carlisle only once, through the windows of a car. On one of the five days in the week when the bus doesn't run, a taxi had driven me to the studios of Radio Cumbria next to the museum and across the road from the castle. We had taken the shortest route, which is not the finest approach to Carlisle. In 1973, a four-lane inner ring road cut the city off from its castle. Gesturing at the great sandstone fortress with its moat of modern traffic, the driver had asked,

''Ow long has that been there, d'yer think?'

'About a thousand years?'

'A thousand years and still standin' . . . And 'ow long d'yer think *that* was there afoor it began to fall down?' (pointing to a decrepit concrete and glass pedestrian bridge).

'Not quite so long?'

'I'll give yer a clue: it's called the Millennium Bridge.'

That December morning, I saw a different Carlisle. The bus driver deposited his passengers opposite a Victorian covered market with a roof which briefly reminded me of the former Halles of Paris. Heading for the museum by a roundabout route, I walked through several quarters reminiscent of different places hundreds of miles apart: the cobbled back lanes of a northern industrial town; a cathedral close in the south-east of England; a residential district of Georgian town-houses and shrubby gardens which might have been a down-at-heel suburb of Edinburgh; the medieval square of a market town in the Midlands. In English Street, the biting wind and squabbling seagulls were reminders that Carlisle was once an inland port. Even with snow on the ground, pavement cafes testified to the hardiness of North Cumbrians.

I entered the museum by the older of its two entrances, under the city council's coat of arms with its motto from Shakespeare's *Henry VIII*: 'Be Just And Fear Not'. At the top of a staircase, the automatic doors swung open.

There were two compartments from an Edwardian railway carriage. A little girl was settling in to the plusher of the two, rummaging in her handbag and preparing for a long journey. The chugging of a locomotive came from a small ventilation grid above a recreated guard's van filled with packages and suitcases. This was the soundtrack of the 1936 documentary film, *Night Mail*, whose director had preferred to show the crossing of the border forty miles to the north of Carlisle – the fleeing scarf of steam rushing through the dawn-dappled fells of the Beattock Pass rather than over the wetland wastes of the Solway Firth where the actual border lies.

A further gallery, devoted to the social history of Carlisle, conveyed the impression that nothing much had happened in the twentieth century. A video screen displayed the main events – floods, railway closures, pageants and mayoral parades, visits of royalty and pop stars. 'You were up in Carlisle fairly recently,' an interviewer was reminding the Beatles in November 1963. On the pavement outside the theatre, the fans looked sturdier and less awe-struck than their southern counterparts, and I wondered whether the skinny lads from Liverpool would have survived a stampede of Cumbrian lasses.

The exhibit I had come to see was an introduction to the world of the Border reivers. A map showed the geographical distribution of all the reiving clans. These kinship groups of the borderlands were referred to as 'surnames' or 'clans'. They first emerged in the fourteenth and fifteenth centuries, at about the same time as the clans of the Scottish Highlands. (It was only much later that the term 'clan' was reserved for Highlanders.) The area where we now lived had been occupied mostly by Armstrongs and Forsters, with Routledges, Nixons and Nobles to the east, Grahams and Storeys to the south, and Elliots to the north. I recognized the surnames of several of our neighbours and of people who had lived in our house in the late nineteenth century: John Armstrong the blacksmith, John Graham the labourer, John Elliot the printer.

The shires on either side of the border had been policed by government officials known as wardens. Their duties consisted of defending the Border forts, administering justice and obtaining redress from their opposite numbers after a Scottish or an English raid. The first wardens were appointed in the early fourteenth century, and the office was maintained until the Union of the Crowns in 1603. They received no salary: it was expected that, as landowning borderers, they would naturally defend their own property and thus the national frontier. Eventually, the Border shires were grouped into six

marches: West, Middle and East (fig. 1). As an extreme case, Liddesdale had been treated as a march in its own right.

I picked up a worksheet for schoolchildren titled 'Nasty Nixon's
Reivers Trail'. 'Nasty Nixon' was a cartoon sword- and gun-wielding
maniac in a steel helmet and a leather jack (a quilted doublet reinforced with plates of horn or metal). On my copy of the worksheet,
the questionnaire had been correctly filled in as follows:

Wardens.

What criminal activities did the March Wardens (like our modern police
force) try to stop the Reivers from performing? Tick any that you see.

Murder	☑
Kidnap	☑
Theft of cattle and possessions	☑
Blackmail	☑

A diorama in a glass case smeared with small fingerprints showed
a band of reivers with raised lances galloping across a river towards a
pele tower made of stones the size of Rice Krispies. 'Peles' or 'peels'
were originally the pales (stakes) used to construct the earlier, even
less congenial towers of timber and clay. The stone towers were
nearly windowless and their walls so thick that they took up almost
half the ground plan. In that miniature world of modelling clay,
herdsmen were chasing hairy cattle into the walled courtyard known
as a barmkin or barnekin, which also contained some wattle-and-
daub cottages.

As I peered at this absorbing scene of naked banditry, the sound
of screams and clanging metal came from a darkened room around the
corner. A video had begun to play.

Like a child's nightmare, the faces of reivers with jagged teeth
and terrible hair floated out of a blasted landscape of bog and ruin.
These were the medieval Armstrongs, Elliots, Nixons and Nobles,
some of whose descendants were presumed to be watching the video.
The satanic night-riders of the borderlands, the Scottish voiceover
explained, spent their worthless lives stealing their neighbours' animals, setting fire to their farms and lopping off their limbs. In sunless
towers of stone, women cowered night and day, awaiting the inevit-

able. The only female face in the rain-drenched inferno was that of a
tear-streaked widow lamenting the murder of her husband:

> Nae living man I'll love again,
> Since that my lovely knight is slain;
> Wi' ae lock of his yellow hair
> I'll chain my heart for evermair!

The Border reivers 'blighted the life of the whole area'. To them,
according to the voiceover, we owe the words 'blackmail' and
'bereaved'. They were such a rampant evil that the Archbishop of
Glasgow excommunicated them en masse in a Great Monition of
Cursing issued in 1525. (Though I didn't know it at the time, the curse
was commissioned from the foul-mouthed, heretic-burning Archbishop by Cardinal Wolsey, who must have assumed that the borderers
attended church and cared about their immortal souls.) A long
excerpt is inscribed on a boulder placed in the pedestrian underpass
which leads from the museum to the castle. Some local people have
called for its removal, blaming it for the floods and the poor performance of Carlisle United football team. It still has an air of potency:

> I curse thair heid and all the haris of thair heid; I curse thair face, thair
> ene, thair mouth, thair neise, thair toung, thair teith, thair crag . . . and
> everilk part of thair body, frae the top of thair heid to the soill of thair feit,
> befoir and behind, within and without.*

And so on, for fifteen hundred words, in which wives, children,
servants, household goods, farm tools and 'all that is necessary for
sustenance and welfare' are bundled up in the same Christian execra-
tion and committed 'perpetualie to the deip pit of hell, to remain with
Lucifer and all his fallowis . . . first to be hangit, syne revin and ruggit
with doggis, swine, and utheris wyld beists, abhominable to all the
warld'.†

---

* 'I curse their head and all the hairs of their head; I curse their face, their eyes, their
mouth, their nose, their tongue, their teeth, their skull . . . and every part of their body,
from the top of their head to the soles of their feet, in front and behind, within and without.'

† Committed 'perpetually to the deep pit of hell, to remain with Lucifer and all his com-
panions . . . first to be hanged, then torn and pulled apart by dogs, swine and other wild
beasts, abominable to all the world'.

The conclusion of the film would probably not comfort a traumatized child but it does provide a cathartic moral. The mayhem and carnage are attributed to the weakness of national government. The stateless reivers – 'Scottish when they will, and English at their pleasure' – were a creeping fungus which thrived on the blood-sodden moors of Anglo-Scottish strife. The suffering of the innocent ended only when the two nations were united under one monarch and 'the lion and the unicorn lay down together in peace'.

The screen turned black. I turned round and, in the theatrical murk, saw something I had missed when entering the gallery: a magnificent animatronic sculpture of a Scottish lion and an English unicorn. Their flesh had fallen from their rusted bones, yet the horn of one and the tail of the other were still erect. Prisoners of their own aggression, they seemed to have hammered one another into scrap metal. The fact that the mechanism had ceased to function made it all the more poignant.

These were the reivers I had read about in books. The film had evidently been properly researched. The region in which we were intending to live for at least as long as it took to forget the ordeal of moving had been inhabited by what sounded like a distinct species, 'from their cradells bredd and brought up in theft, spoyle and bloode', their only trade and livelihood 'stealing, which they accompte not shame, but rather a grace and creditt unto them'. This was the view of the third Earl of Cumberland, who, to his dismay, was granted the lands on the edge of the Debatable Land where our house now stood.

The Earl was writing in 1604, when the Union of the Crowns under James VI of Scotland seemed to promise an end to the anarchy. In 1759, when the memoirs of one of the last English wardens were published, the Border Reiver was well established in British history as the natural denizen of a remote frontier zone on which the sun of state had shone but weakly:

> . . . a set of wild men, who, from the time when the Romans left our island, till the death of Queen Elizabeth, kept the southern part of Scotland and the northern part of England in a perpetual civil war, and seem to have equalled the Caffres in the trade of stealing, and the Hottentots in ignorance and brutality.

The term 'Debatable Land' or 'Debatable Lands' referred, both in the film and in the written sources, to the blackest, goriest region of the Borders. For five hundred years, the Debatable Land had been universally perceived as a festering vestige of ancient barbarism in the heart of Great Britain: 'ane spelunc and hurd of thewis'* (1537); 'the sink and receptacle of proscribed wretches' (1787); 'a land of contention, rapine, bloodshed, and wretchedness . . . uncultivated and desolate' (1794); a 'degraded piece of land' and 'scene of butchery' (1802); 'the sewer of abandoned men' (1912); 'a monument to the intractable character of the natives' (1975).

✻

Outside, on the icy streets of Carlisle, the descendants of the Armstrongs, Elliots, Grahams and Nixons were going about their everyday business. None of them was dripping blood or screaming murder. Considering the savage weather and the boarded-up shops, they seemed remarkably high-spirited. In Oxford and London, shoppers would now be staggering under the weight of presents; here, they were relatively unburdened and it was hard to tell that Christmas was approaching.

In Oxford or London, a pedestrian was primarily a person who might get in the way. Civilized public behaviour consisted of not making eye contact, except to initiate evasive action on a crowded pavement. In Carlisle, groups of people stood around exchanging news and, despite an apparent lack of warm clothing, complaining cheerfully about the cold. Several men were wearing T-shirts. Young and not-so-young women sported bronze or 'summerglow' tans. In the south, the high minimum walking speed ensured the general unpopularity of babies, small children and anyone slowed by age or disability: the street was not a place for families. Here, it was common to see four generations of the same family embarked on a leisurely shopping expedition. When someone shouted, it was to hail an acquaintance, sometimes at quite a distance, as though across a field on a windy day. Shop assistants working in dreary jobs smiled at their

---

* 'A den and hiding place of thieves'.

customers and seemed to be unaware that they were living in a depressed northern city.

The typical Cumbrian was defined by the novelist George MacDonald Fraser, a native of Carlisle, as 'suspicious and taciturn'. This might have described a typical traveller on the London Underground, but most of the Cumbrians I met in the early days, as well as later, tended to be voluble and confiding, though they might well have been taciturn and suspicious towards a man who expected to find them so.

The readiness of locals to talk to strangers can be disconcerting to visitors from the south. Having an hour to spare before the bus left from Devonshire Street, I walked over towards the railway bridge where Victorian buildings frame the mountain panorama to the south. A shabbily dressed man sidled up to me and asked, in a low voice, 'Are yer lookin' fer *steam*?' Out of habit, I assumed him to be either insane or engaged in criminal activity. Perhaps 'steam' was the local name for a street drug. '*Steam* sometimes comes through here,' he explained, and I realized to my shame that he was trying to alert me to the fact that the Romantic Victorian panorama was sometimes complemented by the billowing plumes of the Flying Scotsman running a special cross-border service.

There was only one obvious connection between these modern Cumbrians and the 'wild men' depicted in the museum: the noticeable homogeneity of the population. It was not hard to imagine them as members of a small number of clans. The telephone directory for Carlisle and North Cumbria shows that the surnames of only fourteen reiving families account for one-sixth of the population. In and around the Debatable Land, the ratio is even higher. Certain types of face and physique were already becoming familiar. I had found George MacDonald Fraser's comments on the borderers' 'racial composition' better suited to the Victorian settings of his Flashman novels than to the study of medieval history, but, remembering his evocation of the American presidential inauguration of 1969, when three 'Border types' lined up on a podium in Washington DC, I had begun to notice Billy Grahams, Lyndon Johnsons and Richard Nixons sitting on benches, sweeping the streets and smoking outside pubs.

❉

The 127 bus lurched down Lowther Street and swerved onto the Eden Bridge. Momentarily mounting the kerb to overtake a slow car, the driver headed for the black Border fells like a reiver making off with stolen sheep. As I looked through my notes on the reiver exhibition, one question kept recurring: if the 'Debatable Lands' were such a hell on earth, why did anyone live there?

Livestock trucks – locally called 'wagons' – thundered past in the darkness. As the Cumbrian removal man had told me, the area has a long tradition of haulage. Several firms were founded by descendants of reivers – Armstrongs, Grahams and Robsons – who carted goods and animals over long distances. Even in the Middle Ages, this was a highly mobile society. Yet generation after generation of border farmers and their wives chose to live in a war zone, knowing that, every year, once the harvest was in, their houses would be burned to the ground and their animals driven off. The same question occurred to the English military commander, Sir Robert Bowes, who surveyed the Anglo-Scottish border in 1550. The land was largely 'waste' and unproductive, yet 'the people of that countrey (specially the men) be lothe to departe forth of the same but had rather live poorely theire as theaves than more wealthyly in another countrey'.

Forty minutes after leaving Carlisle, but well ahead of schedule, the 127 bus slewed to a halt halfway down a steep hill in the middle of nowhere. Clinging to the thin beam of the torch, I set off for home and the frozen river.

6

Mouldywarp

The question posed by the reiver display was one that we were often asked in the first months of living on the border. A young man whose family would be considered neighbours though they live four miles away came up to Margaret while she was parking her bicycle outside a village hall. 'Are you the American lady?' he asked. She confirmed his identification, adding that she came from Chicago via Nashville, Tennessee. 'So if you wanted to,' he suggested, 'you could live anywhere you liked in America? You could live in *New York*!' 'Yes, I suppose I could,' she agreed. His face creased up with incredulity: 'Then *why* did you decide to live *here*?'

Later, the question changed. Instead of, 'Why did you come up here?', it was, 'You're still here, then?' To people born locally, the decision seemed bizarre because of the scarcity of sun and what they saw as the inconvenience of not owning a car. But they understood a love of the country, and the thought of riding a bicycle in the rain was not as amazing to sheep-farming folk as it had been to some of our friends in the south.

The same question was asked by quite a different group of people with something more sinister in mind. To many southerners, 'Cumbria' means the Lake District – that miniature Scotland-without-Scottish-people, associated with Romantic poetry, happy holidays and relatively inexpensive retirement homes. Liddesdale, which straddles the border, is a long way from the tourist-thronged Lakes and there is no community of wealthy English 'ex-pats'.

Friends of friends from southern England warned us about the world we had entered. Those fortress-like farmhouses were the lairs of unreformed reivers. One farmer was said to have 'accidentally' and repeatedly severed the electricity cable connected to the house of his new neighbours. Another Liddesdale miscreant had sprayed the outside of his neighbour's house with slurry. The nearest inn, which could pass for a lonely smugglers' tavern, was said to be reasonably safe, but only 'until nine o'clock'.

This was the Cumbrian 'breed' I had read about in books and magazine articles, some of which were written by people who claimed to be, however distantly, Cumbrian. There was certainly evidence of feuds and clannish loyalties, grudges spanning generations, and a good deal of mischievous gossip. I have lost count of the number of local people reported to have been found drunk in a ditch. Far more complicated webs of enmity are spun through the suburbs of a city. Here, the effect of gossip is less pernicious. Stand on a deserted road away from any dwelling, and there is a good chance that, within half an hour, a small group of people will form. News of illness or accident spreads with astonishing speed. That winter, Margaret fell off her bike on a patch of black ice. She picked herself up and pedalled home unhurt. No house has a view of that stretch of road and no one was about. Over the next three weeks, a dozen different people asked if she was all right and still cycling. The news had spread as far as Longtown, nine miles to the south.

Was this an example of the rural telegraph which made the march wardens' work so difficult? Catching a reiver unawares was practically impossible. The sophisticated noblemen who served the state were accustomed to ciphered letters and cleverly concealed post bags. Confused by their enemy, they watched tinkers and horse-dealers cross the border passes and thought of 'spies and lookers into the privity [secrets] of the country'. They heard the cry of a barn owl or a curlew, spotted marks cut in a smooth patch of turf or in the bark of a tree, saw fires blazing on the tops of pele towers and suspected the existence of a complex communications network. The bedsheets spread on hedges and hillsides by the housewives of Liddesdale, 'washed wi' the fairy-well water, and bleached on the bonnie white gowans [daisies]',* were believed to be signals to alert the entire valley to a government raid.

Such subtle devices might have been used but they were not

---

* Walter Scott, *Guy Mannering* (1815), ch. 24.

strictly necessary. Where nothing much happens, news travels fast. As one of the English wardens noted in alarm at the shrinking of distances, 'rumours are swift messengers'. These days, postmen spend the morning driving up and down dead-end lanes, increasingly laden with news as the postbag grows lighter. School buses collect children from remote, deserted crossroads; shepherds lean on walls and gates, scanning large areas of hillside. Within twelve hours of a violent storm, some people are able to provide a comprehensive damage report covering about eighty square miles.

The effect is magnified by the web of family relations, but the main factor is physical geography and local government. The Cumbrian 'breed' is a product of environment, not genetics. Many of the people I thought of as Cumbrian turned out to come from elsewhere. I happen to know that the two local women mentioned in a recent book about the border line, who seemed to exemplify that Cumbrian taciturnity, moved to Cumbria from counties far to the south. The most notorious reivers, who might have sprung from the bogs and bentgrass of the Borders, had migrated from other parts. The Grahams probably originated in Fife and most of their 'English' tenants were Scots; no one knows for certain the origins of the Armstrongs, who arrived in the Debatable Land in the early sixteenth century.

The independent spirit of borderers, which 'offcomers' can mistake for effrontery, is inseparable from remoteness and the lack of services. The nearest police and fire stations are more than eight miles distant, but the police station is unstaffed and when the fire trucks arrived recently in Nicholforest to put out a fire large enough to be seen from a village several miles away in Scotland, no working fire hydrant could be found and the water had to be drawn from a stream swiftly dammed with hay bales and sucked up from a fish pond two miles down the road. 'You could see Rodney's fish flying into the flames,' said the man whose property had been destroyed.

Southerners tend to view the native population in terms of social class, which usually entails a moral judgement. Borderers are more likely to consider people from the point of view of their social function. This can be as confusing to outsiders as the activities of the reivers were to government officials. The need to adapt to difficult conditions, the relative freedom from class constraints and a potent dislike of pomposity can make even the most candid of Cumbrians seem shifty and elusive. A gamekeeper in the wild looks very different from the same man dressed to guide a visiting party of pheasant-shooters, just as a reiver strolling through Carlisle on market day might have been hard to identify as the man who, the night before, had been setting fire to a warden's house.

✣

One of the locally famous 'characters' of Liddesdale – a man well loved by his neighbours and respected for his professionalism – might have appeared to be an enigmatic, disconcerting specimen of the human fauna of the Borders. Sometimes, he could be seen crawling over a field. At other times, dressed in a dapper moleskin waistcoat and an elegant hat, he would be pushing a bicycle along a street in Newcastleton. I first met him that winter when returning from Carlisle. The 127 bus slowed unexpectedly and stopped at one of the invisible bus stops in open country. A stocky, elderly man clambered aboard, weighed down by his muddy tweeds and a misshapen sack. 'Only one caught,' I heard him say to the driver. He tottered down the aisle, the bus remaining motionless until he reached his seat, then sat in front of me, facing away from the driver, and went on, as though the change of interlocutor were immaterial, 'But only two traps set.'

Several months later, riding to Newcastleton over the edge of Carby Hill, we saw a hunched figure in a red bandana kneeling in a field near the top of the climb, high above the valley. He appeared to be conducting a small burial. Something resembling a giant clothes peg jutted out of the ground in front of him. I thought of a gypsy performing an obscure rite. As we drew closer, I recognized him as the man from the bus. By then, I knew him to be Wattie Blakey, the master mole-catcher with more than seventy years' experience of ridding farmers' fields of the inexorable 'mouldywarp' or 'mowdy' which damages ploughs, breaks horses' legs, spoils the silage and spreads disease to sheep.

Mr Blakey grew up in Newcastle upon Tyne but was evacuated to Cumbria during the Second World War. He does not drive a car. The bus service is inadequate and yet he manages to serve an area stretching from Longtown to the edge of the Kielder Forest. The fruits and proof of his labour can be seen, hooked by the snout onto barbed-wire fences, like sacrifices to a local god.

We stopped to say hello. Noticing our bikes, he pointed to the junction at the brow of the hill where the road drops down to New-castleton. 'I had a bike stolen from there,' he growled. We expressed our sympathy at this alarming news. Was nowhere safe? ... He explained that the driver of a recycling truck, spotting a discarded heap of old metal, had heaved it into his truck and carted it off to the dump. This is how we learned about the mole-catcher's solution to the lack of public transport. Over the years, he had acquired seven old bicycles, which he left in various locations along the sparse bus lines. This greatly expanded his field of operations. He had, in effect, invented his own bike-share scheme long before the idea came into use in cities all over the world.

7

Beachcombing

Just before dawn one morning, a deep shuddering came from outside the house. I rushed out into the dark, half-expecting to see a mechanical digger at work. The river was coming back to life. Within minutes of the first tremor, gigantic slabs of ice were see-sawing downstream, buffeting and mounting one another like stampeding animals. Gaining speed, they scoured the banks, felled trees and smashed some steps which had led down to the river. Hundreds of them stacked up on the inside bend, dwarfing the willow and the alder and creating the perfect illusion of a polar sea.

Since the big freeze, only moles had been able to pierce the ground. Their hills had frozen instantly into heavy, crumbless cakes of black earth. A few days after the thaw, when the banks were still littered with ice, it became possible to dig the soil, and for the first time, I had a sense of the remoteness of which concerned friends in the south had spoken. But they had been referring to remoteness from mobile-phone masts, railway stations and restaurants. This was remoteness in four dimensions.

Oxford had been thick with history. A hole dug almost anywhere in the garden would turn up artefacts from several periods of human settlement. The evidence of continuity in the earth conveyed a sense of unshakeable comfort, of occupying a place designed and prepared for human beings. In Liddesdale, any remnants of ancient or modern civilization had been carried off by the tide of boulder clay. No burnt flints or Roman roof tiles were filed away in the soil's archive, only unworked stones transported by glaciers.

When the river began to perform its cycle of changes, I discovered its power of revelation. Unlike the concrete-jacketed rivers which flood Carlisle, the Liddel is exactly where it wants to be. As a result, it has made a pact with human beings. Invasions are punished with destruction, but in exchange for being left alone, the river brings treasures which can simply be gleaned without the need for excavation.

In the middle of the night, after several days of rain, a cavernous rumbling would begin, punctuated by a thudding reminiscent of a demolition site. I looked out at sunrise one day to see a brown arm of open sea churning past the house six feet above the usual level of the river. There were crashing waves and a nasty-looking undertow where the river seemed to be swallowing itself. A fallen tree, stripped of its twigs, stood up as the base of its trunk caught against a boulder. A wooden bench weighted with stones was waltzing up towards the house. The shingle beach had disappeared.

When the flood had subsided, the beach was reconfigured, spread out into a thin strand with a curving headland but with an extra foot of material on top, neatly sorted, as though by a builder's merchant, into fine sand, coarse sand, grit, gravel, pebbles, stones and boulders. A two-foot-wide embankment of thatch, ripped from the river banks, stretched away into the alder carr and marked the high point of the flood. Rocks which had teetered along the skittering gravel sat in mid-stream like small islands where nothing had been before.

After each flood, the shingle beach offered a fresh selection of archaeological evidence, culled from twenty miles of river. The artefacts had been smoothed, smashed and smoothed again. '*Price 1/3 . . .* PREPARED . . . LINCOLN &' was all that remained of a pot of Clarke's Miraculous Salve (c. 1910), probably from the same period as the broken neck of a blue ink bottle and a similarly softened shard of a Wilson's Tonic Beer flask.

As a general rule, the heavier the object, the longer its trip down river and thus through time. A wrought-iron bootscraper and a tie plate (used to attach a rail to a railway sleeper) belonged to the mid-nineteenth century, as did some pipe fencing of a variety I later discovered, falling apart but still in situ, upstream at Kershopefoot. This rule is not absolute. Some weighty objects are naturally well equipped for a river journey. A post-war tennis umpire's chair, corroded but still usable, had cartwheeled downstream for nine miles to be followed a few decades later – but arriving at about the same time

– by a tennis ball, a shuttlecock and a nylon sock embroidered with the word 'Sport'.

These items indicated human habitation to the north, though few pre-dated the twentieth century: brackets and hinges, corrugated asbestos roofing, a Bakelite vent and a piece of vinyl flooring, pathetically uncamouflaged by its shingle-beach print. A pink rubber hand-grip from a child's bicycle still enclosed the rusty conglomerate of its handlebar. Agriculture was represented by the metal wing of a tractor, endless twisted ribbons of black plastic used for wrapping hay bales, an assortment of sheep bones and a small cow, bloated and flayed, which lingered for less than an hour before rolling on to the sea. A year later, another flood cast up a large yellow tag marked '109' which, given its size, must have been clamped to a cow's ear. The only sign of deliberate animal activity was the corpse of a salmon skilfully filleted by an otter. Human predators were represented by a gun cartridge and a waterproof pouch for freshly killed game.

None of this river-borne rubbish is particularly noticeable, and the Liddel is probably as clean as it was three centuries ago, when the poet-physician Dr John Armstrong said of its 'sacred flood' in his inexplicably popular poem, *The Art of Preserving Health* (1744), 'not a purer stream . . . rolls toward the western main'.

> May still thy hospitable swains be blest
> In rural innocence; thy mountains still
> Teem with the fleecy race; thy tuneful woods
> For ever flourish. . . .

The rubbish described above must have been generated by a very small number of people, and it would not be surprising if a local reader of this book remembered learning to ride on the pink-handlebar bicycle or came to claim the umpire's chair. The 'swains' and artisans of Liddesdale occasionally use the river as an industrial conveyor belt but they are not unusually prone to dropping litter. The largest settlement upstream is Newcastleton (home to eight hundred and fifty people), and the total population within jettisoning distance of the Liddel's banks is certainly less than one thousand. If this equation of detritus and population density is reliable, the amount of garbage transported by the Tyne, the Trent or the Thames must be truly colossal.

In one respect only, the Liddel is an archaeological treat. After three years of sporadic beachcombing, I had assembled a small museum of bricks which I embedded in river sand to form a pavement. Each brick was stamped with the name of the brickworks and sometimes its place of origin. They had come from all over northern England and southern Scotland. There were astoundingly heavy bricks from Accrington in Lancashire, marked 'NORI' ('Iron, whichever way you put it'), noted for their use in the foundations of the Blackpool Tower and the Empire State Building. There were bricks from the Pentland Hills and the Cumbrian coast. Many of them had probably tumbled into the river when the Waverley Line was demolished after its closure in 1969.

The oldest bricks, from the 1870s and 80s, were those produced in Corbridge on the Roman Wall and at the Buccleuch Terra Cotta works in Sanquhar. The name 'Sanquhar', imprinted on the bricks, comes from the Celtic '*sean caer*', referring to the 'old fort' above the town. These were the only river-borne reminders of Roman or Celtic civilization. Everything older than the mid-nineteenth century had long since been atomized or ferried off to the Solway Firth, and perhaps those bricks and bottles will turn out to be the last pre-war items to make the journey this far down the Liddel. Eventually, all evidence of human life will have been evacuated from the catchment area, and only the scratched and rounded stones brought by ancient glaciers will remain.

I relished that sense of emptiness, unaware that more substantial treasures would come to light in other ways. The historical coordinates of the place were plotting themselves on a mental map, and soon, that silent fourth dimension would seem more populous and busy than the present.

❖

A few weeks after the melting of the ice, the roads were clear of snow and floodwater no longer filled the ditches. Winter seemed to have exhausted itself for the time being. Before it could recover or change its mind, we decided to set off towards the river's source, up the valley of the Liddel and into the heartland of the reivers.

Food was prepared and information collected: I had assembled various scraps on the history of Liddesdale, its inhabitants and early explorers. The idea was simply to provide mental sustenance on the journey, and perhaps to recreate a past discovery of that world within a world. I had learned about the expeditions of Mary Queen of Scots in 1566 and Walter Scott in the late eighteenth century: they seemed to be the only historical personages to have ventured into that valley with something other than destruction on their minds. Their itineraries would give the ride a goal; the rest would be left to chance and the weather.

We checked the roadworthiness of the bikes and watched the changing sky. Ideally, we would have hired a pair of ponies, but the whispering and ticking of the chains on the sprockets suggested the precision of a time machine, and the light shower which fell from a gleaming sky as we left the house guaranteed a certain authenticity.

PART TWO

8

Blind Roads

In the late summer of 1792, a young lawyer from Edinburgh who was practising at the circuit court in Jedburgh entered Liddesdale from the north. A few days before, he had been exploring the 'savagely romantic' country to the east, gazing in wonderment at Latin inscriptions on stones built into walls and used as gateposts: 'These have been all dug up from the neighbouring Roman wall, which is still in many places very entire, and gives a stupendous idea of the perseverance of its founders.'

Walter Scott had then returned to Jedburgh, but since the weather was holding good and he had recently made the acquaintance of a reliable guide, he set off again, this time into the 'wild and inaccessible district of Liddesdale, particularly with a view to examine the ruins of the famous castle of Hermitage' – 'that grim and remote fastness' – 'and to pick up some of the ancient riding ballads, said to be still preserved among the descendants of the moss-troopers'.

There was not a single inn and only one permanent bridge in all of Liddesdale. A reluctant visitor who had been commissioned to write a 'statistical account' of the parish, noted that 'for about 16 miles along the Liddal, the road lay rather *in* the river than *upon its banks*, the only path being in what is called *the Watergate*, and the unhappy traveller must cross it at least 24 times in that extent'. The alternative was to take to the bogs and mosses, and to scan that smiling landscape of sinkholes and quagmires for the 'blind roads'. This peculiar variety of upland way was defined by Scott as

> a tract so slightly marked by the passengers' footsteps, that it can but be
> traced by a slight shade of verdure from the darker heath around it, and,

being only visible to the eye when at some distance, ceases to be distin-
guished while the foot is actually treading it.

Few people came into Liddesdale from Carlisle and the south.
Drovers and tinkers usually passed farther west, by way of Gretna.
The northern route was reputed impassable, though, by then,
road-builders had started work. It was Walter Scott who, in a sense,
declared the road open by appearing in Liddesdale in an open carriage. His little gig was the first wheeled vehicle ever seen in the
valley, and 'the people stared with no small wonder at a sight which
many of them had never witnessed in their lives before'.

Until Scott published the ballads he collected in the isolated
farmsteads and placed that remote valley on the map of European
Romanticism – from which it has long since disappeared – Liddesdale
was still recognizable as the bastard realm of reivers to whom 'England
and Scotland is all one' and who, as an English warden had noted, 'fear
no officers of either side', being 'so well provided with stolen horses,
and the strengths they lie in so fortified with bog and wood'. The
young lawyer found his sheep-farming and smuggling hosts warm and
generous with their devilled ducks and whisky-punch. He gamely
subjected himself to the 'hideous and unearthly' sounds of 'riding
music' with which the natives of Liddesdale recounted the deeds of
their dubious ancestors. According to Scott's guide, he 'suited himsel'
to everybody'; he 'never made himsel' the great man, or took ony airs
in the company'.

The twenty-one-year-old barrister from Edinburgh who had the
motley horde of sheepdogs eating out of his hand was probably the
first officer of the law ever to be made welcome in Liddesdale. His
private descriptions of what had been, almost within living memory,
'the bloodiest valley in Britain' are written with the indomitable
cheerfulness which served him as a suit of armour, but his novels and
ballads express the fear that was felt by every visitor and which was
only partly inspired by the inhabitants and their history.

✻

In summer, along the upper reaches of the Liddel twinkling over the
tree-shaded shingle of its gentle bends, the empty land can appear so
green and fertile that it seems to have suffered some inexplicable

depopulation. I first saw it through the windows of the X95 bus to Edinburgh. The X95 is the kind of bus normally found only in a city. It has no seat belts and, despite the length of the journey, no toilet. An illuminated panel indicates the next stop and the final destination with figures calibrated to an urban time scale: '*Next stop: Albert Street. Terminating at Edinburgh bus station in 217 minutes.*' Once out in open country, it looks like a runaway bus and the printed banner above the windows sounds a sardonic warning: 'X95 – Make Each Journey An Adventure.'

That morning, thrown off course by a landslip, the X95 headed up the Liddel, following the line of the old railway towards the col of Whitrope Hass, known locally as 'the Edge'. This had been, according to an 1883 article on 'English Express Trains', 'undoubtedly the hardest of all the routes in the kingdom along which any train runs at express speed'. The driver hustled his unwieldy bus up the narrowing valley, twisting it over humpbacked bridges, until the hills seemed to crowd in with a menacing, beggarly appearance. The moors stretching away on either side still deserve the epithets used by William Camden in 1600: 'leane, hungry, and a wast'.

The next bus stop lay twenty miles to the north in the town of Hawick. We descended into a gloomy valley which, despite unfolding views of deserted heath, gave a curious sense of claustrophobia. 'The Edge' itself is the northern limit of Liddesdale. It stands on a watershed line, which, though both sides are in Scotland, forms a more substantial boundary than the political division of the two nations. I later heard a bus driver complaining about the traffic in Carlisle: 'It's better on the other side of the world' – by which he meant, not the Antipodes, but the land which lies 'ower the Edge'.

The man at the wheel of the diverted X95 that day was a skilful and experienced driver, but he was visibly unsettled by the lack of progress and the bleakness of the hills, and when at last we re-entered the modern world, he tottered out of the cab with an ashen face, held out his arms to the colleague who was to take the bus on to Edinburgh, and said, 'Look at this – ma hands're shakin'! Twenty miles o' single-track road!'

✻

On the day we cycled up into Liddesdale, I was hoping in particular
to find the route by which medieval travellers from the outside world
had entered that 'den of thieves'. The sparsely populated Liddesdale
route had been used by invading armies from Scotland – Áedán of Dál
Riata in 603, William Wallace in 1297 – but their exact itineraries
are unknown, and this might have remained a 'blind road' of British
history without the evidence of a journey undertaken into that dark
dale during the blackest days of the reivers.

The twenty-three-year-old Queen of Scotland rode out from
Jedburgh early on the morning of 16 October 1566 with her maids
in waiting and a detachment of soldiers. After presiding over the
circuit court in Jedburgh, Mary Stuart had decided to obtain a first-
hand report from her lieutenant on the border, the Earl of Bothwell,
who, in Mary's words, '[employed] his persoun to suppres the insolence of the rebellious subjectis inhabiting the cuntreis lying ewest
[adjoining] the Marches of Ingland'. The Earl had been unable to
travel, having suffered a near-fatal sword wound at the hands of a
Liddesdale reiver called Little Jock Elliot. He was recovering in bed
inside the charmless fortress of the Hermitage, which guarded the
valley and which he had recently been forced to reconquer from a
jeering gang of Elliots.

It was a round trip of fifty miles, to be completed in a day: the
Hermitage was no place for a young queen to spend the night. This
was the height of the reiving season and Liddesdale was 'the most
offensive' of all the border regions. Fortunately, quite a few Armstrongs and Elliots had just been massacred by Bothwell's troops, and
it was twelve days yet to the full moon, when reivers were at their
most active.

The Queen's route can be pieced together from several accounts
and a trail of clues on the Ordnance Survey map: Queen's Mire,
Lady's Knowe, Lady's Sike and Lady's Well. These names are said to
mark the stages of her journey, though another Queen's Mire on an
entirely different route through Eskdale suggests that the name is the
Scots word 'quean', meaning 'young woman'. More tangible evidence
was provided by the archaeologist's favourite animal: two and a half
centuries after Mary's epic ride, a shepherd spotted an incongruous
object protruding from a molehill on the boggy moor of the Queen's
Mire above Hermitage Castle: a small, silk-lined case containing a

sixteenth-century French pocket watch. In such an inaccessible place, it was assumed, this glinting token of civilization could only have fallen from the baggage of the Queen.

*

We cycled along the English side of the Liddel to cross the border at Kershopefoot. Below the road to the west, sheep grazed peacefully on the disused railway line. They covered the distant hillsides like giant daisies. A farmer and his dog came rushing towards us on a quad bike and squealed to a halt. ' 'Ave yer sin any sheep?' he asked – meaning, of course, had we seen any sheep which were not where they should have been.

There was no sign of any fleecy renegades and nothing to show that Liddesdale had ever been a war zone. Of the pele towers which once dotted the valley, only a few piles of rubble now remain. The handsome stone mansion of Stonegarthside Hall (pronounced 'Sting-erside'), a mile from Kershopefoot, is associated with the reivers, but it was built for the Forsters in 1682, and its large windows and conveniently crow-stepped gables would have left it entirely defenceless.

The only intact monument from reiving days is a stone cross on the Scottish side of the Liddel. It stands on the outskirts of the village of Newcastleton. The Milnholm Cross is thought to commemorate an Armstrong laird who was foully murdered at Hermitage Castle in about 1320, but the monument which dominates the scene, higher up the hillside in the cemetery of the defunct parish of Ettleton, is an obelisk erected in 1852. Here, on the edge of what I assumed to have been a defiant bastion of Scottishness a few miles from England, was another clue to that cross-border community:

IN

AFFECTIONATE REMEMBRANCE

THIS MONUMENT

IS ERECTED

BY A NUMEROUS BODY

OF FRIENDS

ON BOTH SIDES OF THE BORDER

The deeply etched letters tell the tale of William Armstrong, a popular local man known as 'Sorbytrees' from the name of his farm

below Carby Hill across the valley. Returning late one evening from
Brampton market in April 1851 with his friend, Mr Elliot, Sorbytrees,
in a gay mood, had tapped at a window of the vicarage on the edge of
Walton Moss near the Roman Wall, hoping to speak with an old servant of his family. The vicar, precisely identified on the monument as
'the Revd Joseph Smith, incumbent of Walton, Cumberland', possess-
ing the valour of a mouse and a six-barrelled revolver recently
purchased in Carlisle, took aim at the darkness and, 'to the great grief
of the neighbourhood', shot William Sorbytrees 'without challenge or
warning'. The English judge acquitted 'the reverend gentleman' and
scolded the deceased for frightening honest people 'by making noises
at untimely hours'. The case was widely reported, even – under the
heading ' "Killing No Matter" in English Courts' – in the *New York
Times*, whose readers included a fair number of emigrant Armstrongs
and Elliots.

The flexed arm of the Armstrong family crest on the Milnholm
Cross suggests the threatening gesture of a ruffian. The obelisk, too, is
a giant finger raised in anger and defiance by friends 'on both sides of
the border'. The enemies of the Armstrongs and the Elliots were not
men from a rival country: they were the unfeeling agents of a power
seated in a distant city who owed their authority to nothing but paper
and ink.

Beyond the mile-long main street of Newcastleton, at the confluence of Liddel Water and Hermitage Water, the road turns off towards
Jedburgh and then, growing ever narrower, along a hedge-lined vale,
until a strangely hideous spectacle appears.

✤

Walter Scott is sometimes accused of having exaggerated the horrible-
ness of Hermitage Castle, presumably by people who have seen it
only in photographs or driven to it on a sunny day and heard the
hypocritical tinkle of its little burn. Under the usual glowering skies,
with the torrent raging and the great bulge of bare moorland behind,
its blank walls and the maw of its arch are the emotionless face of a
torturer or an executioner. In that desolate spot, in the months when
the castle is open to the public, a young woman sits in the shack which
houses Historic Scotland's ticket office like an Andromeda chained to
a rock in the ocean.

The fortress has tales to match its demeanour. It once belonged to the Douglas family. In 1342, Sir William Douglas (a.k.a. the Black Knight of Liddesdale) endungeoned his former friend and brother-in-arms, Sir Alexander Ramsay, and left him to die. Immediately above the dungeon was the granary from which, now and then, a grain would drop through a crack in the floor, enabling the prisoner to prolong his miserable life for another few days.

A short distance west of the Hermitage, at Braidlie Farm, a track leads off towards the Queen's Mire. It stumbles over the stony braes of a narrow glen to a ruined farmhouse, where, needlessly, we hid the bicycles. From there, it heads coaxingly up the hillside in the direction from which the Queen arrived, before disappearing into a sea of tussocks on a bed of black, peaty mud.

Only the drystone sheepfolds broke the monotony of the moor. For every foot gained in altitude, there were several feet to climb – onto and down from each tussock. On the skyline, the cols of Windy Swire and Moss Patrick Swire were as clear as beacons, but the process of negotiating the mire was so engrossing that, whenever we stopped to look up, the twin cols seemed to have shifted their position. The sun was sinking and it began to look as though we would have to turn back if we were to reach home before dark, when suddenly we found ourselves on a firm and grassy surface running like the wake of a ship through the mire.

The track had been invisible from a distance, and although we lost all trace of it for about fifty yards, we picked it up again closer to the top of the ridge. Certain types of boulder clay, compacted by rollers or, in this case, by hooves, become solid enough to form a road embankment or even an airstrip – unless the clay dries out completely, which is unlikely to have happened on the Queen's Mire. This must have been the old way over the hills to Teviotdale and the towns of Hawick and Jedburgh.

There was only one obvious discrepancy with the tale of Queen Mary's journey: for miles around, not a single molehill was to be seen. The flint-packed soil was no more than ankle deep and, where subsidence had exposed a cross-section, quite wormless. Even assuming that a watch case might have been excavated by an animal which rarely turns up anything larger than a walnut, what would a mole have been doing fifteen hundred feet above sea level on a tussocky morass when its relatives were hard at work in lower Liddesdale, clearing out their tunnels to the despair of Mr Blakey's clients?

Some months later, in the Mary Queen of Scots House museum in Jedburgh, where furry toy moles peep out from every corner, I learned that, apart from the watch, the Queen or one of her maids had also dropped an enamelled thimble case on the mire. The same display cabinet contained a stirrup of iron and leather 'found on the route taken by Mary to Hermitage Castle and attributed to the royal party'. Other relics of the same journey were preserved in private collections: a silver spur, several bronze spurs and a gold signet ring. Over the ridge at Priesthaugh, a hoard of gold coins was unearthed, six of which bore the image of the Queen. They came into the possession of a Mr Elliot in 1795 and were 'supposed to have been deposited by some of the attendants of Queen Mary, when she visited Bothwell at Hermitage Castle'. I found no relics to add to this impressive total, but I did notice several half-buried fragments of old sheep trough. On that stony avenue, it clearly took a long time for objects to disappear.

Perhaps Liddesdale had not been such a backwater after all. Unless the Queen's attendants were extraordinarily bad at packing, the route over the reputedly impassable mire must have been extremely well travelled. Walter Scott himself observed that this 'pass of danger [exhibited], in many places, the bones of the horses which have been entangled in it'. The route to the Hermitage had been a highway, which would explain how Mary and her party, with only twelve hours of autumn daylight, managed to cover fifty miles on horseback, leaving enough time for refreshments and a meeting with Bothwell at the Hermitage.

Having only occasionally sat on, rather than actually ridden, a horse, I had overestimated the difficulty of journeying through the medieval borderlands. I later met two horsewomen who regularly ride across the bogs and mosses of Liddesdale and the fells to the north of Hadrian's Wall. One of them, a former lecturer in equine studies, finds the principal inconvenience to be the lowness of the gates, which, being designed for bog-trotting ponies, require most modern horse riders to dismount. The other woman, who sometimes drives the 127 bus, has often ridden her retired racehorse across the Bewcastle Waste and Walton Moss, where many a reiver escaped from a warden's posse. The horse, which is devoted to its mistress, will happily traverse the boggy terrain, even if the black water comes up to its fetlocks. If allowed, it will find its own way through the mire.

This is the kind of horse riding that the Catholic Bishop of Ross, John Lesley, described in the authoritative account of Border life included in his *Historie of Scotland* (1578). Reivers fleeing from government troops would 'entice their pursuers into some of the most intricate parts of the marshes',

> . . . which, though to appearance they are green meadows, and as solid as the ground, are nevertheless seen, upon a person's entering upon them, to give way, and in a moment to swallow him up into the deep abyss. Not only do the robbers themselves pass over these gulfs with wonderful agility and lightness of foot, but even they accustom their horses to cross many places with their knees bent, and to get over where our footmen could scarcely dare to follow; and, chiefly on this account, they seldom shoe their horses.

✻

The more I saw of the wilds where the reivers had lurked and plotted mischief, the more implausible the hellishness of the border badlands appeared. Indoors, in an urban setting, pictures of dark skies and rain can make the imagination quail. Even for a borderer, it goes against the grain to leave a warmish house and ride out into a rainstorm. But if the downpour comes gradually, introducing itself with sporadic drizzle before the incessant chatter of rain and hail, the mind and body can adjust to the inescapable companionship of the elements.

Adaptation is more a question of habit than equipment. In 2013, I witnessed the Scottish stage of the Tour of Britain. The peloton, coming from the direction of Newcastleton, was to pass along the southern edge of the Debatable Land above the Liddel. About fifteen local people had gathered at an exposed crossroads to see the riders whizz by. Many of the spectators were estate workers and sheep farmers. There was also a man in a wheelchair. A powerful gale was blowing up the valley, in precisely the wrong direction for the riders. The heavens opened and torrents began to rocket off the hillside. No one moved: they stood waiting patiently, all without umbrellas and some without hats. Twenty-five minutes later, it was still raining and there was still no sign of the riders. At last, the wretched peloton came into view down the road, moving more slowly than I have ever seen professional riders move. For once, it was possible to make out every grimacing face – the streaming stubble of Wiggins, the gleaming mask of Quintana. The sopping spectators waited for a few more moments then slowly dispersed, apparently quite happy to have seen the race pass through.

Even two centuries ago, this mental weather-proofing was an impressive sight to an outsider. The author of the 'statistical account', who found Liddesdale 'an extremely wet district', was shocked to meet a farmer riding over the hills from Teviotdale without a greatcoat on his back. 'I ken very weel,' the farmer explained, 'though I were to tak twae, they wad be wat through, and it's needless to burden baith mysel and the beast wi' wat claith.'*

Changing perceptions of simple physical realities can have a significant distorting effect on the writing of history. Both Bishop Lesley in the late 1500s and Walter Scott in the late 1700s noticed this 'odd prejudice . . . in favour of riding'. 'Every farmer rides well,' said Scott, 'and rides the whole day.' 'The truth is undeniable; they like to be on horseback, and can be with difficulty convinced that any one chooses walking from other motives than those of convenience or necessity.' According to Lesley, it was even considered 'a great disgrace' to go on foot. 'If . . . they be possessed of nimble horses, and have sufficient wherewith to ornament their own persons and those of their wives, they are by no means anxious about other pieces of household furniture.'

Scott's claim to have been the first to enter Liddesdale in a wheeled vehicle evokes a world of barbaric inconvenience, but that incongruous contraption manufactured in a city was no more a sign of the region's backwardness than the Ferrari which a prospective buyer of our house had apparently tried to drive down the lonning only to have it towed back to the tarmacked road by a very large and muddy tractor.

---

* 'I know full well that if I took two coats, they'd be wet through and there's no point burdening both myself and the animal with wet clothing.'

9

Harrowed

I had planned the trip to the Queen's Mire out of simple curiosity, having no thought of writing a book about the region in which we happened to have found a home. One of its attractions was its emptiness, in time as well as space. Queen Mary's expedition to the Hermitage seemed to be the only connection with the highways of British history. It was a reminder that the great events which would form the modern nation had all taken place elsewhere – the political and dynastic struggles, the English and Scottish Reformations, the first developments of an empire.

But in that emptiness lay an invitation or a challenge. Beyond a ridge that was no more distant than the horizon of a child's world, I had seen an unsuspected realm within the borderlands. Beneath the bog, there had been a road which joined towns in the north to the valley which slopes down to the Irish Sea. The few texts I had read for the trip suggested that the historical irrelevance of border society was an illusion, just as the moorland had seemed devoid of life until a plover or a curlew shot up from its nest.

In the writings of Bishop Lesley and Walter Scott, I had the first inklings of a world with a history of its own. Though it was too exceptional in many ways to serve the purposes of general historians, it belonged to the history of Britain. It might even call into question the coherence and completeness of that history. The borderers had been considered important only in so far as they could be conscripted as footnotes into the national narrative. Serious misconceptions had resulted: the notion that a borderer must have been, at heart, either English or Scottish and that the Debatable Land was the unviable remnant of an otherwise extinct world. But it was the other great divide in British society – between Catholic and Protestant – which first opened a door into that world and showed how much persistence and luck it would take to recover it.

In apparent contradiction of the ghastly facts, Bishop Lesley had asserted in 1578 that a reiver never wilfully shed the blood of his opponents,

> ... for they have a persuasion that all property is common by the law of nature, and is therefore liable to be appropriated by them in their necessity, but that murder and other injuries are prohibited by the Divine law. ... They think the art of plundering so very lawful, that they never say their prayers more fervently, or have more devout recurrence to the beads of their rosaries, than when they have made an expedition, as they frequently do, of forty or fifty miles, for the sake of booty.

The Roman Catholic bishop's unexpected portrait of devout and principled reivers has often been dismissed as a deliberate lie. George MacDonald Fraser, understandably incensed by romantic portrayals of those homicidal 'merry men', found the bishop's account suspect in the extreme and wondered whether Lesley himself had taken part in a raid ... One of Lesley's main sources was his friend, Mary Queen of Scots, whom Fraser considered equally suspect, both as a woman and as a Catholic: 'In our time, she would probably have been a highly successful fashion model and jet setter', but 'her perception and handling of affairs was on a par with her taste in men, which was deplorable'.

The bishop's error was one of interpretation rather than fact. Assuming that adherence to a moral precept must inevitably be religious, he misconstrued the reivers' code of honour as an expression of Christian faith. Walter Scott's informed opinion was that, if the borderers 'remained attached to the Roman Catholic faith rather longer than the rest of Scotland', this was probably the result of 'total indifference upon the subject'. The reivers were neither Catholic nor Protestant nor even, in an orthodox sense, religious. For a reiver, the greatest disgrace was not excommunication but ostracism: if a man failed to keep his word, one of his gloves or a picture of his face was stuck on the end of a spear or a sword and paraded about at public meetings. This 'bauchling' was considered a punishment worse than death.

The Great Monition of Cursing (p. 33), which was written to be recited from pulpits throughout the Borders, would have fallen on deaf ears if it fell on any ears at all. Reivers occasionally burned churches along with barns and cow sheds, while priests and curates, or people claiming to be such, took part in raids. The only sign that reivers attended religious ceremonies is an unconfirmed report that the right hand of a male child was held during baptism so that, untouched by holy water, it would be able to 'deal the more deadly or "unhallowed" blows to its enemies'.

As everywhere else, there was a belief in fairies, witches and ghosts, and in the efficacy of magic wells and potions. There was either no concern about the fate of the soul after death, or no understanding of a minister's purpose. One of the few men who tried to convert the heathen northerners, in the 1560s and 70s, might just as well have been a missionary in a foreign land:

> [Bernard] Gilpin did preach at a church in Redesdale where there was neither minister, nor bell, nor book, but one old book which was set forth in King Edward's time, and an old psalter torn to pieces, and he sent the clerk to give warning he would preach. In the meantime there came a man riding to the church style [the churchyard gate] having a dead child laid before him over his saddle crutch, and cried to Mr. Gilpin, not knowing him, 'Come, parson, and do the cure', and laid down the corpse and went his way.

The borderers' beliefs seem on the whole to have tended to the practical. Several local people have told me that, in the days of the reivers, only the women were buried in consecrated ground. The existence of female-only graveyards is considered plausible because a man is always more likely to be seen tippling in a pub than kneeling in a church. This shows the unreliability of what is loosely termed 'oral history'. Most local people have read at least one book on the reivers, and several books recount the traditional tale of a visitor to Bewcastle who, remarking on a curious (but unattested) dearth of men's names on the gravestones, was told by an old woman, 'Oh, Sir, they're a' buried at that weary Caerl' – meaning that all the

men had ended up on the gallows in that confounded ('weary') city
of Carlisle.

❉

A stone slab inside the entrance of the Armstrongs' pele tower at Hollows (p. 86), known as 'the dead stone', is said to cover the tomb of
several Armstrongs, though the thresholds of other towers are believed
to conceal the remains of enemies, placed there so that they would be
trampled on every day. I despaired of finding any real evidence of this
pagan practice until, one afternoon, I was cycling along a quiet back
road near a boundary of the Debatable Land.

For some distance ahead, the entire width of the road was filled by
a flock of sheep. The flock had divided itself into two contingents: the
able-bodied had clip-clopped on ahead while the sick and the lame,
some of whose relatives were already rotting in the hedgerow, hobbled
along so slowly that the sheepdog was able to perform two functions
at once, spraying every gatepost and returning in time to chivvy the
invalids.

The owner of the sheep apologized for the delay. As we waited for
the animals to progress, we talked about the weather and the landscape. He pointed to a farm in the middle distance:

'That's mine,' he said.

It was the first time I had seen the place, though its name was
familiar from a sixteenth-century map which shows it as the site of a
stone house or a pele tower, and so I asked, 'Wasn't there a tower there
once upon a time?'

'Aye,' he said, 'there used to be a water tower in that field, but it
wasn't needed any more.'

'*Before* that, I mean. Wasn't there a pele tower or something?'

His eyes lit up. 'The reivers! Aye, there was – and it's us that found
it! We was puttin' in a new door, but the wall was that thick you
couldn't drill through it . . . They had to be careful in them days, didn't
they? People comin' to steal the sheep and a' that.'

He paused, then continued in a conspiratorial tone, talking to a
stranger on a bicycle who was probably a tourist passing through the
region: 'We found somethin' else as well . . . '

'What was that?'

'Bodies! All lined up one aside t'other.'

'*Human* bodies?'

'Aye, but not exactly bodies. Skellingtons, y'know, from back then. Naught but banes.'

A few years before, the ploughman had turned up a burial where no chapel had ever stood and stopped the tractor to show the farmer. He pointed out the place to me: 'Up yonder, in front o' the house.'

'And is that known?' I asked. 'I mean, did you report it?'

He had the gleeful, slightly guilty expression of someone who has got the better of the authorities.

'Well, y'know 'ow the police can be aboot such things . . . '

'Mm, yes,' I lied. 'So what did you do?'

He looked around at the empty fields as though a constable might be concealed in a ditch or watching from a bush, and then, with raised eyebrows and teeth bared in a grin, said, in a surprisingly loud voice, 'I harrowed them under!'

Perhaps noticing something in my expression, he added, in order to excuse himself or to invite me to join him in the historical joke, 'Onyways, it was prob'ly Armstrongs from ower there, come to steal the sheep!'

By the time I reached home an hour later, I knew that something would have to be written about this neglected region where nature and humans conspired to destroy the evidence of the past. In the weeks that followed, I discovered the great treasure of border history in the archives of the Scottish and English border officers, and those empty landscapes began to be populated with identifiable individuals.

Only the stone footings of their towers remained, the people themselves had been illiterate and many of their ballads had probably been written by Walter Scott or professional balladeers, but the thousands of documents preserved in the State Papers of Scotland, England and France were a stupendously detailed record of that dark age of British history. There were minute accounts of reiving expeditions and official raids conducted by the wardens; there were verbal 'maps' describing the location of every hidden settlement and reiver's lair; there were the reports of spies and diplomats, the letters of kings and queens, cries for help from the beleaguered frontier and disquisitions on the ancient laws and customs of the Borders.

Historians had plundered those records for examples of the chaos and the moral vacuum which seemed to be caused by the lack of central government, but in that medieval Babel of squabbling, frightened, laughing and sinister voices, a world came to life with its own battles, feuds and dynasties, its peculiar patterns of settlement and internal migration, its history and legends, and even its own laws. And at the heart of that world was something stranger than even the best-informed wardens had suspected: a land incalculably older than Scotland or England, known only to the people who buried the dead on their doorsteps and who recognized no lords or nation but their own.

10

'Loveable Custumis'

It is one of the joys of studying history that first impressions are always wrong. Truth is proverbially stranger than fiction, but only because no guiding mind has contrived to make it credible. The truth is that the lawless borderlands of the Middle Ages had a fully developed, indigenous legal system. A civil and criminal code administered by reivers sounds like an ironic euphemism, yet it was described in almost identical terms in documents spanning several centuries and adopted, with few modifications, by the governments of England and Scotland.

The laws and customs of the borderers were first written down in 1249, after the perambulation of the forty-eight Scottish and English knights. The *Leges Marchiarum* (March law or Border law) were distinct from the laws of Scotland and England and had remained in use throughout the Borders for many generations:

> The lawis of marchis . . . are antient and loveable custumis, ressavit [accepted] and standing in force as law, be lang use, and mutual consent of the Wardans and subjectis of baith the realmis, as fund be [found by] experience to be gude and proffitabill for the quietnes of the bordouris, and gude nichtbourheid amangis the pepill, inhabitantis of baith the natiounis.

The fact that these 'loveable' (commendable) customs were the same on both sides of the border suggests a very early origin: March law might have been the last and still lively remnant of the remote period when the post-Roman kingdoms of Strathclyde and Northumbria had straddled the future frontier.

One of the few consistently sensible policies of both governments was to codify and, in principle, uphold those laws and customs from a Britain which no longer existed. Instead of imposing 'foreign' legislation passed in Edinburgh or Westminster, they recognized the usefulness of rules which were 'commoun and indifferent to the subjectis of baith the realmis' and which, far from being an imposition, reinforced the community which adhered to them. Some of the worst disasters in the administration of the frontier were caused by a failure to apply or to comprehend the efficacy of March law.

It provided a system of justice and compensation involving complex financial calculations and the use of hostages or 'pledges', which prevented criminal acts from igniting feuds and reprisals. It set procedures for the recovery of stolen goods and, in effect, established a domestic police force. It regulated the traditional days of truce on which conflicts were resolved, and it ensured compliance with the courts' decisions. Despite its antiquity, it was flexible enough to cope with the imposition of a national frontier: no man could be found guilty unless the allegations were supported by at least one of his compatriots.

It was obvious that an individual warden, who might be lazy, corrupt or cowardly, could never bring lasting order to a region controlled by rebellious clans, but I was surprised to find such institutional orderliness behind the mayhem. The home-grown system of laws was so effective that a legal historian has recently proposed it as a model for policy makers hoping to bring stability to zones of long-standing conflict. This 'unique and decentralized system of cross-border criminal law' proves that, 'contrary to conventional wisdom', even when the two sides are 'bitter enemies', 'central authority is not needed to create or enforce a legal system governing intergroup interactions'.

Since the reivers of the Anglo-Scottish border had burned and plundered far and wide, the question itself seemed questionable: were the reivers restrained and anarchy held at bay by the power of the two nations, or was it thanks to those 'ancient and loveable customs' that the Marches had been able to function as a buffer zone? Those respected traditions might explain why some hardy individuals had been able to live in this blighted zone, but was it really possible that the borderers' boisterous society had helped the two nations to coexist and in this way laid the foundations of a united kingdom? It was only when the reivers themselves emerged from the records that this fantastic vision began to look like the historical truth.

✲

Some of the reivers whose outlandish names appear in the official papers of England and Scotland have become quite famous: Archie Fire-the-Braes, Buggerback, Davy the Lady, Jok Pott the Bastard, Wynkyng Will and a hundred other colourfully named members of the merry band. These Cumbrian cowboys were the hell-raising night-riders who terrorized the frontier and cocked a snook at the authorities for a century or more. Plucked from their particular time and place, and labelled 'the much-feared' or 'the scourge of the borders', they look like miniatures in a museum battle scene. These spine-chilling felons are the stars of reiver tourism. Who could fail to tremble at the thought of 'Nebless Clem' or 'Fingerless Will' or even (if they knew what it meant) 'Dog Pyntle Elliot'?* These, it is supposed, were the medieval Armstrongs, Elliots, Grahams and Nixons whose modern equivalents make honest people's lives a misery and who appear in the *News and Star* and the *Cumberland News*, branded with the *bons mots* of magistrates and judges: 'a danger to society', 'a one-man crime-wave', etc.

The friends and relations of Archie, Clem, Jok and Will would have been amazed and perhaps delighted. The startling fact is that, unlike their twenty-first-century descendants who break into garden sheds, steal farm gates, rustle sheep and elicit groans of recognition from court officials, most of these reivers took part in only one raid. The majority of individuals named in the records never went reiving at all. The records are certainly comprehensive, since no one was likely to miss the ransacking of several farms or a small town. Yet 'the Bastarde of Glenvoren', 'Ill-Drowned Geordie', 'Ill-Wild Will'† and dozens of other notorious reivers are mentioned only once. These names were not titles bestowed by an awestruck society, they were simply 'to-names', to distinguish, for example, 'Gleyed John' and 'Jock Halflugs' from all the other John Nixons and Jock Elliots who did not have a squint or mutilated ears.

---

* 'Nebless' = noseless; 'pyntle' = penis.
† 'Ill-Wild' = ill-willed.

For most of these men, the reiving expedition was a once-in-a-lifetime adventure and, as in other cattle-raiding societies, a rite of passage. For every ballad commemorating a famous raid, there must have been a thousand well-worn tales of the glorious, hectic day when grandfather earned the right to be called a man by burning down a Tynedale barn or making off with a Cheviot farmer's sheep. The distant voice of the reivers can be heard not only in the polished ballads but also on the terraces of Brunton Park, home of Carlisle United football club, where the insults still travel in the same direction, from North Cumbria, 'the land that's mountainous and green' (as the chant has it) towards Newcastle and the north-east, the home of 'Geordie scum'.

An entire season's reiving by men of the West Marches in 1589–90 is recorded in a list of 'bills' or official complaints compiled for the English and Scottish wardens. The biggest raid was carried out by two hundred and four riders, mostly Armstrongs and Elliots. A typical raiding party was much smaller. The document lists a total of fifty-three raids, involving more than a thousand reivers, and in all those perilous, high-speed excursions over moonlit moorland, only three men were killed and two 'maimed'. Another document lists unresolved complaints relating to offences committed by men of Liddesdale between 1579 and 1587. As 'unredressed' offences, these may well have had an element of malice. A total of one hundred and twenty-three houses were burned by more than two thousand reivers in seven raids. Eleven men were killed, but all eleven perished in two raids led by the exceptionally violent and remorseless Kinmont Willie, whom we shall meet again.

By comparison with medieval sporting events, reiving of the traditional kind was a remarkably safe activity – even by comparison with the lively local tradition of jumping off the single-arch bridge on the border at Penton into the shallow pools of the rock-strewn Liddel, which several inhabitants of Carlisle have described to me with a mixture of nostalgia and amazement at their youthful stupidity. The object of a reiving expedition was not to kill another man but to take his animals and whatever else came to hand, preferably with stealth and cunning. Sometimes, the owner himself was stolen so that he could be held to ransom.

Some of those expeditions were like major house removals, and perhaps reiving expertise is the origin of the haulage and removal businesses which are still a mainstay of the Cumbrian economy. One of the largest raids in the winter of 1589–90 was directed against a wealthy servant's house on the estate of Sir John Forster in Hethpool, two miles inside England in the northern Cheviots. On the night of 3 November, thirty riders arrived from the west and set about preparing eighteen animals and almost a hundred household items for a thirty-mile overnight journey: 'a steil cap', a sword, a dagger, some knives and spears; breeches, doublets, shirts, a cloak and a jerkin; a complete woman's wardrobe, including nightgowns and ribbons; some sheets and coverlets, a cauldron, a pan, a bolt of hemp, a pair of cards (for carding wool), four 'childrens coates', six shillings, a shroud and, impressively, 'a fetherbed'.

Their ponies laden with kitchenware and underwear and, somehow, the feather bed (probably a mattress rather than a frame), the cackling band turned for home with a wonderful tale to tell. This was a time-honoured and, in some ways, orderly enterprise. While the reivers celebrated the haul and their wives and sisters tried on the garments, the 'bereived' made a careful note, as though for an insurance company, of every stolen item and its monetary value. The list was then submitted to the wardens, who would present it at the next day of truce.

Most cases were satisfactorily resolved, but some were not, and here, when all the records are indiscriminately lumped together under the same heading, is the source of the great and lasting confusion. On the one hand, there were the once-in-a-lifetime reivers who usually returned the stolen goods or paid remuneration. Then there were the murderous reiver armies of a few petty warlords such as Kinmont Willie, hardened by military experience in the service of one nation or the other. These were men who cynically exploited a tradition, in the same way that knife-wielding hooligans masquerade as football supporters.

Others were engaged in long-running family feuds which were invariably bloody but constrained by the sharp focus of their hatred. These in turn could become confused with the wardens' punitive raids, some of which were inspired by greed or revenge. And finally, in the years of famine at the end of the sixteenth century when order broke down as far south as Penrith, there were wandering gangs of desperadoes and professional thieves whose names were known to no one and who came from much farther afield. An especially gruesome example, which has often been quoted as a representative episode of reiver history, took place at Caldbeck, ten miles south of Carlisle, in the winter of 1592–3. Six thieves broke into the house of a man called Sowerby.

> They sett him on his bare buttockes upon an hote iron, and there they burned him and rubbed him with an hote gridle about his bellie and son-dry other partes of his body to make him give up his money, which they took, under £4.

This brutal burglary was described in the report as 'a speciall outrage', in other words, as an exceptional event occurring outside the usual run of reiving and well beyond the zone controlled by the reiving clans. In the borderlands north and east of Carlisle, a band of sadistic thieves would have found it impossible to operate with impunity.

These records which seem to paint a picture of unremitting violence are full of unexpected vistas like the side-valleys of the Liddesdale hills. Perhaps the most surprising is the fact that, apart from organized reiving, practically no crimes were reported. In 1599, the English warden of the East March, Robert Carey, correcting Queen Elizabeth's assumption that reiving occurred 'in the dead of winter', explained that reivers were active only from Michaelmas to Martinmas (29 September to 11 November), when the fells were 'good and dry' and the cattle strong enough to be driven. Outside the reiving season, he wrote, there was 'great quiet and little or no stealing'.

Some crimes were almost unknown. In his first year as warden of the Middle March, Robert Carey arrested and hanged two 'gentlemen theeves' who 'robbed and took purses from travellers on the highways'. The incident, which he recalled in his *Memoirs*, would have been scarcely worth mentioning elsewhere in England, but highway robbery was 'a theft that was never heard of in those parts before'. A medieval borderland crossed by major north–south routes but devoid of highwaymen is a curious image and the absence of ordinary felonies on the wild frontier is almost as intriguing as the clue to a crime.

✤

On the day we cycled back to England from the Queen's Mire, past the hamlet of Hermitage where Walter Scott met his first Liddesdale sheep farmer, and the solitary cottages with their warning 'Farm Watch' signs, I wondered whether criminal behaviour inevitably occurs near borders, where one jurisdiction meets another. Kegs of contraband liquor found their way from inlets on the Solway Firth into the depths of Liddesdale, where the young lawyer from Edinburgh often breakfasted on 'run brandy'.

Even in a united kingdom, a border between constabularies or a minor difference in the law can give a small advantage to a thief escaping with a piece of farming equipment or a sheep. In the summer of 2015, on the road from Longtown to the border, I noticed a tall, neatly dressed man kneeling in the verge. He had roped off a small area as though it was a crime scene. Inside the cordon was a square block of carved sandstone bearing a round, wrought-iron plaque marked 'Carlisle – 12 miles'. It might have been a picture in a book of obscure occupations: 'The Milestone Mender', with his paintbrush, scrubber, bag of gravel, some weed matting and a hammer.

I remarked on the almost complete sequence of milestones on the old turnpike road and said that, where I used to live, they would all have been stolen long ago. 'Ah!', he said, 'but they *do* get stolen.' This is why he was setting the plaque deeper in the stone and reinforcing the metal bolts which hold it in place. He explained that while English scrap-metal merchants now had to obtain written proof of each item's provenance, the trade was still unregulated in Scotland. Only recently, on the road to Brampton, one of those historical treasures had been prised off with a crowbar and spirited across the border to a Scottish merchant a few miles away who would ask no questions.

Twenty-first-century Liddesdale is hardly a den of thieves. In the absence of any visible police presence, a certain amount of local policing helps to maintain order. A local farmer whose animals had a tendency to wander onto a neighbour's property opened his front door one day to discover an errant sheep attached to the door-knob with a rope. In another, legally more complex incident, an estate owner erected a small fishing hut on land over which he owned the fishing rights. A group of anglers from another part of the country, traipsing over a field and idling away the time on a riverbank, is not usually a welcome sight to a working farmer. The hut mysteriously caught fire, its fireproof replacement fell into the river and, as though the matter had been settled once and for all in a court of law, no further attempt was made to provide shelter for the anglers. This might sound criminal to a city-dweller, but it has a powerful echo of the old law according to which no man shall 'set stob and staik' (erect a permanent structure) in the Debatable Land (p. 118).

On that day, we reached Newcastleton from the north, where the mile-long street stretches away in a straight line towards England. Stopping at Elliots the butchers, we picked up a copy of the latest *Copshaw Clatter*.* This useful publication contains a regular police report. Sometimes, in exceptional circumstances – for example, after the sighting of a 'suspicious vehicle' – local people are advised to lock their doors when they leave the house. The following, untypically dramatic list of incidents is taken from the September 2015 issue:

> 8th June – Sudden death in the village.
>
> 19th June – Theft of fencing from field at bottom of village.
>
> 22nd June – Vehicle blocking road at Signal Box Cottage: lorry became stuck while attempting to turn.
>
> 24th June – Alarm activation at Health Centre. Accidental.
>
> 1st July – Alarm activation at Costcutter. All in order.
>
> 21st July – Report of concern for a person's well-being.

Then came the following litany:

> 31st July – Theft housebreaking, Riccarton Farm.
>
> 31st July – Theft housebreaking, Hewisbridge Cottage.
>
> 31st July – Theft housebreaking, Mountain View.
>
> 31st July – Theft housebreaking, Steele Road End Cottage.
>
> 31st July – Theft housebreaking, Dinlabyre.

The sequence of places shows that the burglars were following the old reiving route from Teviotdale, crossing the watershed by Note o'

---

* Copshawholm is the older name of Newcastleton (pp. 27–8n). 'Clatter' = gossip.

the Gate pass and down into Liddesdale along Liddel Water. The crimes are as yet unsolved, and it seems likely that the thieves were heading either for Langholm in the next valley or for the English border and the city of Carlisle, where stolen goods will always find a buyer. After this latter-day Liddesdale raid, the crime list returns to normal:

2nd August – Two youths annoying residents. Youths traced and spoken to.

6th August – Vehicle accident in Saughtree area. Minor injury to driver.

6th August – Request assistance with dog. Advice given.

11

Accelerated Transhumance

After the excursion to the Queen's Mire, the dense drizzle cum sea-fog called a 'Liddesdale drow' settled in, defying the waterproof guarantees of cycle-clothing manufacturers. A 'Liddesdale drow', pointedly defined in a Scottish dictionary of 1841 as 'a shower that wets an Englishman to the skin', is a phenomenon easily observed. I have often looked down over Liddesdale from the high roads in the east to see a dense bank of cloud funnelling up the valley, while the hillsides remained clear, and returned, quite dry, to find the lonning awash and the woods loud with waterfalls. This is the natural wonder which the warden of the West March Henry Scrope described to Queen Elizabeth's principal secretary Sir Francis Walsingham in 1584. He and his troops had stumbled into a dream world and become totally lost:

> I set furthe, the weather being verie fayre everie where in all the coun-trie, till we came to the boundes of Lyddesdale, wher their was growen suche a terrible and foggie myst as is wonderfull to be uttred . . . wherin my companye were mervelouslie seperated and dispersed from me . . . and all guydes who were there verie well acqueynted, were utterlie voy-de of any knowledge where they were! . . . The strangenes of this myst is the more, for that besydes that they of Lyddedales them selves, who had gathered them selfes togeather to have done some injorie to our people, were in like sorte in that countrie wholly dispersed one companye from an other – all the other countries rownde about everie waye bothe in England and Scotland . . . being verie cleare and fayre without either myst or rayne.

Perhaps the climatic conditions explained why there had been so little crime, apart from in the months of reiving.

The river sang its tireless song of the open sea. We went out every day, either to dig drainage channels on the lonning or to cycle up to the high peaks of the area in the hope of rising above the 'drow' to glimpse the Solway in the west and the sodden green pastures of the Debatable Land gleaming below the pine-blackened ridges.

The questions now took a different form. Reiving had been a crucial part of border society, but how had this kleptocratic system actually worked? Stealing other people's property hardly seemed a firm basis for an ordered society. For the ancient Celts, too, cattle-raiding had been a vital tradition. The Gauls had honoured Hercules the cattle thief as a founder of their race. In the early Irish epic 'The Cattle-Raid of Cooley', rustling was associated with the heroic deeds of a demi-god. A sixth-century poem of 'the Old North' (northern England and southern Scotland) celebrated the reiving prowess of Urien, King of Rheged. Other pastoral cultures had comparable myths and legends.

The border reivers have only a geographical connection with the 'Celtic' world. Few of them would have understood (still less uttered) the Gaelic phrase 'Fàilte gu Alba' which appears on signs welcoming drivers to Scotland at Kirkandrews and Gretna Green: Gaelic has not been widely spoken here since the fourteenth century. But as habitual cattle-raiders, they pose the same questions, and the records of their deeds offered some hope of answers.

Why, for example, did the human population of this ravaged zone increase throughout the years of reiving? Why was there no catastrophic decline in the domestic animal population? For that matter, why did all the livestock not end up in the West Marches, crammed into the overstocked barmkins of the Armstrongs, Elliots and Grahams? How – and why – were fresh sheep, cattle and oxen continually produced in the regions which suffered most from the reivers' predation?

When summer drew to a close, the mother of a 'riding' family is reputed to have said to her son, 'Ride, Rowley, hough's i' th' pot,' meaning that the last of the meat (the hock) was now being cooked and it was time to go and steal some more. An ancestor of Walter Scott made the same point by serving up a dish of spurs as a heavy hint to the menfolk. These tales may be folklore but they do express the apparent lopsidedness of the reivers' world.

Where was the incentive to spend every waking hour rearing animals and growing their fodder when their fattened limbs would only end up on someone else's table? Was this the incurable disease of optimism or simply the mindless comfort of an inherited way of life? 'I don't know why I bother' is a phrase on the lips of many a Cumbrian farmer. The reiving supermarkets have their own code of conduct which allows them to pay dairy farmers less than it costs to produce the milk. But even if the farmer's tax return shows zero profit, life can go on as before in the tiny farmhouse within its fortress of barns and sheds.

In a pastoral society unsupported by European farming subsidies, the answers to such conundrums usually lie with the animals themselves. Sheep and cows are transhumant. Instinct propels them from one meadow to the next. If a hedge or a fence has a gap, a sheep will find it, however small the gap or large the sheep. Cows migrate around a field with such inconspicuous slowness that, unless they are watched, they seem to teleport themselves to different parts of the field as though in a time-lapse film. Worshippers at the church of Kirkandrews near the Scots' Dike sometimes arrive for a service through meadows which appear deserted, only to find, when they leave the church, that the parking area is besieged by stationary cows.

Where the land is poor, the transhumant animals have to be driven, often great distances, to fresh pastures. Eventually, they are driven to market or, as usually happened in the borderlands, slaughtered before the onset of winter. Under the reiving system, cattle and sheep were forced to perform athletic feats of endurance and subjected to an intensified process of natural selection. Some grew stronger, the weak died and, over time, the stock improved. This accelerated transhumance is perhaps not unusual in frontier societies. The Texan cowboys of Larry McMurtry's *Lonesome Dove* are, in the natural way of things, rustlers as well as ranchers:

> Every now and then, about sundown, the Captain and Augustus and Pea and Deets would strap on guns and ride off into that darkness, into Mexico, to return about sunup with thirty or forty horses or perhaps a hundred skinny cattle. It was the way the stock business seemed to work

along the border ... Some of the skinny cattle spent their lives being chased back and forth across the Rio Grande.

In the Anglo-Scottish borders, this system was underpinned by March law. On the days of truce, the livestock producers would receive the value of their stolen animals – in money, corn or merchandise – exactly as though they had been sold at market. In many cases, the guilty party would pay twice the value of what had been stolen, along with what is now termed a 'victim surcharge', for all the time and trouble caused, equal to the original value. The attendant festivities – gambling and football, bartering and haggling, gossiping and courting – proceeded without the distraction of flocks and herds, while, at the assessor's table, every last sheep, cow, ox, horse and donkey, as well as all the household goods, were carefully recorded by a scribe. If anyone convicted of reiving tried to escape punishment and refused to pay, he would be subjected to the ignominy of 'bauchling' (p. 62): 'They think there cannot be a greater mark of disgrace than this, and esteem it a greater punishment even than an honourable death inflicted on the guilty person'.

It goes without saying that reiving was not a system deliberately devised by committees and upheld by general agreement. But for all the aggravation, fear and suffering it caused, it allowed a particular society in a remote, impoverished region to survive for many centuries. Seen from a distance, the movements of border livestock have a logic as elegant as that of a flight of geese. The natural crossroads of the West Marches, and especially the region of the Debatable Land, were an obvious destination. It is no coincidence that Longtown, which visitors from the south might mistake for a one-horse town, is home to the biggest sheep market in Britain.

✻

The reiving economy flourished at a time when one period of economic history was ending and another beginning. The pre-medieval world in which cattle were treated as common property was adapting to the modern world in which personal property had a specific, transferable value. The days of truce served to regulate the ebb and flow of assets. Especially when the wardens were in control, justice could be slow in coming, but in the meantime, the effects of reiving were mitigated by the much-maligned institution of blackmail. This was protection money or, more often, payment in kind to a powerful neighbour who assumed the responsibility of organizing a 'hot trod' whenever anything was stolen. A band of swift and tested reivers would set off in pursuit of the thieves, crossing – quite legally under March law – into Scotland or England to recover the goods.*

'Blackmail' is often cited as one of the reivers' two lasting contributions to the English language. The other is 'bereaved', said to have referred originally to a person who lost a loved one to a reiver. 'Bereaved' (or 'bereft') simply meant 'robbed'. It was not applied to the loss of a loved one until the mid-seventeenth century, long after the heyday of the reivers. Neither 'bereaved' nor 'blackmail' were peculiar to the Borders, yet both are repeatedly held up as proof of the reivers' unique depravity, as though a society which exists independently of a larger, neighbouring state must inevitably be criminal.

The word 'blackmail' acquired its nefarious meaning only when the traditional practice had been turned into a protection racket by thugs such as Johnnie Armstrong. In July 1596, the writer of an ignorant official report on 'the decayes of the Borders' assumed that 'black' was the colour of the reiver's soul: 'this bribenge they call Blackmeale, in respecte that the cause for which yt is taken is fowle and dishoneste . . . and is paid in meale corn or victuall'. 'Mail', from the Old Norse '*mal*', meant 'tribute' or 'rent' – which *was* sometimes paid in meal or grain – while 'black' was the common collective noun for cows, bulls and oxen, which were usually black. 'Grassmail' was money paid to a landowner for grazing rights; 'blackmail' paid for the protection and recovery of cattle.

These institutions were as much a boon to border farmers of the Middle Ages as insurance was to their descendants. A medieval farmer of Redesdale or Tynedale could expect to have his property returned or to be compensated when his house was burned down. Even in the early twentieth century, before the advent of affordable insurance, similar disasters were likely to spell the end of a farmer's career.

---

* The 'hot trod' allowed for deadly force if the thief was caught 'red handed'. Alternatively, he could be held to ransom. The trod was announced 'with hound and horn, with hue and cry' to proclaim its legality and to encourage others to join in. If action was delayed for six days or more, the pursuit would be a 'cold trod' and subject to the wardens' permission.

1. 'North East View of the City of Carlisle', by Robert Carlyle (1791): the cathedral, the castle and the Eden bridges, from the vallum of Hadrian's Wall, looking south to the Lake District.

2. A Northbound freight train on the Waverley Line near Riccarton Junction, in June 1965, climbing to 'the Edge' (the northern limit of Liddesdale). Photograph by Maurice Burns.

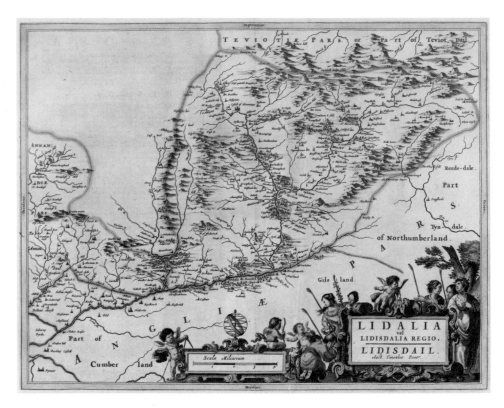

3. Joan Blaeu's map of 'Lidalia' (Liddesdale), 1654, based on Timothy Pont's survey, conducted c. 1590.

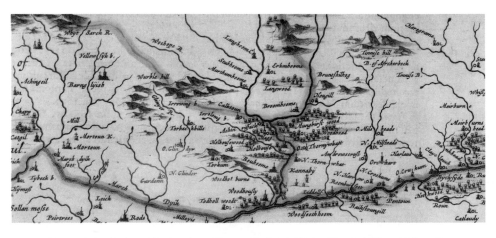

4. Part of the Debatable Land on Blaeu's 'Lidalia'. Right: Tinnis Hill and Mere Burn descending to the Liddel. Bottom left: the Scots' Dike.

5. Liddel Water in early December 2010: England on the right, the former Debatable Land (now part of Scotland) on the left.

6. The Solway Firth near the Lochmaben Stone, looking south to the Lake District, August 2014.

7. Statue of King Edward I in Burgh by Sands, commemorating the seven hundredth anniversary of his death on the Solway Sands in 1307.

8. 'Gilnockie [*sic*] – or Johnny Armstrong's Tower (Dumfries-shire)' by Henry Adlard from an original study by Thomas Allom, 1837. The true name of Armstrong's home above the Esk is Hollows Tower. Both banks of the river lie in the former Debatable Land.

9. Statue of 'Lang Sandy' in Rowanburn. 'Lang Sandy' (Alexander Armstrong) was hanged in 1606 for the murder of Sir John Carmichael, Warden of the Scottish West March.

10. Hermitage Castle, seen from the ruins of its fourteenth-century chapel, April 2016.

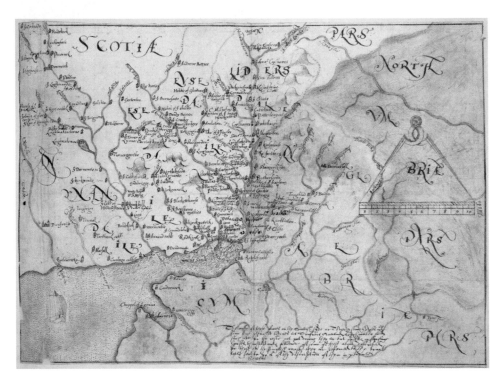

11. 'A Platt of the opposete Borders of Scotland to ye west marches of England', drawn by an anonymous cartographer for William Cecil, Lord High Treasurer of England, in December 1590. The map shows the towers and bastles of the clans or surnames of Liddesdale, Eskdale and the Debatable Land.

WALTER SCOTT ESQ^R

12. 'Walter Scott Esqr'. Engraving by Charles Turner after Henry Raeburn, 1810.
The ruin in the background is Hermitage Castle.

13. The Lochmaben Stone near Gretna, the ancient, wordless monument to inter-tribal and Anglo-Scottish relations at the south-western tip of the Debatable Land.

Blackmail became a burden only when the beneficiary was forced to pay additional rent to a feudal lord, a corrupt warden or a gangster.

In answering various accusations, the laird and outlaw Richard Grayme (Graham) of Brackenhill tried to explain the practice to the English warden, Thomas Scrope, in 1596. (The letter was written by a lawyer since Graham himself was illiterate.) Blackmail was the remuneration of 'such money as he had expended in redeeming the tenants' goods'. If Scrope did his duty as a warden and saved him the expense of protecting 'his poor neighbours' from 'Scottish' invaders, there would be no further need for blackmail.

A weak man buckling under heavy responsibilities, Scrope failed to exploit the potential of the system. He saw only its criminal abuse – the bullying of tenants and the nailing of demands for payment to church doors in Canonbie and Arthuret. Having decided that there was only one remedy for unruliness, he came up with the idea of making blackmail a capital offence and thereby helped to destroy the institutions which, in spite of Anglo-Scottish animosity, had kept the Borders in a strange state of peace.

12

Skurrlywarble

The weather finally improved. The last snows were washed out of the woodland. Boulders which had been arrested by the frozen clay came crashing down, dividing a waterfall into two torrents or resting against pliant stems of hazel. A band of surly sheep which had occasionally passed through the woodland like ghosts headed for the grassy banks of the Liddel, munched then spat out the snowdrops which the river had brought and wandered off in the direction of Longtown.

Among the oak, the alder and the birch, unidentifiable trees were coming into leaf. More than a hundred exotic specimens had been planted by Nicholas Ridley in the 1980s. Most had long since succumbed to the conspiracy of boulder clay and wind, but some had made themselves at home and even flourished, finding North Cumbria a fair approximation to the Caucasus Mountains or the Himalayas.

One evening, a fire rose behind the forest. I grabbed a torch and scrambled up along the side of a gully to the top of the ridge: a huge red moon was darting its flames between the branches. A few lights glimmered to the north where a row of small houses sits in the lee of Harelaw Pike on the eastern edge of the Debatable Land. Just below the ridge was a small level area where a hare or a roe deer had rubbed the ground and exposed the earth. Sheltered by two low embankments, it formed a kind of parapet like the roof-walk of a pele tower. Fifty feet below, two headlights were inching towards the house. I saw a figure emerge. It knocked at the front door, waited for a minute, then returned to the car. There was no time to scramble down the slope. At that distance, the gleam of a torch would have been either invisible or baffling, and no voice, especially one directed downwards, could compete with the river's fortissimo.

This was terrain which lent itself to stealth and private sociability. Reivers returned from raids to unobtrusive towers and bastles which might have escaped the attention of a passing horseman but where a watch could be kept or a beacon lit that would alert a whole family network to approaching danger. In the enclosing wall of the barmkin, the reek of peat smoke and the fug of warm animals were the heart of an independent community, and each of those microcosmic settlements was contained within another, wider world of secluded cleughs and surprisingly open valleys.

✻

The reports and letters of the wardens showed how much sifting and arranging of the evidence it took to produce the traditional image of the reiver: the satanic riders of the museum in Carlisle were based on a handful of thugs who exploited their neighbours; the tearful widow of the ballad was the victim of an official raid by King James V of Scotland, not of a band of reivers. No single voice could be trusted, especially not that of the ecclesiastical windbag who so memorably cursed the Border reivers along with their children, animals and household goods in his 'Great Monition' of 1525.

That curiously ordered world was coming into view as a country in its own right, with its own laws, institutions and traditions, and the quiet enclave at its heart looked less like 'the sink and receptacle of proscribed wretches' and more like the key to an otherwise impenetrable society. The Debatable Land had been misrepresented and misidentified. Its name was not a general term for the blackest parts of the Borders: it referred to a precisely defined area in which no permanent building had been allowed. Animals could be pastured there, but only between sunrise and sunset, and the soil was not to be cultivated, ploughed or 'opened' in any way. For the reivers themselves, the name was practically the opposite of 'debatable'. As Lord Dacre reported in 1517, 'there is no strife for the boundes' of the Debatable Land, 'but it is wele knawne by the subjects of bothe the realmes'.

I was amazed to discover that the true meaning of the name had been lost. The Debatable Land was sometimes referred to, especially in the earliest documents, as the 'batable' or 'battable land'. The more usual terms for disputed territory were, in English, 'threpe' or 'threap' lands – a word which survives in several place names – or, in Latin, '*terra contentiosa*'. 'Batable' *was* a common abbreviation for 'debatable', but it also had an entirely different meaning.

'Batable' comes from the obsolete verb 'batten'. Batable land was rich, fertile land on which livestock could be pastured and fattened up (or 'battened'). By the 1800s, the word had fallen out of use.* Walter Scott knew it only as the shortened form of 'debatable', modern historians are unaware of it, and it was already unknown to most of the sixteenth-century officials who governed the Borders. Yet this is clearly its original sense and the reason why the Batable Land had endured:

> There is a grounde ... betwene the realmes of England and Scotland [which] allweyes has been used and accustumed to pasture upon the same grounde with bit of mouthe, from the sonne rising to the sonne setting, with all maner of cattell, for the subjects of bothe the realmes.

This 'batable land' had been a world apart for several centuries or, as the documents said, since 'ancient' times. Despite the commercial value of its woods and grasslands, its integrity had been respected. The law which stated that no building should be erected within its boundaries nor any animals pastured there between sunset and sunrise would be broken only in the 1510s, by the Grahams and Armstrongs, and even they would restrict themselves to its perimeter and a narrow corridor along the Esk.

Its uniqueness was a sign of its antiquity. Unlike the cantref or hundred of Arwystli in the Welsh Marches, it was not disputed but recognized as neutral by both sides. It was not 'common land', which is to say private land over which certain rights such as pasturage could be exercised, since it was not owned by a manor or the crown, and its

---

* *Holinshed's Chronicles* (1577 and 1587) mention 'two fertill and plentifull regions' in eastern Scotland 'both verie notablie indowed with batable pastures, and by reason thereof are verie full of cattell'. British pasture in general is 'verie fine, batable, and such as either fatteth our cattell with speed, or yeeldeth great abundance of milke and creame'. The term 'batable' made a late appearance in Jonathan Boucher's *Glossary of Archaic and Provincial Words* (1833): 'land ... such as is rich and fertile in nutrition, grass and herbage, calculated to *batten*, or to make fat, the animals that graze on it.'

fields and other resources were not recorded in title deeds. As its later history would prove, it was not waste ground to which no one thought it worth staking a claim.

At that point, we had crossed the Debatable Land only once, on a shopping expedition to the town of Langholm. On that eighteen-mile round trip, there had been so much climbing and descending that the food carried back in the paniers was barely enough to supply the calories expended. In two hours of cycling, we saw not a soul, only wooded ravines cut by the torrents of Archer Beck and Tarras Water, a half-felled pine forest which looked like a battlefield after the battle, a few farms on the edge of high moorland, the deep gorge of the Esk and a hamlet with a telephone box and the remains of a Roman camp. The terrain was so varied and the road so treacherously pot-holed that it left the impression of a journey ten times as long. Now that the spring was shyly venturing forth, it was time to explore the land across the river and to find out what remained of the last unconquered part of Great Britain.

✿

At 6.30 a.m., the radio emitted the faint crackle of a switch being thrown. Then came silence, as though the Glasgow studios of Radio Scotland were being taken over by a band of rebels. This was the usual introduction to five minutes of local news from Dumfries and Galloway. On this northern edge of England, the Scottish forecast is often more pertinent than its Cumbrian equivalent and less likely to make a fuss about gale-force winds and torrential rain. 'A fine day is in store, with only occasional showers, some of them heavy, and a strengthening wind towards evening.'

After news of protests at job losses and wind farms, the non-reopening of a long-abandoned railway station and the wide-scale disruption to traffic caused by a fallen tree in Ayrshire, came the cheery-sepulchral tones of the weather woman. She delivered the familiar litany in the clear, strong voice of a kindly nurse administering a painful remedy. At certain times of the year, the weather is so dependable that a listener can guess the forecast with a fair chance of being in perfect unison with the forecaster: 'It will be a chilly start, with icy patches on untreated roads . . .'

A perusal of maps and guidebooks had suggested that two or three bike rides would be enough to cover the entire Debatable Land. In the event, even with icy patches, it took less than a day. The usefully sign-posted 'Reiver Trail' created by the Clan Armstrong Trust includes only four sites in the Debatable Land:

1. GILNOCKIE HALL. A metal-clad shed in near-total isolation, this village hall without a village boasts a large painting by a retired local art teacher which shows the reiver Johnnie Armstrong splashing across the Esk on a horse to reach his riverside tower (see no. 3).

2. 'LANG SANDY'. In the long linear village of Rowanburn, the statue of a reiver stands on a raised flower-bed near the bus stop. 'Lang Sandy' was one of the nastiest and, as his name implies, tallest of the reiving Armstrongs. This giant chess-piece of a figure is a sandstone copy of the original sycamore log which was carved by members of the local Smith family. I have heard it said that it bears a striking resemblance to Mr Smith Sr.

3. HOLLOWS TOWER. Commonly but incorrectly named Gilnockie Tower, Hollows Tower (pronounced 'Hollus') rises behind a hedge-row on a section of the old A7 which used to carry the heavy traffic from Carlisle to Edinburgh. The pele tower of Johnnie Armstrong is one of the architectural gems of the Borders. The almost complete absence of windows other than gun loops shows that this is a genuine relic of reiving days. The roof-top walk, but not the parapet, has sur-vived, and so has the beacon lantern. At the time of writing, a notice pinned to the oak door informs the public that guided visits have been curtailed 'due to a bereavement'.

4. CANONBIE KIRKYARD. Above the Esk, an army of massive red grave-stones – typical of the region – introduces the main surnames or clans: Elliots and Grahams are the best represented, followed by Armstrongs, Bells, Carruthers, Davisons, Dixons, Forsters, Jardines, Littles and Nichols. None of the departed were reivers. The oldest stones date only from the late eighteenth century. Many were removed by their owners. In the 1920s, a woman of the village was seen entering the churchyard accompanied by a carter. Asked her business, she explained 'that the front door-step of her cottage having been worn down, to remedy the defect, she had come to take away her grannie's tombstone'.

There is only one other obvious guidebook sight in the Debatable Land: a pele tower in an elbow of the Esk near the church of Kirkandrews. It was built by the Graham family, which explains its absence from the Reiver Trail devoted to the Grahams' rivals, the Armstrongs. This is probably the older of the two towers: a map of 1552 shows it as a sturdy stronghold, while the site of Johnnie Armstrong's tower is occupied only by a pair of crooked cottages. Purists can be sniffy about the later additions to Kirkandrews Tower, but many original features are preserved, including the remains of its barmkin. With the mansion of Netherby across the river and the Georgian church, it forms 'a wonderful group', as Pevsner's guide to the buildings of Cumbria observes. 'The Grahams' private railway station', mentioned in the 2010 revised edition of the guide, unfortunately closed more than half a century ago.

This initial reconnaissance of the Debatable Land produced the unsurprising information that there was very little to see. The pickings were bound to be poor in an area where no permanent settlement had been allowed and which had been regularly ravaged by the troops of two nations. Apart from the two pele towers, the main attraction is the village of Canonbie (population: 390). Canonbie grew up around a priory which was founded in about 1153, but it was probably never a part of the Debatable Land. In 1531, it was said to share a border with England but not with Scotland since it was 'three parts surrounded by the Debatable ground'. It stood on a 'holm' or peninsula between the Liddel and the Esk and formed a separate, religious enclave, neither Scottish nor English nor even 'debatable'.

The Debatable Land itself seemed at first to be an empty chapter in Border history, but now, without the distraction of notable 'sites', certain corners of the landscape began to insist on their own significance, and it was in this emptiness that the ancient territory came to life. Nothing suggested, however, that its exploration would take years rather than a single day.

❋

We returned home that afternoon along the old turnpike road which runs parallel to Liddel Water but too far inland for the river to be visible. Looking over towards Scotland and the hills around Langholm on the Debatable Land's northern edge, I happened to notice, at the far end of a narrow strip of neglected woodland, the grey gable of a small house. A few days later, I saw it again through the steamed-up windows of the 127 bus, but on the next journey, it seemed to have vanished, and even once I had seen it, I was never sure of its location. It was a strange place for a house in any case: there was no sign of any path that might have led to it, and the sky behind suggested that the land must drop steeply down to the Liddel.

A local man had pointed out the strip of trees to me as the charmingly named Skurrlywarble Wood. 'Skurrlywarble' is occasionally mentioned as a 'funny' name but it has never been explained. 'Skurr' is the Old Norse word for 'shed' or 'shieling'; 'warble' comes from 'Warb Law' – sometimes 'Warbla', 'Warblowe' or 'Wurble' – meaning 'look-out mountain' or a hill from which a watch is kept. (A 'watch' was kept by night, a 'ward' by day.)

A month later, I squelched for nearly half a mile through the marshy wood, stumbling over its clogged-up drainage ditches, until I reached the gable end of what turned out to be a ruin. The sandstone cottage, according to the 1871 census, had been the home of a gamekeeper on the Netherby Estate. The old cast-iron fire surround was still in place and even the huge roof slates. In a more accessible location, they would long since have been removed or stolen. Among the rubble of the two tiny rooms was a trace of weaponry from the ancient war of humans and animals – a tub labelled 'Mole Mines' (mole-activated phosphorus bombs). But the real revelation was the view.

From that wind-blown edge, I saw a great stretch of the Liddel valley and the fields and fir plantations on the other side. There were the low white houses of Rowanburn and Canonbie, and beyond them the Langholm hills, one of the highest of which, Warb Law, looks over to its namesake at Skurrlywarble. From that magnificent, unsuspected belvedere, it was easy to picture the Debatable Land as a country in its own right. Its entire northern half was encompassable at a glance, with its woods and grassland and all the natural resources of a nation in miniature. It was striking how clearly, at a range of several miles, the dots of sheep and cattle showed which pastures and hillsides were being grazed. As daylight waned, it would have been obvious if a crime of encroachment was being committed or if the land after sunset was still, as it had been for centuries, as quiet as a shrine.

13

Exploratores

After that first, unfruitful foray into the Debatable Land, I decided instead to trace its boundaries, since these are its incontrovertible historical treasure. They were so minutely recorded that they seem to rise from the darkness of Border history like gold leaf on a medieval parchment.

Until the mid-fifteenth century, knowledge of the boundaries was passed from generation to generation and no one seems to have felt the need to record them in writing. In 1517, the warden-general Thomas Dacre noted that there was complete agreement on both sides: the boundaries, which had 'always' been there, were disputed by no one and were 'wele knowne by the subjects of bothe the realmes'. Within the Debatable Land, almost nothing seems to have been named in any legal document until the seventeenth century (p. 108).

Surveys were conducted in 1494 and 1510, but the first surviving description of the boundaries dates from 1550, when Sir Robert Bowes published the results of a survey of the Anglo-Scottish border in *A Book of the State of the Frontiers and Marches Betwixt England and Scotland*. The surveyors had ridden the entire length of the border, along the ridge of the Cheviots, noting all the boundary stones and earthen dykes, the 'rakes' and other tracks, listening to tales of ancient times and recent disputes. Not to miss the opportunity, they 'wasted and destroyed in our passage' the crops which had been illegally 'sown by the Scots within the ground of England'.

Following the watercourses down towards the Solway Firth, logging every crossing point of the border, they came at last to the Debatable Land, whose boundaries, though intricate and different in nature from those of the national border, were etched in local memory as though on a map. Sir Robert's informants were well aware of the limits within which livestock could be pastured, which is probably why his report uses the older, more accurate term, 'Batable Land':

> The said bounds and meares [marches or boundaries] begin at the foot of the White Seyrke where it runs into the Sea, and so up the Water of Seyrke until it comes to a place called Pyngilburnefoot which runs into the Seyrke, then up the Pyngilburne till it comes to Pyngilburne Know and from Pyngilknow to the Righeades, and from the Righeades to Monke Rilande Burn, and thence down Hurvenburne until it falls into the Eske. Then across the Eske to the foot of Terras and so up Terras to the foot of Reygill, and up the Reygill to the Tophous, and so to the Standinge Stone and to the Mearburne head, and down the Meareburne till it falls into Ledalle at the Rutterford, and down Ledalle till it falls into the Eske, and down the Eske till it falls into the Sea.*

The only doubtful section is the westernmost quarter of the northern boundary: 'Righeades' and 'Monke Rilande Burn' can no longer be identified for certain, but the gap is filled by two other documents. The magnificent 1552 map of the Debatable Land (p. 135) shows the boundary crossing 'Cocclay rigge', now called Cockplay and distinguishable by a sheepfold and a small plantation. A delineation of the 'Bateable grounds' in 1597 describes this section as a 'dry march' – a boundary marked by something other than a watercourse. This must be the old straight highway from Annandale. The road is now a rubbly track below Cockplay ridge, but it is still raised above the moorland on its *agger* and oriented directly on the 'Standinge Stone' below Tinnis Hill.

These and other documents prove that the term 'Debatable Land' had a precise geographical sense. Today, the term is routinely misapplied to all of Liddesdale and the West Marches, and even to any area in which reivers were active. The misconception existed five hundred years ago. When King James VI marvelled that his 'favourite cow',

---

* Spellings are modernized for clarity but the place names are unchanged. This text probably reflects the 1542 survey. It is followed by a description of the English and Scottish portions of the Debatable Land, anticipating the division of 1552 but following watercourses rather than the geometrical line of the final settlement.

after becoming separated from the royal party en route to London, made its own way back to Edinburgh via the Debatable Land without being stolen, he seems to have been thinking of the borderlands in general. Recently, the English parish of Kirkandrews on Esk appended the words 'Debatable Land' to its official signs, though the parish covers only one-third of the territory and the part which includes the village of Moat never belonged to the Debatable Land at all.

Tracing every inch of these boundaries exactly would have meant keeping to the middle of three rivers. As I knew from a battered and slightly hysterical party of would-be canoe instructors who were forced to abandon their canoes and leave by the lonning, this would have been, at best, a waste of time. Twice, when the river was low, I have seen people in the Liddel, usually in or beside a two-person kayak, bumping into hidden boulders or even trying to stagger along the river bed and slipping on the stones, so painfully engrossed in the business of staying upright and alive that the house and anyone standing on the riverbank were effectively invisible to them.

Fortunately, most of the Liddel, the Esk and the Sark can be followed at a short distance on a road or a path. The smaller streams can also be followed quite easily, except when they wander off into the bogs and mosses, where there is only a slight risk of being sucked from the light of day but a real danger of having to walk home in bare feet. Pieced together in this way, the whole journey is just under fifty miles. The Debatable Land itself might appear to be almost devoid of antiquarian interest, but its margins are wonderfully rich in historical events, both notorious and obscure, as though, for two thousand years, that empty space had acted as the black hole of border history.

❁ ❁ ❁

The eastern edge of the Debatable Land is still an important boundary. The stream called Muir Burn or Mere Burn, whose name means 'boundary', flows into the Liddel at a place once known as Rutterford or 'cattle crossing'. It can be reached by a private estate track running down from the old North British railway to a clutch of huts at the upstream end of a fishing beat. On one side of the ford is Cumbria, on the other, the boundary of Roxburghshire and Dumfriesshire or, since 1975, of the two oversized divisions of southern Scotland: Dumfries and Galloway and the confusingly named Scottish Borders.

No cow will now be seen attempting to cross the Liddel at this point, and there is little to show that it was once a significant boundary. Ancient territorial divisions often have no apparent raison d'être. Perhaps it marked the mid-way point between two tribal centres. The only material clue is the grass-covered walling of a medieval chapel which stands in total isolation about one mile upstream in a bend of the burn, as close as possible to the Debatable Land without being in it.

Between this ruined chapel and the Liddel, the Mere Burn passes through a culvert under the B road from Newcastleton. This is the route of the 127 bus, which, on Tuesdays and Fridays, offers the most convenient clockwise tour of the Debatable Land's southern perimeter as far as Longtown. It passes the site of Hector of Harelaw's tower (p. 147), gives a fleeting view of the Lake District, then drops down to the border. On the English side of the Liddel, it passes Skurrlywarble Wood and the tiny village of Moat. Just beyond the milestone marked 'Carlisle – 12 miles', the road descends into a ravine which is currently patrolled by an untethered Alsatian, a friend neither to walkers nor to cyclists. At the top of the rise on the other side is the unnoticeable hamlet of Carwinley.

Carwinley, which now consists of three houses, was the site of one of the very few battles of the Dark Age which can be located with some confidence. According to several early medieval sources, in AD 573, a thousand years before the reivers, a great battle was fought between two of the British kingdoms which rose from the ruins of the Roman Empire. One of the kings was Gwenddoleu, whose 'caer' or fortress gave its name to Carwendelowe (Carwinley). The battle is stated in the *Chronicles of the Scottish People* (late 1300s) to have taken place '*in campo inter Lidel et Carwanolow*'. This 'field' or 'plain' between the Liddel and Carwinley is the site of the castle mound called Liddel Strength or Liddel Moat (p. 136).

The name of the great struggle which opposed pagan and Christian armies is the Battle of Arfderydd. 'Arfderydd' is plausibly identified with Arthuret, the parish to which Longtown and Carwinley belong. 'Arthuret' in turn is identified less plausibly with King Arthur. As a result, Arthurian pilgrims are occasionally seen in Longtown. Perched on a cliff below two wooded knolls within sight of a Roman road, the church of Arthuret does seem to occupy a typical Iron Age or Dark Age site, but its name, locally pronounced 'Arthrut', probably has no etymological connection with 'Arthur', whatever the nearby Camelot Caravan Park might suggest. For historians who find the wilful credulity of Arthurmaniacs exasperating, it must be an irritating coincidence that the early medieval sources identify the bard of King Gwenddoleu, who went mad and fled from the Battle of Arfderydd, as Myrddin, the prototype of the Arthurian Merlin.

✿

After Carwinley, a stately mansion appears across some cow-grazed parkland on the right. This is Netherby Hall, which was built and rebuilt between 1639 and 1833 around the original stone tower of the reiving Graham family. It used to be famous as the setting of a poem by Walter Scott, in which the dashing knight Lochinvar crosses the Esk on his horse and gatecrashes a wedding feast to steal away his beloved. I once recited the relevant section to the horse-riding driver of the 127 as we passed Netherby, but she had never heard of the poem.

> While her mother did fret, and her father did fume,
> And the bridegroom stood dangling his bonnet and plume;
> And the bride-maidens whisper'd, ''Twere better by far
> To have match'd our fair cousin with young Lochinvar.'
>
> One touch to her hand, and one word in her ear,
> When they reach'd the hall-door, and the charger stood near;
> So light to the croupe the fair lady he swung,
> So light to the saddle before her he sprung! . . .
>
> There was mounting 'mong Graemes of the Netherby clan;
> Forsters, Fenwicks, and Musgraves, they rode and they ran:
> There was racing and chasing on Cannobie Lee,
> But the lost bride of Netherby ne'er did they see.

Netherby has always been a place of disappearances: the clan of Grahams who were dispossessed and transported to Ireland in 1605; the ghosts of two children whose footprints were seen in the dust of a spiral staircase, starting halfway up and ending just as suddenly; Lady

Graham's prized jewellery which was snatched by a murderous 'ladder gang' in 1885. But the greatest vanishing of all, and a crime of far greater consequence, was the complete eradication of the 'strange and great ruins of an ancient Citie'.

The antiquary John Leland visited Netherby in 1539, when the West Marches were in an unusually peaceful state. All around the Grahams' pele tower on the south bank of the Esk lay the vestiges of Roman greatness. 'Ther hath bene mervelus buyldinges, as appere by ruinus walles'. Inscribed stones, urns and altars littered the ground, and in the fields sloping down to the Esk, the foundations of streets and houses were clearly visible. A Roman fort had been established there in the first century AD. In the third century it was known as Castra Exploratorum.

The most curious find was reported to Leland by some local people: 'Men alyve have sene rynges and staples yn the walles, as yt had bene stayes or holdes for shyppes.' The fact, surprising at first sight, is that Netherby had been an inland port. Ships had sailed up the Esk almost to its confluence with the Liddel. Two centuries after Leland's visit, the 'great marks of a ruinous Town' were still in evidence and an elaborate bath-house had been uncovered, though most of the stones had already been absorbed by the growing mansion.

The name 'Castra Exploratorum' – the 'camp of the scouts' – is usually interpreted as a sign that this part of the world has always been a backwater. Few people travelling through North Cumbria would naturally imagine a sophisticated urban settlement in which the barbarian ancestors of today's borderers wore togas and spoke Latin. The 'exploratores', however, were not the creeping pathfinders of a remote and fearful outpost nine miles north of Hadrian's Wall. The name did not refer to the untamed frontier but to the busy river and the sail-flecked sea. 'Scafae exploratoriae' were boats used to intercept convoys and to spy on the enemy. The 'scouts' themselves would have been the crews of reconnaissance vessels which patrolled the Solway from Castra Exploratorum and protected the merchant shipping. The place to conjure up an image of Roman Netherby is on the thrillingly springy suspension bridge which connects Netherby Hall to the church of Kirkandrews, where the broad and confident Esk stretches away like a highway to the coast.

A safe inland port on the Esk was a vital strategic asset. A line of forts and earthwork defences – many of them still in evidence – continued Hadrian's Wall along the Solway Firth and down the Cumbrian coast. At Netherby, the road from Luguvalium (Carlisle) led north to the rich mining and agricultural lands of southern Caledonia. Another road, crossing the Esk here or at the southern edge of the Debatable Land, headed west to the forts of Blatobulgium and Burnswark Hill. This was an important and well-connected settlement which thrived for at least three hundred years. To judge by the many native Celtic finds, it had been a major tribal centre before the Roman invasion. A Roman lady called Titullinia Pussitta, who left the Danube for the Esk and was buried at Netherby under a red sandstone monument, might have been appalled at the progress of barbarism had she seen the place in the eighteenth century: 'As for the houses of the cottagers, they are mean beyond imagination; made of mud, and thatched with turf, without windows, only one story; the people almost naked.'

When William Stukeley wrote this in 1725, almost nothing remained of the 'ancient Citie'. A succession of Grahams, repairing the sins of their reiving forefathers, 'improved' Roman Netherby out of existence. The cemetery was swallowed by a shrubbery. A miscellaneous, muddled collection of sculptures, coins and inscribed stones – some from Netherby, others from places unknown – was eventually acquired by the museum in Carlisle, where one of the most popular exhibits from Netherby is a pair of .38 bulldog revolvers used in the famous jewel robbery.

✳

Eradication of the past is a constant theme of border history. On 17 November 1771, after three days and nights of heavy rain, the Grahams of Netherby woke to find their view to the south-west greatly extended. Distant fields and woods, previously obscured, could now be seen beyond the great bog of Solway Moss. Sodden with rain, the bulging morass had heaved itself up, burst through its crust of peat, and, in a belch of black slime engulfing cottages and cattle, deposited half its mass on four hundred acres of farmland until finally it surged into the raging Esk, leaving behind a huge, foul-smelling basin.

The eruption of Solway Moss is as much an emblem of the Borders as the pele towers and the salmon rivers. Nothing here is timeless, not even the hills which subside and the rivers which change their course, and especially not loyalties and deep-rooted traditions – traditionally associated with 'remote' populations – unless, like the Debatable Land, they served an enduring practical purpose. Rain and floods were ably assisted by human beings. Almost as soon as the Romans stopped maintaining their towns and infrastructure, the great Wall and its forts were pillaged for nicely dressed stones and lintels. The building of Lanercost Priory in the late twelfth century sucked in Roman stone from miles around. The fort of Camboglanna, where 'several foundations of houses [were] still standing pretty high' before 1789, was lost to the blight of landscaping when Castlesteads House was built in 1791.

The tyranny of the weather, the needs and habits of farmers, and, probably, the scarcity of witnesses foster a utilitarian attitude to the natural and historic environment. The woman who took her granny's gravestone from Canonbie kirkyard and the man who scattered the bones of buried reivers are not entirely exceptional. The inhabitants of a certain Roman site near the Wall have assembled a collection of Roman artefacts known only to themselves and their dinner guests. Stories of marauding reivers are valued more than their material traces. A local man explained to me how he came to acquire some useful stone from a well-known Roman fort on the Wall. Another Liddesdale man, who happens to have the name of a reiver, told me about his garden landscaping which includes a feature referred to by his wife, with good reason, as 'Hadrian's Wall'. As a road engineer observed to me, when complaining about a law which forbids him from scooping stones from gravel beds and shingle beaches, 'It all ends up back in the river anyway, doesn't it?'

14

Windy Edge

From Netherby, the road follows the Esk, which forms the boundary of the Debatable Land. After Longtown and the busy A7 from Carlisle comes a region where the Border hills are a distant memory. Here, the farms are like islands in the muddy plain. Smells of cowsheds and manure hang in the air and the puddly roads zigzag between hedges towards the sea.

A Roman road led to a temporary marching camp above the river Sark. It was obliterated by the bunkers of the munitions depot between Longtown and Gretna. The whole area seems to have been given over to infrastructure. As the Solway delta comes into view, so do the railway and motorway bridges, the electricity pylons and, straddling the national border, the remnants of the nine-mile-long First World War cordite factory.

Though its name is associated with natural scenery, this, too, is the Debatable Land: 'the greatest factory on Earth' where twenty thousand workers kept the British army supplied with shells, the biggest sheep market in Britain, the trunk roads to Edinburgh and Glasgow, and the west-coast main-line railway which divides on the boundary of the Debatable Land at Gretna Junction. This is a scene to test the resolve and the high spirits of the English couples who come to be married romantically at Gretna Green.

Where the Esk pushes into the Solway Firth, the world comes to an end. Far out across the sandflats, the tenuous lines of wading birds and their thin cries give a more accurate measure of distance than the shifting sandbanks and shallow river channels. At low tide, it is still possible to splash across the Solway on foot, but the Eden, the Esk, the Kirtle and the Sark change their courses through the sands and it is hard to say exactly where reivers and drovers crossed the border with their cattle. The crossing on the edge of the Debatable Land was the Sulwath or Solewath, a Norse name meaning 'muddy ford'. Long after the days of reiving, whisky was smuggled across the Solway in carts with secret compartments, hollowed-out cheeses and bladders strapped to dogs and 'pregnant' women.

The English end of the Solewath probably lay near the incongruously perpendicular monument to Edward I on Burgh Marsh. On that spot, in July 1307, the ailing King of England stared out from his tent over the watery sands at the country he was hoping to ravage one last time. Dissolving with dysentery, 'the Hammer of the Scots' watched his strength ebb away into the mud and the silt. Even on a clear day, with the sun high in the sky, the hills over the water look like a mirage of the Scottish Highlands.

The Scottish end of the Solewath is marked by something less antagonistic than a tribute to the genocidal 'greatest King of England' (so named by the inscription). A ten-ton lump of glacial granite in a field of cows is not the most obvious memorial to international cooperation, yet the Lochmaben Stone, where England, Scotland and the Debatable Land come together, was for centuries the meeting place of ambassadors and wardens. In the presence of the stone, prisoners were exchanged, legal disputes settled and truces discussed. It was first recorded in 1398 as the 'Clochmabanestane'. The name itself is a monument to Anglo-Scottish harmony – Gaelic '*cloch*' and Old English '*stane*', both meaning 'stone', on either side of '*Maban*' or Maponus, a Celtic god whose name appears on several inscriptions in the region.

The Lochmaben Stone was once surrounded by a prehistoric stone circle. The attendant menhirs were buried some time before 1841 by a farmer who found them a hindrance to his plough. The meeting point of nations is now quite hard to find. Seen from a distance, it imitates a large hay bale. The footpath sign points implausibly to an area of oily runnels and knee-deep chasms strewn with agricultural rubbish. It may be the low point of a Debatable Land tour in more than one sense, but this mute witness to several centuries of British history is an impressive testament to the durability of tradition and a stern lesson to planning committees and developers. In 2015, when much of Carlisle was under water, the Lochmaben Stone was

standing proud on the ocean's edge where it has stood for five thousand years.

✻

The Debatable Land is a plateau tilted up towards the north. From the
Lochmaben Stone, its western boundary rises four hundred feet in ten
miles, following the corkscrew windings of the little river Sark.* After
the Old Toll Bar tearoom at Sark Bridge in Gretna ('First House in
Scotland / Last House in Scotland') and the 130,000 painted stones of
the 'Auld Acquaintance' or 'Hands Across the Border' cairn inaugu-
rated shortly before the Scottish Referendum by Rory Stewart,
member of parliament for Penrith and the Border, nothing indicates
the existence of a major frontier. Small roads run along the field
boundaries on either side of the Sark towards the worn velvet of the
border hills. Apart from the occasional tractor, there is rarely any
traffic. Buzzards and curlews are a more common sight than human
beings.

Six miles north of the Solway, a long barrier of trees stretches
towards the horizon. This is the embankment called the Scots' Dike
or March Bank, which, since 1552, carries the national border across
to the eastern boundary of the Debatable Land at Kirkandrews.
Even in these flat and marshy moorlands, the Debatable Land looks
like a crossroads of different regions. The hills of four counties
create a panorama almost worthy of a mountain-top viewing platform: the granite bulk of Criffel guards the gateway to the Galloway
peninsula; the North Pennines mark the edge of Northumberland;
the Cumbrian Mountains mass like storm clouds on the horizon; and
the hills of Eskdale form the backdrop of the Debatable Land's
northern perimeter, ending at its North Pole, the tawny pyramid of
Tinnis Hill.

Beyond the Scots' Dike, the road rises gently to a farm called
Tower of Sark. The tower, which no longer exists, was the stronghold
of the unjustly venerated reiver, Kinmont Willie (p. 154). Across the

---

* Older maps show the Sark entering the Solway much closer to the Lochmaben Stone,
which was then the south-western tip of the Debatable Land. The diminutive Sark is entitled to be called a river because it flows directly into the sea, unlike Liddel *Water*, which
flows into the Esk. The same distinction exists in French: the Esk would be a '*fleuve*' and its
tributary the Liddel a '*rivière*'.

road, on a cliff above the Sark, a small, weed-strangled cemetery crouches behind crumbling walls. The oldest stones are being eaten by slime and fungus; most have fallen or are stacked in mouldering heaps. In the 1830s, a raised arm brandishing a sword was spotted on one of the stones. This was the crest of the Armstrongs. The name on the stone was William Armstrang of Sark, and the place is still identified as 'Kinmont Willie's Grave', though the William in question was probably born after the death of the old reiver. The verses are now illegible but were recorded before they disappeared:

> Grass decays and man he dies
> Grass revives and man does rise

For some of the cemetery's inhabitants, this mystical rebirth has taken a literal form. The badly eroded gravestone of the Beattie family of Sark would be completely indecipherable if rain and dew had not collected in the dimples of the letters and allowed a perfect relief inscription of their names to be raised in mossy tufts.

A greater mystery is written in all the religious ruins of the Debatable Land. The cemetery at Tower of Sark belonged to a twelfth-century church. Two miles to the north, at the Debatable Land's north-western tip, another vanished chapel gave its name to Barnglies, from Gaelic 'eaglais' ('church'). On the Mere Burn above the Liddel, where this tour began, the boundary was marked by yet another small chapel, and at least three other churches stood on the eastern perimeter: Kirkandrews (replaced by the present church on a modern, north–south orientation), the Church of Liddel at Canonbie and the original church of St Michael at Arthuret.

Why were these chapels and churches sited on the boundaries of the Debatable Land? Parish churches normally occur near the convenient centre of a parish rather than on its perimeter. Were the Debatable Land chapels intended to guard its sanctity and prevent its occupation by miscreants and evil spirits? Perhaps these perimeter chapels are proof of a steady and ancient state of concord protecting the pastures of the 'batable' land which only later became 'debatable'. Carvings, place names and Viking burials show that many Cumbrian churches were already established in the ninth century. In 1517, when the Armstrongs and Grahams began to build within the hallowed precincts, how much weight of history and tradition was pushed aside and consigned to oblivion?

✾

From Barnglieshead, the northern boundary strikes out across a region of peat bogs and plantations which might be in deepest Galloway. The breeze from the Solway and the Carlisle Plain brings the oceanic sounds of a vast landscape. After a formidable forestry gate, which an Olympic-strength acrobat with extendable arms would have no trouble negotiating with a bicycle, the tarmacked road becomes a wide track surfaced with fist-sized gravel. It cuts straight across a heathy bog from which almost the entire Debatable Land can be seen.

On just such a moorland highway, the hero of John Buchan's *The Thirty-Nine Steps* flees across Galloway on an old bicycle. For a fugitive reiver, the long views might have been reassuring, but that was before technology had given the advantage to the oppressor:

> I was on the central boss of a huge upland country, and could see everything moving for miles ... Half a mile back, a cottage smoked, but it was the only sign of human life. Otherwise there was only the calling of plovers and the tinkling of little streams. . . . Then I saw an aeroplane coming up from the east ...

This magnificent, empty road is the 'dry march' of the 'Bateable grounds' mentioned in the 1597 description of the boundaries. Until the mid-nineteenth century, it was the main road to Langholm from the south-west. For hundreds of years, this would have been a familiar sight to travellers bound for the border passes and the Scottish Lowlands: an arrow-straight road pointing directly at the peak of Tinnis Hill, whose Cumbric name means 'hill fort'.

On the unmarked boundaries of the Debatable Land, time seems to thicken like the boggy moors after heavy rain: it is easy to forget not only in which country one is travelling but also in which age. Long before the days of the turnpike, this was an artery of the northern Roman road system centred on the fort and tribal capital at Newstead on the river Tweed. Like many Roman roads, it probably followed the trajectory of an earlier, British road. This spectacular orientation on a prominent hill fort is typical of native tracks adopted by the Romans.

As though to confirm its ancestry, when the road spirals down to the confluence of the ravinous Irvine Burn and the Esk, beyond the embankments of the A7, it offers another view from ancient Britain: a grassy plateau suspended high above the river. Even on a dull day, the luminous meadow of Broomholm Knowe catches the sun. In 1950, a Roman fort was discovered there. It had been built on an earlier settlement of the native British.

Placed at the northern end of the Esk corridor, the boundary fort of Broomholm mirrors the fort and settlement of Netherby at its southern end. Here again, in the obvious and exact relationship between an ancient site and the medieval boundaries of the Debatable Land, a geographical coincidence took on the appearance of a clue.

✿

Beyond Broomholm, the nightmare section of the Debatable Land tour begins. On a map scaled to journey time instead of distance, the northern section would be many times larger than the rest. I first approached the north-eastern corner from Broomholm, following the torrent of Tarras Water to the edge of Bruntshiel Moss. Tarras Water surges out of Tarras Moss, where the outlawed Armstrongs took refuge from the English warden Robert Carey in the summer of 1601 (ch. 21). They camped with all their possessions on dry 'islands' in the bog. 'Tarras . . . was of that strength, and so surrounded with bogges and marish [marshy] grounds, and thicke bushes and shrubbes, as they feared not the force nor power of England nor Scotland, so long as they were there.'

The torrent itself used to be famous as the subject of a cautionary rhyme –

> Was ne'er ane drown'd in Tarras, nor yet in doubt,
> For e'er the head can win doun, the harns are out

– meaning that you're in no danger of drowning in Tarras Water because it will dash your brains out first.

A rough-looking man was striding down the track towards Broomholm and, unusually in these parts, passed without a greeting. He seemed to be staring at a mental image and moved at such a speed that I instinctively looked at his hands for the bloodied weapon or the poacher's trap. As it wound up from the burn, the track ran alongside

a stock fence, and a herd of similarly wild-eyed Galloway cattle galloped away at the shock of seeing a human being on two wheels. After
that, the only signs of life were the forest finches which dart at waist-
height from one gorse bush to the next.

The goal of this stage of the expedition was the haunch of Tinnis
Hill beyond Bruntshiel Moss. On the edge of the Tinnisburn Forest,
the 1552 map of the Debatable Land shows a dark-green eminence
called 'Toplyff hille' and then the highest and northernmost point of
the Debatable Land: a monolith labelled 'Standyng stane'. On modern
maps, the area is named Windy Edge.

I gave up the attempt to reach Windy Edge from the south-west
and eventually took a more easterly route, which proved just as damp
and arduous. Where the track petered out, I laid the bicycle down
among the bentgrass. It disappeared from view within a few steps and
so I memorized its location using as reference points a hilltop, the
straight edge of a distant fir plantation and a fallen tree, which was the
only useful landmark for half a mile.

Now that the Ordnance Survey updates its cartographic data from
the air, nothing on the map distinguishes the Queen's Mire from the
peat bog below Tinnis Hill. While the former had been exhausting but
manageable, the latter was soft and intimidating: it sparkled like a
jewel box and yielded like a trap door. It did not have the simple
colour coding of mountain bogs with their gleaming, light-green
morasses. A tip for borderline bog-walkers, which I discovered by trial
and mostly error, is that the muscular thistle which suggests solidity
grows on a suddenly descending platform of moss, whereas the reeds
and rushes, normally to be avoided, are firmly rooted in stubborn
tussocks. The real danger is not the clinging quagmire but the likeli-
hood of a twisted ankle. The whole process is so absorbing that it is
easy to walk a long way into the bog without noticing how far one has
travelled.

It was obvious why the wardens and their troops never followed
the reivers into the mosses, but how had a reiver's pony ever managed
to totter across these peaty pools and crevasses? To recreate a journey
in the past, it is usually necessary to imagine all sorts of additional
discomforts, but the mosses are more treacherous now than they were
five hundred years ago. Non-native conifers planted for profit have
covered most of the mountain's lower slopes. The trees are planted so

close together that their branches interlock in the lifeless gloom like the bars of a cage. Where the giant machines called harvesters have snatched up the trunks and shaved them, the brash lies on the bog like the covering of an elephant trap. The peat built up over millennia has been gashed at unpredictable angles and intervals by ditches which drain the sphagnum and cottongrass of their moisture and send the water rocketing down into the brown, swollen rivers.

Tinnisburn Forest is a 'sustainable resource' in the sense that the devastation can be sustained indefinitely. No bog-trotting pony would ever have traversed those moats and entanglements. It was strange to think that barely two miles separated this forest Armageddon from the roads from which I had often seen the mountain looking down over Liddesdale. Only two patches of the original terrain have been spared. One surrounds a small stone which commemorates the death of a slater from Castleton who was struck by lightning on 29 July 1805. The other is a stretch of heath at the top of the forest on Windy Edge, where the Debatable Land reaches its highest point, one thousand feet above sea level.

The standing stone depicted on the 1552 map leans heavily at the end of a long scatter of grey rubble. This is the ruin of a 'chambered cairn' or 'gallery grave' of a type found in Ireland and south-western Scotland. When the stone became a boundary marker of the Debatable Land, like the Lochmaben Stone thirteen miles to the south-west, no one would have known its original purpose. Celtic civilization reached Britain in about 800 BC, by which time this burial site of a forgotten ruler was already more than three thousand years old. Perhaps, like other such monuments on the Anglo-Scottish border, the cairn and the stone always marked a boundary, but there are, of course, no prehistoric documents to tell us, and the landscape is unreliable. In this part of Britain, it can change from one week to the next, when a plantation is felled, or over several years, when the black wall of spruce slowly blots out the view which a previous generation had taken for granted.

On Windy Edge, commercial forestry has eradicated one of the most valuable clues to the historical meaning of a site. Near the chambered cairn, a narrow swathe in the forest gives a blinkered view south towards Canonbie. I could see the mists processing up Liddesdale and the grey veil of the Solway at high tide, but nothing else. The bare summit of Tinnis Hill lay just behind to the north, looking much higher but also closer than the map suggested: from there, the view must be tremendous ... But since Tinnis Hill lies outside the Debatable Land, I postponed the pleasure of making its acquaintance and returned through the forest to find the bicycle not yet swallowed by the bog. Nearby, a forestry track leads down along the Mere Burn, where the ruined chapel marks the boundary, and finally to the B road from Newcastleton to Canonbie. The burn then descends through native woodland to the broadening Liddel, which enters the Debatable Land with a serenity that belies the cataracts to come.

15

'In Tymis Bigane'

This circumambulation of the country between Scotland and England had consisted of several coincident journeys to very different periods. Roman roads ran along three sides of it and in one case formed the boundary itself. Two Iron Age British settlements stood at its main entry points in the north and south. The Roman forts which replaced them had been vital links in the northern British network. One of those forts – Castra Exploratorum – had controlled the road to Luguvalium (Carlisle) as well as the north-western seaboard. Only two or three centuries after the Romans had abandoned Britain to the barbarians, chapels were built on the boundaries. Some of the streams forming those boundaries had Old Norse or Old English names – '*rae*', '*mere*', '*har*' – suggesting that they had marked off a distinct territory long before the earliest written records of the Debatable Land.

This varied realm of moor and meadow was quite unlike the other 'debatable lands' of the Borders. It was not a small, anonymous patch of ground far from any settlement but an extensive zone of great strategic importance. For a thousand years, armies had fought on its perimeter. The Debatable Land had been the eye of the storm, an unpopulated but well-managed country, governed only by ancient tradition. The sloping plateau with its panoramic corniches under high ridges might almost have been designed to be visually policed. Some of the terrain was wild and inaccessible, but much of it was indeed 'batable': the cattle and sheep which grazed its woodland and grew fat on its pasture had always known its value. Most of it had never been 'waste'. Even in the 1980s, farmers in the former Debatable Land considered the old, unimproved fields near the original farmhouse to be of greater worth than the modern, artificially fertilized land.

The unexpectedly sharp outlines of the Roman and pre-Roman Debatable Land suggested that the clues to its unique significance might lie in a very distant past. But the idea of discovering the earliest origins of the Debatable Land in the infinity of unrecorded history was, of course, a pipe dream. How far back would it be possible to go in a land whose illiterate inhabitants destroyed more than they preserved and whose principal legacy consists of ruined towers and historically dubious ballads? Before the 1400s, written documents are sparse. In 1297, the archives of Scotland were seized by Edward I and taken back to London, where most of them disappeared. When the national archives were finally returned to Scotland in 1948, they consisted of barely two hundred documents.

The boundaries of the Debatable Land, however, had been vivid and consistent. They were invariably described as 'ancient'. The word sometimes meant 'former', like the French '*ancien*', but in the fifteenth century, it already had the modern sense of 'far back in time'. The oldest documents which mention 'the landez called batable landez' (1449–57) refer to a very long-standing agreement that the region was to remain unoccupied: the boundaries had 'always' been there, 'aforetyme' or 'in tymis bigane'.

In 1580, they were said to stand where they had stood in the reign of Edward VI, which takes us back to 1550. But in 1550, the Debatable Land was already believed to have 'remained undivided' since the days of Robert the Bruce. This was a reference to the treaty of 1328, in which the border was dated to the days of Alexander III, who acceded to the throne in 1249. No doubt it was 'ancient' even then. In 1245, the knights who walked along the border line were following a document or a verbal 'map' from 'the time of King John and his predecessors'. This was presumably an allusion to William Rufus, the son of the Conqueror, who had driven the Scots out of Cumbria in 1092.

At this remote extremity, where the trail of documents ends, the Debatable Land itself becomes wonderfully eloquent. That oddly persistent western boundary, the tiny river Sark, is such a paltry obstacle that it can easily be crossed on foot. This was clearly a boundary set by consensus rather than conquest. As a national border, it seems out of place in the early Middle Ages, when frontiers were marked by the great rivers of Esk, Liddel, Tweed, Forth and Humber.

The Sark, with its obscure Brittonic name, belongs to an even earlier age. The main river of the Debatable Land is the Esk, but it lies at the heart, not on the confines of the little country. This may reflect the way in which rivers were used by the people who lived along their banks: they were often shared thoroughfares rather than obstacles, impossible to demarcate and fence. The trickling Sark, by contrast, is a thread of steel, its integrity maintained for centuries by something even stronger than a body of raging water.

Only then, when I tried to trace the Debatable Land beyond the age of its notoriety, did it occur to me that in all the early medieval charters and land grants which list every hill, stream and farm of the surrounding baronies and estates, I had never seen any of the place names of the Debatable Land. A few were shown on Bullock's map of 1552 (p. 135); most were not recorded until 1605. The only exception was a vaguely located corner of land called Brettalach (p. 110).

This absence from the legal record is intriguing. Before the 1500s, no one ever claimed possession of that useful tract of land. Neither the Barony of Liddel, created in the early 1100s, nor the older parishes of Canonbie and Kirkandrews – apart from the holm between Liddel and Esk – explicitly included the Debatable Land. The northern boundary of the later parish of Canonbie is quite different from that of the Debatable Land. Parish boundaries, in any case, meant nothing to the natives who could trace the limits of the Debatable Land in minute detail. In 1604, when its boundaries were as familiar to local people as a mother's face, 'the bounder of the forest of Nicholl' (the parish of Nicholforest) was 'not knowne by anie of the antient [people] ther dwellinge, neither have ye Commissioners anie meanes in ye Countrie to decide the same'.

*

The Debatable Land is so closely tied to medieval history that I had not thought to look deeper into the past by consulting the archaeological rather than historical records. I knew something of the Roman remains, but the pre-medieval Debatable Land belonged to a different stage of civilization. What possible connection could it have with the world referred to as 'the modern period' (from the early sixteenth century to the present)? Now, as I picked through the wordless relics of the pre-modern borderlands, I began to see, as though approaching a familiar place from an unfamiliar direction, the uncanny depths of the Debatable Land's foundations.

Before the first pele towers in the early 1500s, there were the medieval or Anglo-Saxon chapels and the two Roman forts and British settlements which had stood on the perimeter. In the Debatable Land itself, there were not only no settlements, there was practically nothing human at all. From the end of Roman rule (c. AD 400) to the age of the Armstrongs and Grahams – a period spanning more than one thousand years – in all thirty-three thousand acres of the Debatable Land, the archaeological record is almost completely blank (fig. 6). The only signs of human activity between the Roman conquest and the 1500s are a bronze jug with three legs, two dead animals and a hoard of miscellaneous treasures.

The jug was unearthed at Whitlawside near the Debatable Land's eastern boundary. It has been dated roughly to the period AD 1100–1499, though it may have been handed down as an heirloom and reached its final resting place in the Debatable Land only later. The two animals were cows whose remains were found in a peat bog a short distance east of the river Sark. The archaeologists' report gives a radiocarbon dating of 'between AD 684 and 947' and suggests 'a ritual motive'. Ritual or not, the remains are consistent with the ancient law which allowed livestock to be pastured on the Debatable Land between sunrise and sunset. To judge by the name of the nearby Drownedcow Moss, they were not alone in meeting a soggy end.

The only definite human traces in the pre-1500s Debatable Land are those of a man or a woman who must have scrambled up from Canonbie Priory through the decayed Roman camp of Gilnockie to the point where the Solway Firth gleams in the distance and the view opens up in all directions. Some time after 1307, a hole was dug in ground which now belongs to the farm of New Woodhead. A hoard of rings, brooches, beads and coins was buried. The newest coins were pennies and halfpennies bearing the head of Edward II (r. 1307–27). The owner or purloiner of the treasure then left the scene, never to return.

This extraordinary absence of material traces over such a vast stretch of time suggests a remarkable, perhaps unprecedentedly long-lasting observance of a rule by a supposedly unruly society. In all those years, in the ebb and flow of conquest, with the great tides of Strathclyde and Northumbria sweeping in and being driven back, the Debatable Land had remained intact and unspoiled. For century after century, when the setting sun had turned the Solway into a shining sea of blood, the pastures, moors and hills of the Debatable Land must have been one of the quietest parts of Britain.

The 'batable' land, I now knew, had not been uninhabited because it was uninhabitable. The tracts of 'wasteland' lay beyond its boundaries, and even its mosses and moors had been grazed by livestock. But who were the people whose laws and traditions had preserved its integrity? Among the Old Norse, Old English, Gaelic and Brittonic place names of the Debatable Land, there are two which contain the relatively uncommon word 'Brettas' or 'Bretar'. In 1190, a certain area – perhaps the flood-prone meadows by Canonbie – was referred to as Brettalach. Some higher ground to the north, around Windyhill, was recorded in 1661 as Wobrethills. 'Bret' place names first appeared in the ninth century. They were given to enclaves of the surviving native population which was there when the Vikings and Anglo-Saxons arrived. The Romans had known these people as 'Britanni' or Britons. Since 'Briton' now has a wider sense, they are usually referred to as Celts.

There is no direct connection between Border clans and ancient Celtic tribes. The family names of the borderers are Anglo-Saxon rather than Celtic. But in the organization of the Debatable Land itself, there are distinct features of ancient Celtic society: the cattle-raiding economy, the creation and maintenance of an extensive neutral zone, the use of tiny streams as major frontiers and the adoption of prehistoric monuments as boundary markers – the standing stone below Tinnis Hill and the Lochmaben Stone at the mouth of the Sark.

Were these the people who first drew the boundaries of that undefended and unassailable fortress? If so, could its origins be traced back to the days of the Romans and even beyond? Perhaps the siting of those Roman roads and forts and their British predecessors at Netherby and Broomholm was not coincidental but a sign that the boundaries had been respected even then. This time, returning to the archaeological records, I pursued the search as far as it could go . . .

There it was again: the strange, yawning gap. Apart from the temporary Roman camps, there was a void of more than two thousand years. The Stone Age and the Bronze Age were represented by cairns and stone circles, weapons, tools and utensils. But the entire Celtic Iron Age (c. 800 BC–AD 600) had nothing to show but a small copper terret (a rein-guide) discovered in a field to the west of Canonbie. The Iron Age had been an age of technological innovation, of agricultural improvement and population growth, yet the ancient Celts appeared to have left the Debatable Land almost completely unlittered and unoccupied.

✻

That curious alcove of British history now looked like a vast and unexplorable cave system. The chronicle would have to begin in the early sixteenth century with the mountain of maps and official documents. How and why the Debatable Land had come into existence would, I thought, remain obscure, and its verifiable history would be the story of its disappearance and destruction.

Yet I still half-believed that those silent landscapes might contain an unnoticed lesson, like some Dead Sea Scroll of the borderlands concealed in the enfolding hills, and so it was with a lurking sense of unfinished adventures that I finally made it to the top of Tinnis Hill. Having failed to reach it from the south-west and the south-east, I tried the northern approach from the single-track Langholm–Newcastleton road over Tarras Moss and found it even swampier. What should have been a morning's walk took on the complexity of an Everest expedition. A woman who lives by one of the burns which rise on the hill told me of an old route to the summit known only to shepherds and hunters. This proved to be a false lead, but it was likely that such a route did exist: the '*dinas*' or 'fort' of the mountain's name implies habitation of some kind, if only a temporary refuge.

Base camp turned out to be Whisgills, two miles west of Kershopefoot on the lower slopes of Tinnis Hill. More than two weeks had passed without rain. I left the bicycle near Windy Edge and headed for the shoulder of the mountain. The white, wind-combed grasses were dry and crackly on their bed of liquid peat. I had often seen the light pass over that hillside like a hand stroking soft deer hide.

Now, walking into the postcard scene, I stumbled over knee-high tussocks and plotted endless diagonals through the maze of gullies.

After more than an hour, the rubble of an unidentifiable circular structure emerged from the bentgrass. Some of its stones had been heaped up on three sides of the Ordnance Survey triangulation pillar at the summit. A cloud of flies buzzed around the droppings of animals which had taken shelter there.

The view from the top was so magnificent that my first thought on reaching it was sadness at having to leave. Beyond the summit to the north lay the expanse of Tarras Moss; the only sign of the road which crosses it was the speck of a white van heading for Langholm. Behind, apart from a short stretch of the Esk valley near Canonbie concealed by fir trees, the entire Debatable Land and much of Cumbria were visible. A solitary column of white smoke was rising from the Solway coast.

From that vantage point, in 1517, when history at last intruded on the Debatable Land and its days were numbered, the alarming sight would have been impossible to miss. Far to the south, the beacons of the Lake District occasionally broadcast their fiery warnings of invasion, but closer to hand, the smoke curling up from the once-deserted river valleys showed that another, more local system of communication was developing along the Esk and the Liddel. In their towers of oak and clay, thieves and outlaws sat at hearths where no fires had been lit before, waiting for the full moon to light their way across the moors.

PART THREE

16

'Stob and Staik'

The first recorded trouble in the Debatable Land concerned neither sheep nor cattle but the migratory animals which live on the border itself. 'Have you got the fishing?' is one of the questions most often asked by local visitors to the house. The idea that fishing rights might be devolved to a resident heron, cormorant or otter is not one that should be lightly expressed. Five hundred years ago, it would have been a mark of insanity, and perhaps still is.

The salmon which thrashed their way up the Esk and the Liddel every year in wildly varying numbers to their spawning grounds came close to causing a war between Scotland and England. Some time before 1474, when the matter was discussed at Westminster, the poor cottagers who lived among the ruins of Roman Netherby constructed a 'fish garth' across the Esk. Often described as a dike of sand and pebbles – which the Esk would easily have demolished – the garth was probably a dead hedge or a net held in place by stakes. Since the opposite bank lay in the unpopulated Debatable Land, the garth-builders met with no resistance.

That spring, while the people of Netherby netted, stabbed and scooped up the frustrated fish, the monks of Canonbie and the people of upper Eskdale waited in vain for the salmon to arrive. Drawing the obvious conclusion, they trooped downstream to dismantle the fish garth and struck the first blow in a dispute which sputtered on for nearly three hundred years.

In the days when protein was harder to come by, fish were a vital resource. It was because of fish that the boundaries of the Debatable Land were first surveyed and recorded – in 1494 and 1510 – and no one found anything odd in the report that, before the Battle of Flodden, James IV, in order to avoid unnecessary bloodshed, had proposed to fight in single combat for 'the Towne of Berwicke and the Fisigarthis on the West Marches'.

The first permanent occupation of the Debatable Land in over two thousand years was a murkier business and the motives of those involved are harder to grasp. The only 'fishing' associated with the reivers is the practice of 'scumfishing' (etymologically unrelated), which meant surrounding a pele tower with a smouldering heap of damp straw and smoking out its inhabitants. The ostensible cause of the incursions was an increase in the human population and the system of partible inheritance. As in many upland parts of England, property was divided equally among the male heirs. When the population grew, the system of clans or surnames struggled to cope with this fragmentation of estates. A young man who saw his future livelihood reduced to a thatched hovel and a sodden field, and who had tasted the excitement of war and profited from its spoils, was likely to question his allegiance to a 'laird', who might be nothing but an old farmer with a house built of stone and a bloated sense of his own importance.

The 'broken men' or 'clanless loons' who refused to recognize a laird's authority might retain their surnames and even start their own branch or 'grayne'. If they were strong in numbers, they would be outlaws only in name. The romantic notion of undying loyalty to a hoary clan chief is misleading: this was a relatively fluid system, supported by common Border law rather than by the whims of a feudal lord. But there was something shockingly modern in the irruption of reiving families into the Debatable Land.

In 1521, the Scottish author of *A History of Greater Britain* wrote of a '*terra inhabitata*' between England and Scotland. He must have seen or heard about the Debatable Land in the last days of its independence. By the time his book was published, men who did not share the veneration of their forefathers were creeping along the Esk and encroaching on the ancient boundaries. Ignoring the law which prohibited the erection of any permanent structure, they came like colonists to a new frontier. Although the deeper mosses and the hilly interior remained empty, the fringes were soon dotted with crofts, and ploughs tore into grassland which had remained uncultivated for countless generations.

✲

These interlopers felt allegiance neither to Scotland nor to England, but their encroachment on the Debatable Land inevitably had international implications. A Scottish army had recently invaded England. The plan had been to distract Henry VIII from his attack on northern France, in accordance with the 'Auld Alliance' between France and Scotland. The result was the Battle of Flodden (1513), at which James IV and thousands of Scottish soldiers lost their lives.

This military disaster still looms large in the national consciousness, but it was spectacularly untypical of Anglo-Scottish relations. Fourteen years after the defeat of Edward II by Robert the Bruce at the Battle of Bannockburn, Scottish independence and the existing border had been recognized by the Treaty of Edinburgh–Northampton (1328). When James IV invaded England in 1513, he was breaking a more recent treaty of 'Perpetual Peace' signed with England in 1502. Until Henry VIII began to devastate the borderlands there was hostility but little open warfare. The battles of Otterburn (1388), Sark (1448) and Flodden (1513) were border raids rather than full-scale invasions. Some Scottish historians have tentatively suggested that more attention should be paid to 'evidence for peaceful Anglo-Scottish accommodation and exchange'.

Before and after Flodden, both countries pursued a defence policy of harrying and dissuasion. It was cheaper to launch punitive raids than to maintain a barrier of fortresses from the Solway Firth to the North Sea. (A later proposal to build a new Hadrian's Wall on the borderline was never seriously considered.) Since the Debatable Land was respected by the borderers themselves, it had proved to be a useful buffer zone. The ancient local law had been repeatedly confirmed by parliamentary decrees: 'the Landes callid Batabil Landes or Threpelandes' were not to be occupied in any way, 'nor by lande nor by water', except in times of truce, and even then, 'as it hath been done in time of other truces', there was to be no 'pyndyng' or 'parcage' (impounding or penning of livestock).

The illegal settlements of the 1510s were therefore something quite new. They might have been an effect of the increase in population, but they also suggest a breakdown in the moral order. The occupation of the Debatable Land began not long after the catastrophe at Flodden. Armies did not always dutifully disperse when the fighting was over: their wages consisted largely of plunder, and some of the worst acts of violence were committed a long way from the battlefield. A group of Armstrongs who had fought as mercenaries might have decided to maximize their profits on their way home from Flodden. In the valley of the Esk, they found a fertile realm naturally defended by the river and its cliffs and conveniently devoid of other human beings.

*

The first hint that miscreants had broken into the Debatable Land and set up 'stob and staik'* is a letter to the English Privy Council from Thomas Dacre, Warden-General of the English Marches. Baron Dacre of Gilsland had fought at Flodden: it was he who had discovered the body of the Scottish king on the battlefield. In May 1514, eight months after the battle, Dacre led a raid along '6 miles of the water of Esk from Stabulgorton [Staplegordon, north of Langholm] down to Cannonby'.

Noticing the new settlements along the banks of the Esk, and mindful of the weakness of the defeated Scots, Dacre sensed an opportunity to reinforce the border. More than two years later, in August 1516, he revealed his sly policy in a letter to the new Lord Chancellor, Cardinal Wolsey: 'I have four hundred outlaws and give rewards to them that burn and destroy daily in Scotland, all of them being Scotsmen who should be under the obeisance of Scotland.' Though the surname may have originated in Cumberland and Northumberland, the Armstrongs were nominally Scottish subjects, which meant that England could not be held responsible for their actions . . .

It is unclear from Dacre's letter whether or not any of those four hundred outlaws were based in the Debatable Land. Since the Debatable Land was covered by international treaties, he would have been careful not to mention it in any case. But a few months later, a decree issued by the Scottish Privy Council (18 May 1517) showed that the ancient spell had been broken. This is the first definite evidence that outlaws were operating from inside the Debatable Land. The thieving 'clans and surnames' of Liddesdale were to be granted immunity from

---

* Stobs (or stubs) and staiks were wooden posts used to measure a plot of land and to serve as boundary markers. 'To have stob and stake' is to have a fixed abode.

prosecution for the space of a year in return for pledges of their good behaviour. This offer was extended to the clans 'now duelland in the Debatable Land and Woddis [woods]'.

By 1518, Dacre's policy of 'daily destruction' was an open secret. The Scottish Privy Council was informed that while the Croziers, Elliots, Forsters, Hendersons and Nixons had given pledges, no such guarantees had been received from the Armstrongs: 'Thai ar in the Debatable landis, and agreit [in agreement] with Ingland'. Dacre, still glorious after the victory at Flodden, believed in his influence over the border reivers, but the Scots knew already that the forces which were being unleashed would be hard to control.

✿

Though he wrote with the arrogance of an Allied commander boasting of the long-term cooperation of an Afghan tribe, Thomas Dacre had reason to be confident. While the prolific Armstrongs staked their claim to the northern sector, the southern half of the Debatable Land was being infiltrated by the similarly burgeoning tribe of Grahams. The headman, 'Lang Will', had recently been banished from Scotland for unknown acts of violence. With the connivance of Dacre, who helpfully expelled the previous inhabitants, the Storeys, 'Lang Will' and his eight sons set themselves up on the English side of the Esk and quickly expanded across the river into the Debatable Land to build houses on the edge of Solway Moss.

From Dacre's point of view, this was a happy state of affairs. The West March – along with his own extensive properties in Cumberland – would be safe behind a frontier guarded by ruthless, corruptible warriors. He would hold the Debatable Land by proxy as a no man's land from which attacks could be launched into Scottish territory. He himself could deny any liability for the destruction they caused. He also knew that this was a policy dear to the heart of Henry VIII, who liked to imagine his border patrolled by English war dogs thirsting for Scottish blood and waiting for the royal command, 'Let slip Tynedale and Redesdale to join with Liddersdale to the annoyance of Scotland'.

Dacre's dream of unattributable 'annoyance' was disturbed – momentarily, he thought – on the morning of 23 June 1517, when four hundred Scotsmen, including Herbert Maxwell, the brother of the

Scottish warden, rode out of Dumfriesshire into the newly occupied
Debatable Land and carried off seven hundred cows and oxen which
had been illegally pastured overnight on Hedderskale bog. This robust
official response to the English-funded incursions was followed by
several years of diplomatic bickering, each side claiming that the other
had entered and occupied the Debatable Land, thereby forfeiting any
right to have their property restored.

The impasse soon led to a change of policy, but it would be a long
time before the lessons were learned. The 'dogs of war' attached and
detached their leashes at will. They were, as a later warden observed
in exasperation, 'Scottish when they will, and English at their pleasure' (p. 132). The Armstrongs were just as likely to set fire to a
Northumbrian farm as a Scottish croft. And there would be many
other surprises for the wardens of both sides.

Even after the invasion of Armstrongs and Grahams, few people
apart from cowherds and shepherds had actually seen the interior of
the Debatable Land. It had yet to be discovered, let alone conquered.
The region was considered to be 'wasteland', as it still is today by the
prospectors of electricity and wind-power companies. Yet the sudden
appearance of animal pens and tilled fields showed how productive
the land could be.

More significantly for the wardens who would spend their professional lives trying to root out the 'wilde and mysguyded menn' of
the Debatable Land, its treacherous bogs and trackless moors, its
ancient woods of oak and hazel, its river gorges and panoramic vistas
made it an almost impregnable fortress. Until then, it seemed to
have been protected by a cloak of invisibility; now, it was revealed to
be one of the most formidable strongholds on the frontier. In 1541,
Thomas Wharton, deputy warden of the West March, who had
served on the border for twenty years, ventured into the Debatable
Land to investigate reports that the Scottish warden was encourag-
ing reiving families to settle there. He scanned that long-deserted
land with the eye of a military commander, and what he saw was not
reassuring:

> That same Debatable grounde hath ever been, is now, and is likely to re-
> main, unless it can be reformed, a very great cause of breaches of the
> peace. There could be no stronger place for the harbouring of offenders.

Without the sight I have had of it, I could not have believed it to be so strong as it is.

✻

The Armstrongs having proved untameable, Dacre came up with a new policy, which he presented as a scrupulous application of the law. The ancient edict which ensured the neutrality of the Debatable Land stated that livestock left there overnight could be removed and any buildings demolished. Dacre interpreted this as a licence to wreak havoc. As he put it in a letter to the Council of Scotland – which took much the same view – each side was legally entitled 'to brenne, destroye, waiste, take and drive awcy all suche goods and cattell as there shalbe founde so wilfully kept under cover of night'. Never before had the ancient rule been so vociferously respected and its spirit so blatantly ignored.

Laying waste to the Borders was normal practice for both England and Scotland. After the victory at Flodden, which is traditionally taken to mark the final securing of England's northern frontier, raiding went on as before. Only eight months after the battle, Dacre sent an immodest report to the English Privy Council, detailing the number of Scottish towns he had destroyed, the acreage of crops burned and the livestock captured: the balance sheet showed one hundred cows for every cow lost to Scotland and twice as many sheep.

At no point was there any question of conquering land from Scotland. The idea was simply to maintain a zone of anarchy and devastation. The crofters of the Scottish lowlands and the great landowning families of the Borders – some of whom could be relied upon to make war on one another – would be kept in a state of ruin and distraction, and neither side would ever gain the upper hand. Ideally, there would be no one left to fight and nothing left to fight for, 'except', as Dacre told Cardinal Wolsey in 1524, 'only remnants of old houses from which the thatch and coverings had been removed to prevent their being burnt'.

Thomas Dacre fell from his horse and died in October 1525. His brutal strategy of destabilization was now extended by his son William to the Debatable Land, which, though technically disputed, had been the most peaceful region anywhere between Carlisle and Edinburgh. 'Young' Dacre (who was in his mid-thirties) realized that allowing the Armstrongs to occupy the natural fortress had been a mistake. It gave them a secure base from which to launch their reiving expeditions and it only served to spread the infection of anarchy into England. Meanwhile, the common reivers, who were quite accustomed to dismantling and rebuilding their wooden houses in a day, continued to gallop east along the Roman Wall and across the Bewcastle Waste to reive sheep and cattle from Northumberland. Despite the soldiers at his disposal, Young Dacre found himself impotent even on home ground: 'None of the people of Beaucastell assisted or scoured the field. The garrison of Carlisle refused to come out.'

Early in 1528, behaving increasingly like the king of his own country, William Dacre declared war on the tribe of Armstrongs. He assembled two thousand soldiers 'in secret' (which, as he shortly discovered, was impossible) and marched on the new pele tower at Holehouse (Hollows) on the Esk. Dacre's description makes it clear that this was one of the early 'log cabin' models rather than the stone tower which can be seen there today.* This monstrous, pyramidal protuberance of oak and clay was the home of Johnnie Armstrong, a 'broken' man with no allegiance to a clan chief. 'Black Jock', as he came to be known, practised a perverted form of blackmail, extorting money from farmers who lived far to the east whom he had neither the means nor the intention of protecting.

When William Dacre led his men across the Esk to Hollows, he found a small army of reivers waiting for him. Observing that a house of oak in a slippery 'hole' above a violent river was hard to approach with 'a great host', he retreated to Carlisle and returned with artillery and axemen. This time, in the unexpected absence of defenders, he managed to annihilate it. Rich Grame, who was reported to have tipped off the Armstrong mob, was shackled and locked up in Carlisle Castle. Dacre was able to report to Wolsey that the Debatable Land had been 'burnt and destroyed; and [I] shall not faill, God willing, soo

---

* Sometimes misnamed 'Gilnockie Tower' and confused with 'Gilnockie Castle', which is the earthwork five hundred metres downstream on the opposite bank of the Esk (perhaps the tower or bastle labelled 'Ye Thornwhate' on a map of 1590). Hollows Tower would have been built for a descendant of Johnnie Armstrong, who was hanged in 1530. No tower is shown on the 1552 map by Henry Bullock.

too procede from tyme to tyme, until it be clerly waiste, without one house or holde standing within it'.

The attack on Hollows Tower would have been a complete success were it not for the fact that, while Dacre was blowing it up and hewing it down, its inhabitants were hard at work elsewhere. Eighteen miles to the east, a mill in Gilsland which belonged to the Dacre family was burned to ashes. Then a mass attack was launched on the English side of the Esk. It led to the loss of sixty-one houses and eighty-six cattle all the way from Arthuret to Netherby. Worst of all from Dacre's point of view, the traitorous Rich Grame, having been allowed for some reason 'to go loose up and down [Carlisle] castle', had found his way to 'a privy postern which stood open to the fields' where a rider was waiting with a spare horse.

An exhausted Dacre then left to make a pilgrimage to Canterbury. The result of his father's policy of funding reivers was chaos. He was left with the job of trying to exterminate the war dogs his father had fed. The once peaceful Debatable Land had been turned into a belligerent enclave between the two nations.

While Dacre was away on pilgrimage, a letter reached him from his wife and 'loveynge bedfello', Elizabeth. The daughter of the Earl of Shrewsbury had a firmer grasp of local geography and politics than the menfolk. She told her husband that there were now Armstrongs, Irwins, Routledges, Grahams and Storeys living along the Esk, the Mere Burn on the eastern boundary of the Debatable Land and the fringes of the Solway Moss. She also enclosed a letter from the Scottish warden, Robert Maxwell, 'showing his crafty mind'. Acting on a dubious tip, William's uncle Christopher, the deputy warden, had set off in pursuit of some Routledges, who were allies of the Armstrongs. The Routledges had galloped off towards the head of Tarras Water, 'which is the uttermost part of all the said Debateable Ground', and disappeared thanks to 'the great strength of the woods and mosses'. Unable to take any prisoners, Christopher Dacre had had to content himself with the usual spoils – eighty cows, a hundred sheep and forty goats. On the way home, he had torched the houses illegally erected by the sons of Black Jock Armstrong.

Black Jock was finally disposed of in June 1530, not by Dacre, but by the seventeen-year-old king of Scotland, James V, who combined a hunting expedition to the Ettrick Forest with a purge of the Borders.

Armstrong was hanged along with several of his accomplices for 'common theft and reset of theft' (receiving stolen goods).

History – especially Borders history – is not always written by the victors. The famous ballad of Johnnie Armstrong and his 'gallant cumpanie', which I have heard mentioned and even recited as the authentic cri de cœur of a heroic Scottish borderer, was quite obviously composed by someone who had never paid protection money to Black Jock or seen his wife and children burned to death under their own roof. It is hard to imagine the illiterate Johnnie Armstrong bidding a fond farewell to the charmless hulk of oak in which he plotted his smash-and-grab excursions: 'Farewell! My bonny Gilnock hall, / Where on Esk side thou standest stout!' It is just as hard to imagine jolly Black Jock as a proto-nationalist who, according to the ballad that was tidied up or half-composed by Walter Scott, aspired only to save his 'country deir frae Englishmen!'

One Scotsman in particular was glad to see him gone. A month later, the Scottish warden of the West March, Robert Maxwell, a glorified reiver with a government salary, was granted all of Johnnie Armstrong's possessions, 'movable and immovable' – including whatever remained of the tower, which he claimed belonged to 'the lordship of Eskdale'. Dacre was incensed: 'the Holehouse . . . is no part of the said lordship of Eskdale, but a parcell of the Debatable grounde, as may be evidently proveyd'. He had, therefore, been perfectly entitled to wipe it from the face of the earth.

17

'Rube, Burne, Spoyll, Slaye, Murder annd Destrewe'

For most of the 1530s, a bloody truce prevailed, each side accusing the other of failing to destroy its own future share of the territory. Apart from executing reivers, the two governments had three options: laying waste to the Debatable Land at regular intervals, bestowing land and titles on the leading reivers in the hope that their pele towers would serve as privately funded forts, or dividing the Debatable Land between Scotland and England.

Destroying people's homes and livelihoods had certain disadvantages: it encouraged the reivers to go reiving in order to restock their barmkins, and it tended to provoke revenge attacks on wardens' property. In 1537, a cheaper version of the idea was proposed by the Scots and enshrined in law. (The same law was passed again in 1551, which was quite normal, since proclamations were usually ignored.) The idea, familiar to readers of Caesar's *Gallic War*, was to farm out the labour of destruction to criminal bands who would, in theory, massacre one another like bears and bulldogs in a pit.

> ... all Inglichemene annde Scottesmene, after thys proclamatione mayde, er and shalbe fre to rube, burne, spoyll, slaye, murder annd destrewe, all annd every suche person or persons, ther bodys, heldynges, goodes annd cattalles, as dothe remayne or shall inhabyde upon any partt of the sayde Debatable lannde, witheowtt any redresse to be mayde for the sayme, exceptt for bytt off mowthe betwene son annd son, as an-

ceannt use annd custome haythe beyne to all otheres Inglichmene annd
Scottesmene thatt inhabyttes nott ther witheowtt a stobe or stayke.*

It was stated in addition that if anyone brought to a warden of
either country 'the hede or bodye, deyde or qwyke' (dead or alive) of
an interloper he 'shall have goode rewardes for the sayme'.

The practice of exploiting local conflicts to clear the ground prior
to colonization – either by making social life impossible or by enabling one friendly or easily defeated group to prevail – has a long and
hideous history. In the case of the Debatable Land, it had some moderate success. The following Christmas, Thomas Wharton, deputy
warden of the West March, reported to Thomas Cromwell that 'the
West Marches of England, Scotland and Liddesdale were never so
quiet'. In 1542, no more than twenty or thirty men were living in the
Debatable Land. But by then, the official cross-border raids were
taking on a different character.

✿

That year, the cruellest and best-equipped bully ever to ravage the
borderlands launched a ruthless campaign against the Scots. Henry
VIII sent an army from Berwick across the eastern border into Scotland. As 'the only supreme head in earth of the Church of England',
he was supposedly trying to persuade his nephew James V to break
with the Roman Church. Eight days later, the English went home after
incinerating twenty-one towns and villages, including Kelso and its
abbey.

The Scots retaliated on 24 November. While the Scottish army
moved south towards Arthuret, King James watched from his vantage
point on the table-top summit of Burnswark Hill. At that distance, he
might just have been able to see the smoke pouring from the ruined
towers of the Grahams of Netherby, but he was probably spared the

---

* 'From the date of this proclamation, all Englishmen and Scotsmen are and shall be
free – without the need for reparation – to rob, burn, steal, slay, murder and destroy
any person or persons, including their bodies, property, goods and livestock, which
remain on or inhabit any part of the said Debatable Land, except for the purpose of
pasturing animals between sunrise and sunset, in accordance with the ancient practice
and custom applied to all Englishmen and Scotsmen who do not take up permanent
residence there.'

sight of his soldiers getting bogged down in the boot-sucking mire between the Esk and the Solway Moss.

The defeat of the Scottish army at the Battle of Solway Moss in 1542 belongs to the history of the Debatable Land as well as to that of Anglo-Scottish rivalry, but it introduces a confusion which has often been dispelled by omitting the Border reivers from the serious business of national history or by admitting them only as lawless savages from a bygone age.

There were now three coexisting conflicts: England against Scotland, both nations against the Debatable Land, and the reivers against each other. By far the most destructive began with a full invasion of Scotland by Henry VIII. Two weeks after the Battle of Solway Moss and six days before his death, a child was born to James V. Having decided that the infant Mary Stuart should be betrothed to his son Edward, Henry put his case as forcefully as he knew how. He ordered his commander to turn Edinburgh into a lasting memorial to 'the vengeance of God'. He was to 'sack', 'rase' and 'deface' not only the capital but also 'as many townes and villages about Edinborough as ye may conveniently', in particular, the port of Leith: 'burn and subvert it and all the rest, putting man, woman and child to fyre and sworde without exception, where any resistance shall be made agaynst you'. The campaign lasted seven years, and because the ostensible aim was to win the hand of a baby girl, it came to be known much later by the coy and slightly creepy name of 'the Rough Wooing'.

While Henry turned the Borders into a wasteland, the wardens of Scotland and England continued to treat the Debatable Land as a cancerous growth. English troops set fire to the woods so that cavalry could pass unimpeded, while the Scots used French mercenaries for 'the douncasting of certane houssis upoun the debatable lande'.

The national and local conflicts are sometimes hard to tell apart. At the Battle of Solway Moss, both armies were led by Border wardens acting as agents of the state but with a keen eye to their own property, present and future. The situation is further confused by the opportunistic alliances of reiver warlords with one side or the other and by the English reports of raids and 'damages done to the Scots'. These are easily mistaken for records of reiving expeditions. The crucial difference, in the years of the Rough Wooing, is the phrase *per mandatum* or 'by commandment'. The Armstrongs, Croziers, Forsters, Grahams and Nixons were employed as full-time wreckers and terrorists. They burned entire towns instead of farmsteads and were so efficient that the clerks, who usually made a note of every ruined town, hamlet and barn, every man captured or killed and every animal driven off, sometimes gave up and lapsed into summary:

13th March [1544]

Archebald Armestronge, by my Lord Whartons commaundement.

. . .

Townes, onsettz, graunges and hamlettis spoyled and burnt	124
Oxen and kene brought awaye	3,285
Horss and naggis brought awaye	332
Shepe and gete brought awaye	4,710
Prysoners taken	408
Menne slayne	35

Grete quantity of insight brought awaye, over and besydes a grete quan-tite of corne and insight, and a greate nombre of all sortes of catail burned in the townes and howss, and is not nombred in the lettres, and menye menne also hurt.*

The huge difference between state-sponsored violence and trad-itional reiving was that reiving, though scarcely harmless, maintained rather than wrecked the social fabric. When the Scottish Referendum campaigns pressed Anglo-Scottish history into political service, it became even harder to distinguish the activities of reivers from the clash of nations. But social history does not come to a halt because two countries are at war. In spite of all the death and misery of the Rough Wooing, the society of Border reivers not only survived but became more of a nuisance than before.

✿

It was during this savage campaign that some peculiarly outrageous behaviour of the borderers was first recorded by officers on both sides. The carnage would be well under way – the soldiers having orders to

---

* 'Onsett': farmstead; 'graunge': barn; 'kene': kine, cattle; 'gete': goats; 'insight': furniture, household goods.

kill and to take no prisoners – when some Scottish and English warriors, standing less than a spear's length from each other, were seen to
be engaged in polite conversation. When they noticed the furious eye
of a commanding officer, they began to prance about like novices in a
fencing school, striking, as it were, only 'by assent and appointment'.
Some of those faux combatants eventually left the battlefield with half
a dozen prisoners who seemed quite undismayed by their capture.
This was all the more incredible since these men who seemed to be
treading the planks of a stage rather than a blood-soaked mire were
beyond suspicion of cowardice. These were the English and Scottish
borderers whose reputation for martial skill and bravery was second
to none.

It was observed that some of the Scottish soldiers had tied ker-
chiefs around their arms and that certain significant letters were
embroidered on their caps, so that 'they might be known to the
enemie, as the enemies are known to them . . . and so in conflict each
to spare or to gently take the other'. The English soldiers wore the red
cross of St George, but no image of king or country was engraved on
their hearts: the crosses they wore were flimsy tissues so carelessly
attached 'that a puffe of wynde might blowe them from their breastes'.

These stirring acts of non-aggression on the field of battle belong
to Anglo-Scottish history as much as the slaughter of Bannockburn
and Flodden. The loyalty of these men was to each other and their
surname. As soon as the foreigners from Edinburgh and London had
departed, when the cattle had been retrieved and the cottages
rethatched, life would go on as before.

A state of union existed in the Borders more than a century before
the Union of the Crowns in 1603. Scots and English traded with each
other illegally without obtaining a licence; they met at markets and
horse races, hunted together and played football. Sport inevitably
conjures up images of national rivalry as though the flight of a ball can
be followed through several centuries of history. A notorious game
which took place in 1599 is mentioned by George MacDonald Fraser
as 'the fore-runner of the Scotland v. England internationals'. Fraser's
text is quoted on the information panel which stands in front of the
Armstrong pele tower at Hollows: 'The final score was two dead and
thirty taken prisoner!' The game in question was a six-a-side contest
between the Armstrongs of Whithaugh (the away team) and the men

of Bewcastle. It was announced in advance and, having been properly organized, was to be followed by a post-match 'drynkyng hard at Bewcastle house'.

The bloody battles of nationalistic hooligan armies in Glasgow and London led to the abandonment of the annual Scotland v. England football match in 1989. In 1599, the violence had nothing to do with chauvinism. The first account of the incident, signed by eight members of the Ridley family, turned out to be grossly inaccurate. The Ridleys, who were at loggerheads with the Armstrongs, misrepresented the local-league football game as an invasion of England. Alerted by the Ridleys, the English soldiers stationed at Bewcastle were ordered to 'catch [the Armstrongs] in English ground' and thus avoid the offence of 'entering Scotland'. Unfortunately for the Ridleys, 'secret intelligence' of their plot reached the Armstrongs. The result was an ambush instead of a football game. Three Englishmen were killed, thirty taken prisoner, and 'many sore hurt, especially John Whytfeild, whose bowells came out, but are sowed up agayne, and is thought shall hardly escape, but as yet lyveth'.

✿

It is typical of the lopsidedness of reiver history that we know almost as much about their football matches as we do about their women. The world of the reivers is one of swords and lances, guns and helmets; it has the stench of sweat and carnage, of wet leather and rough whisky. Its sounds are not the flutter of a spindle or the creak of a cradle but the thud of galloping hooves, the crack of burning thatch and breaking bones, the cursing and grunting of men driving cattle, kicking footballs, beating the life out of a warden's trooper.

In the remnants of a vanished society, the smallest fragment of a woman's life is worth a fortune, but the details have to be teased out of a mass of masculine detail. The published sources have very little to say about women. Excluding royalty, the ratio of men to women in the books I consulted on the subject is about fifty to one. There are the 'wild' women of Kielder, who 'had no other dress than a bed-gown and petticoat'. There are fleeting glimpses of domestic lives in the pots and pans and bedsheets carted off by reivers, but individual women are almost entirely missing. Most are widows and nearly all appear as victims – an Isabell Rowtledge whose livestock and possessions were stolen by a thirty-strong mob of Elliots in 1581; a Margaret Forster of Allergarth who lost her livestock in 1588 while Thome Forster of the same place (probably her brother) lost the 'insight of his house' and his 'wrytinges'. We know that Hector of Harelaw had a daughter but not how she spent her days in a tower above the Liddel. The tribe of 'Old Rich of Netherby' was said by one English border official to number twenty-two sons, 'and a nomber more that I cannot calle to memorye', plus all the male offspring of his daughters, 'which alto-geather be more then a hundreth men besydes women'. The latter were evidently not worth counting.

Most of the women who have left a trace are either the implaus-ible phantoms of the ballads or, assuming that they actually existed, women whose behaviour entitled them to be considered honorary men, such as 'fair maiden Lilliard' who fought at the Battle of Ancrum Moor in 1545:

> Little was her stature, but muckle was her fame.
> Upon the English loons she laid monie thumps,
> An' when her legs were cuttit off, she fought upon her stumps.

In this relentlessly masculine world, one document stands out. In 1583, Thomas Musgrave, the Captain of Bewcastle, provided the Lord Treasurer, William Cecil, with a long list of the 'lawless people' living in and around the Debatable Land. His purpose was to acquaint his superior with all 'the riders and ill doers both of England and Scot-land' and to give him a working knowledge of the social geography of Liddesdale and Eskdale. To that end, he included details of the reiv-ers' 'dwellings and alliances'. Although women are mentioned only implicitly and without their Christian names – 'Hobb Foster of Kyr-sope Leys married Will Fosters daughter of Grena in Liddisdaill' – the result is a marital atlas which proves that rampaging bands of reivers were not the only dynamic force in Anglo-Scottish society.

When each bride's journey from her place of birth to her hus-band's home is plotted on a map (fig. 3), the national border disappears like a track though a mire. Far from being exceptional, cross-border marriages were the norm. A Scottish Romeo did not have to brave the wrath of his family to court an English Juliet, nor did the Juliets have to travel very far. The average distance covered by the brides is under six miles. When Miss Foster looked down from her childhood home on the slopes of Greena Hill, she could see the roofs of her husband's house at the confluence of the Kershope and the Liddel. The border was no greater impediment to these couples than it is to the wood-peckers which feed in England and fly back across the Liddel to their Scottish nests. As Thomas Musgrave put it at the end of his letter to William Cecil in 1583: 'Thus your lordshipe may see the vewe of our lawles people ... they are a people that wilbe Scottishe when they will, and Englishe at theire pleasure'.

When James VI in 1604 celebrated 'the blessed union or rather reuniting of these two mighty famous and ancient kingdoms of England and Scotland', he might have been describing the land along the Liddel and the Esk: 'the isle within itself hath almost none but imaginary bounds of separation ... making the whole a little world within itself'.

These marriages were not contracted in naive ignorance of the political reality. A storm cloud hung over every Liddesdale wedding feast: without special permission, cross-border marriages were pun-ishable by death. This was not an idle legal deterrent. In 1587, a young Scotsman, whose English wife had given birth to their child two months before, was arrested by the Scottish warden. In full knowledge of the consequences for his compatriot, the warden handed him over to the English authorities. A few days later, husband and wife saw each other for the last time when they were hanged, one beside the other, in the market place at Haltwhistle.

This was the tight web of kinship, occasionally frayed and torn but as tough as a reiver's jack, which survived three centuries of war and then, when peace had returned to the borderlands, another half cen-tury of brutal state repression. The borderers, who seemed to be the survivors of a distant era, were in this respect ahead of their time. Many couples living in and around the Debatable Land today joined hands across the border, travelling no more than a few miles, from Penton to Harelaw, from Harelaw to Roadhead or from Bewcastle to Newcastleton. When the map of cross-border marriages (fig. 3) was shown to passengers on the 127 bus, several of them could mention long-married couples to whom the border meant as little as it had done to their lawless ancestors.

18

The Final Partition

After the death of Henry VIII in 1547, a nine-year-old boy sat on the throne of England and a four-year-old girl on the throne of Scotland. The Rough Wooing had failed to secure the betrothal of Edward VI and Mary Stuart. By the autumn of 1548, Mary was safely in France, betrothed to the Dauphin, son of King Henri II. When they married, the kingdoms of Scotland and France would be united. The French were already taking a lively interest in border affairs. In September 1550, one of William Dacre's spies reported that the French were urging the Scots not to cede any ground to England and to maintain the neutrality of the Debatable Land. They were offering to pay for the defence of the 'batable land' – 'wherein I perceive the Scots take great courage'.

That small area bounded by the Liddel and the Sark now found itself at the heart of European politics. It was a potential bridgehead of French power on England's northern frontier. If Mary died, English borderers might be looking over to a land that was governed from the European continent. Military force began to yield to diplomacy. The Debatable Land took pride of place in the opening paragraphs of the peace treaty which was signed in June 1551. Only then, when its ancient sanctity had been irreparably defiled, was its usefulness fully recognized.

> It is covenanted, concorded and concluded that the Land variable, common of both the People, called the Debateable Ground, which lieth between the West Marches of England and Scotland . . . shall remain . . . even as it hath been accustomed to be, and was before the beginning of the Wars.

The present occupants of the Debatable Land were to be allowed to stay in their houses until Michaelmas, which gave them three months to 'remove themselves, their wives and children, goods and cattle' and all their other 'things', each into his own country. This vain aspiration shows that the document was drawn up by men who had never tried to flush a reiver out of his den.

Though the peace treaty of 1551 has been described as a milestone on the road to Anglo-Scottish union, it was primarily an acknowledgement of the damage caused by the war. This was not the solution to an intractable problem but an attempt to restore the peaceful realm which had existed between the two kingdoms for centuries. It came far too late. The first generation to be born in the Debatable Land had reached maturity and showed no sign of packing up to leave. At the end of 1551, the Scottish warden, the sixth Lord Maxwell, burned and depopulated the Debatable Land one more time and killed several of the Grahams, but by then, both sides knew that the ancient enclave had ceased to exist and that there remained only the crude expedient of drawing a line on the ground and dividing the Debatable Land in two.

The idea of partition had first been proposed by the Scots in 1510 but never followed up. Drawing a line across the Debatable Land proved to be extremely complicated. In London, clerks were sent deep into the archives but – after what must have been a cursory search – could find nothing 'in any of the Treaties with Scotland' concerning 'the Debatable and Canonbie'. There would have to be much 'perusing of olde writinges and examinacion of old men'. Reliable information would be hard to obtain from the crafty bandits who had overrun the Debatable Land and who would lie about their entitlements. As local landowners, the wardens themselves were scarcely impartial. 'In dede', the Privy Councillors sagely noted in February 1551, 'the lesse pryvey the Borderers be made to the devision hereof, the more likely it is the thing shall take place.' Instead, the commissioners would be forced to seek out illiterate farmers in their cottages and cowsheds and try to make sense of their barbaric dialect.

Then there was the matter of the conference itself. Commissioners would have to be despatched from Westminster at 'muche charge and trouble ... the place being hence so farre distant'. Since there should be equal numbers on both sides, the Scots would have to be prevented from sending a whole parliament of delegates from Edinburgh. The location was discussed repeatedly until, in April 1552, someone who must have seen too many meetings dissolve into inconclusiveness hit upon the perfect venue. The commissioners would meet on the sands in the middle of the Solway Firth at low tide. All around would be the watercolour emptiness of the shallow sea, the clouded peaks of the Cumbrian mountains to the south and, to the north, the sprawling grey pyramid of the mountain called Criffel which seems distant even when approached. There, amid the piping of the oystercatchers, the commissioners would discuss the fate of the Debatable Land and the contours of the two countries' new western border while the sands trickled away between their feet in widening gullies, the flocks rose up and the tide came rushing in.

❊

In the end, the key to the division of the Debatable Land was not the final meeting, which took place on the dividing line itself in September 1552, but the 'juste and true' map that was created for the occasion by an English master mason, Henry Bullock (plate 14 and fig. 4). This astonishingly accurate map was the result of the first official expedition into the Debatable Land which did not have the aim of laying waste to it. Though it looks like the drawing of an imaginary realm, with its exotic place names and unknown rivers winding through a darkly shaded, almost desolate realm, this is the document that was used to divide the Debatable Land between England and Scotland and to establish the new national border. A generation before landowners understood the point of having maps drawn of their estates, Bullock's 'platt' must have been a revelation. That secret domain was suddenly unveiled by the magic of cartography like a landscape illuminated by a full moon.

Some of the sites on Bullock's map are unrecorded anywhere else: Notebery Hill, Toplyff Hill and Petmen Hill are now anonymous features in the lumpy uplands north-west of Canonbie. Many other names are spelled in an antiquated fashion which suggests the thirteenth or fourteenth centuries rather than the sixteenth. This would normally indicate copying from an earlier map, but there *were* no earlier maps and we know that this was the fruit of an exhaustive, on-the-ground survey, so diligently executed that the expense accounts submitted to the Lord High Treasurer include a claim for a horse that was 'burstit of his ryding with the commissioneris at the Debatable land'.

The speech of the 'old men' who alone knew the fields and hills to which their ancestors had always led their livestock had preserved the ancient forms, just as local pronunciation does today: Carby Hill is 'Caerby Hill', Carlisle is 'Caerl', Liddesdale is 'Lid-des-dale' in three syllables. In a land untouched by administrators, the Norse, Brittonic* and Celtic tongues were still alive. 'Tardwoth' and 'Torbrack' would have been recognizable to a Viking; 'Rocley' and 'Greateney' contain the Old Norse 'ey' ('island'), from the days when the high tide cut Gretna and Rockcliffe off from the mainland.

No account has survived of this small but momentous journey of discovery into the British interior at the dawn of the colonial age, but traces of the expedition can be deduced from the technicalities of the map. Though it stands on the edge of the Debatable Land, the mound labelled 'the Mote of Liddall' lies close to the centre. Here, the four compass lines intersect. A tower had been built on the ruins of the ancient castle. It had probably collapsed by the time the map-makers arrived, but even two centuries later, in 1772, when the Welsh scholar Thomas Pennant visited the Borders, the castle mound on the cliff above the Liddel commanded 'a vast extent of view' (almost impossible to imagine today in the neglected woods of Netherby). From there, 'the country might be explored to very great advantage'.

Liddel Moat would have been the initial vantage point chosen by Bullock for his survey. It offered sightlines to four other prominent sites which could be used for calibration or as secondary survey points: Harper Hill above the river Lyne, the tower on Arthuret Knoll (long since quarried away), the triangular peak of Tinnis Hill above the 'Standyng stane' and, in the flatlands along the river Sark, the tower of Sandy Armstrong (son of 'Ill Will' and father of Kinmont Willie), which enjoyed surprisingly broad views to the east, especially once English soldiers had burned down all the woods.

When Bullock and his men rode up to the door of the old reiver

---

* The Brittonic or Brythonic languages (Cumbric, Welsh, Cornish and Breton) developed from the 'insular' as opposed to 'continental' Celtic spoken in Iron Age and Roman Britain south of the Forth–Clyde line.

in the spring of 1552 carrying plane tables and theodolites instead of guns and torches, Sandy Armstrong must have seized the opportunity to assert his dubious claims. A year and a half before, he and his 'associates' had been counted 'faithfull subjectes' of the English king: against two thousand Scots and four hundred Frenchmen, he had defended his tower in the usual way, filling it up with slow-burning peat and making it impossible for the assailants to lay their gunpowder charges. But now he was threatening to transfer his allegiance to Scotland and may well have developed a sudden interest in cartography. For Bullock, the reiver's intimate knowledge of his misappropriated domain would have been a priceless aid: the practice of alerting neighbours to danger by lighting beacons on the rooftops of pele towers would have provided him with a list of mutually visible points from which to take his sightings.*

✤

Apart from the map, the only lasting souvenir of the 1552 survey is the new section of border known as the March Bank in Scotland and the Scots' Dike in England. Two teams of labourers – one English, one Scottish – dug parallel ditches from the Sark to the Esk. The earth was piled up in the middle to form an embankment dividing one part of the Debatable Land from the other. Square stones carved with the arms of England and Scotland were to be placed at either end. These historic monuments are occasionally 'rediscovered' when a walker stumbles on one of the later unmarked boundary stones, but they probably never existed, except as drawings on Bullock's map. The Privy Council found it hard enough to make local people contribute to the cost of the 'diche' without contemplating the expense of an English or Scottish stonemason. One treaty refers only to 'groves and holes' made by the commissioners.

The Scots' Dike is now a three-and-a-half-mile-long barrier of trees – coniferous in Scotland, deciduous in England – running from Reamy Rigg (or Craw's Knowe) on the river Sark to the March Bank Hotel on the A7. Walkers who mistake the dotted line on the map for

---

* See fig. 4. On Bullock's map, north is tilted to the right in order to fit the drawing onto the paper, which explains why the commissioners' 'indenture' (24 September 1552) refers mistakenly to the 'Western' and 'Eastern' halves of the Debatable Land.

a footpath or who deliberately set out to walk along the border between England and Scotland know the Scots' Dike as a muddy, brambly, ankle-twisting exercise in futility. Trampled by animals, strangled by vegetation, its ditches clogged, re-cut and redirected by generations of farmers, the embankment was eventually wrecked by a descendant of the Duke of Buccleuch who planted it with trees and extracted the timber by dragging it behind a locomotive.

The dike is usually assumed to be a testament to Anglo-Scottish strife rather than to the collaboration of the two colonial powers. This would explain why so many false tales have attached themselves to this shambolic monument like burrs and brambles to a walker's clothing. According to one tale, the two teams of dike diggers started at opposite ends and failed by twenty-one feet to meet in the middle. In reality, the western half of the line describes an arc, not because the diggers were uncoordinated, but because they were avoiding marshy ground. There was no attempt to create a perfect obstacle: the dike was symbolic, not strategic.

The Scots were determined to retain Canonbie; the English wanted control of a low ridge called Blackbank which overlooked a useful landing place near the mouth of the Esk; otherwise, neither side was much concerned by the loss or gain of a few acres. Another Scots' Dike fable claims that the French ambassador to England was brought in to make peace between the two squabbling nations: the English drew a line on the map; the greedy Scots drew a second line, much farther to the south. Then the ambassador – with what a recent writer calls 'Gallic rigour' (not a quality much associated with the French in 1552) – diplomatically drew a line between the two.

The ambassador's line was never adopted. Bullock's map shows a fourth line, captioned 'the last and fynal Lyne of the particion' (fig. 5). This corresponds to the actual Scots' Dike which forms the border. On the map, its logic is obvious. In the east, it consigns the tower of 'Tom Greme' (Thomas Graham) to England; in the west, it joins the river Sark just south of the tower of 'Sandy Armestr.' (Armstrong), making the petty domain of that unreliable reiver indisputably Scottish. Some years later, for no known reason, the border line dipped abruptly to the south-west, adding an extra twenty acres to Scotland and, perhaps more to the point, enlarging the domain of Sandy Armstrong's successors.

This separation of Grahams and Armstrongs was one of the main purposes of the new border. It is often said that the Scots grabbed the lion's share of the disputed territory, yet everyone could see from the map that the Scottish portion was more than twice the size of the English. Since the Debatable Land was a source of endless trouble and very little revenue, this unequal division was not necessarily to the advantage of the Scots. The crucial point was that the Debatable Land had ceased to exist as an independent territory. Each nation could now legally lay waste to its own portion of it, and peace would at last descend on the country between Scotland and England.

19

Hector of ye Harlawe

The 'dykes and ditches of the Debatable Land' were finally constructed some time after March 1553. No doubt they were greeted with the same sarcastic hilarity with which expensive public works are often greeted today. The border barrier was no more effective than Carlisle's modern flood defences. That year, the English received almost five hundred 'complaints' from the Scots detailing 'incursions, murders, burnings, mutilations and spoils' committed by 'English' reivers. The list included men who were now nominally Scottish – Hector of Harelaw, Geordie Armstrong of Cadgill and 'the young laird of Gretna' – but who had remained defiantly unaligned.

The new Scottish commissioner, Richard Maitland, who was appointed to settle cross-border disputes, wrote poetry in his spare time and found plenty of 'burning and slaying' to occupy his muse. 'The common thieves of Liddesdale' were still making off with 'spindles, spoons and spits, / Beds, bolsters, blankets, sarks and sheets':

> Thay leif richt nocht, quhairever thay ga,
> Thair can na thing be hid thame fra.*

Meanwhile, more practical steps were being taken to brand the men who 'broke' the new border. The accounts of the Lord High Treasurer of Scotland record the purchase, in September 1553, of 'ane byrnyng irne to byrn the thevis of Lyddisdale on the cheik'.

On the English side, all three marches were placed under the command of a Warden-general. The first post-holder was John

---

* 'Wherever they go they leave nothing behind, / Whatever is hidden they surely will find.'

Dudley, Duke of Northumberland. The Dacre family had fallen into disfavour. The old autocrats of the north who used the upland tribes as a private army were to be replaced by men with closer connections to the Crown. The new deputy warden-general of the three marches was Thomas Wharton, a hard-nosed, war-loving bureaucrat-soldier who had routed the Scots at the Battle of Solway Moss.

Under Wharton's command, the southern half of the Debatable Land began to look like part of England. Its pastures were enclosed and the tracts of black moss were interrupted by paddocks and patches of green corn. The idea, in part, was to attract settlers and to discourage the 'idle and unprofitable' by making farming more efficient. But the double quickset hedges and six-foot-wide ditches were also part of a vast and bewildering fortification: the paths between fields were to be made 'narrow and somewhat crooked so that the enemy or thief might be met at corners and annoyed by crossbow or other means'. Similarly, the Scottish government decreed that, in lieu of fortresses, the Debatable Land would be 'occupyt and manurit in maner of husbandrie'.

In addition, watches were to be kept from the first night of October to the sixteenth of March. The watches along the border were entrusted to the Grahams, who were to be paid by the English government. Two riders would patrol each section from the foot of the Lyne, along the Esk and up the Liddel to Haythwaiteburn, and then four riders on each section from Haythwaiteburn to Kershopefoot, where the river was easier to ford.

The odd thing about Wharton's 'order of watches' is that these are the old Debatable Land boundaries, not the new national border which follows the Sark up to the Scots' Dike. Somehow, in this twilight of its long history, the Debatable Land survived its abolition. Like a coppiced hazel cut to within an inch of the ground, it sent up shoots which seemed more vigorous than ever, as though the attempt to annihilate it only served to reveal the reason and rightness of the ancient agreement.

✻

The idea of using the Grahams of the Debatable Land as a local defence force was inspired by a new English policy which is best described as wishful thinking. The Grahams would be pardoned of all previous offences and encouraged to defend their misappropriated lands along the border. They had been multiplying steadily now for several decades. Old Riche of Netherby, Fargus of Mote, Thomas of Kirkanders, Umfraye 'Shag' Graham and the other pioneers had spawned an impressively large tribe.* In 1561, more than one hundred adult male Grahams were living in and around the Debatable Land, with probably twice that number of subservient tenants.

By the end of the century, these frontier farmers would be able to raise a cavalry force of three hundred men. They would constitute a kind of buffer state, the powerful advantages and equally powerful disadvantages of which were repeatedly aired in official reports: their 'service might be acceptable if they were restrayned in some sort . . . these Grames are not so daungerous to England as others are. But they ride still into Scotland. There is many of them.'

The principal agents of English and Scottish authority were still the wardens, but they would no longer be left to rule the Borders as they saw fit. Until then, both governments had conferred power on local magnates out of necessity. Now, as they tried to exercise more centralized control, their strategies inevitably differed: Edinburgh lay a day and a night to the north, but it took most of a week to reach the West Marches from London. The Scots, therefore, despite finding the English solution unduly optimistic (giving land to reivers 'shall not suffice to make them good men'), continued to use border chieftains whose excesses could, theoretically, be repressed by punitive raids. The result was that the new border was ignored, as it is today, except by administrators and outsiders. The former but still extant Debatable Land was treated, both by the Grahams and by the semi-independent Scottish wardens, as a zone ripe for conquest.

Strict instructions were issued by both governments forbidding the importing and exporting of horses – especially mares – but nothing could stop the interbreeding of the human population. Though the Scots' Dike had separated the 'English' Grahams from the 'Scottish' Armstrongs, a merging of clans had taken place, and when the details were made known in a report to the English Privy Council at

---

* Umfraye Graham had three sons, despite his nickname, 'Shag', which meant 'an ox which has been castrated incompletely or when fully grown' (*Scottish National Dictionary*).

the end of 1583, thirty years after the division, it appeared that an anarchic principality had been evolving all along. No fewer than thirteen Graham–Armstrong marriages were recorded, all in the same generation. Of those thirteen couples, eight lived inside the Debatable Land and the remaining five on its edges.

Some time in the 1580s or 90s, the region was explored and mapped by Timothy Pont, a graduate of St Andrews University who undertook a solitary expedition to almost every part of Scotland. His manuscript maps of the Borders have been lost, but they were used by Joan Blaeu for his atlas of Scotland (1654). The region is named 'Lidalia', in Latin, as though Liddesdale formed a distinct country. On either side of the 'March Dyik', the Debatable Land is sprinkled with little towers representing smallholdings or groups of cottages – twenty-three in England and thirty-nine in Scotland. They are concentrated along the rivers but are already edging up to the Solway Moss and the 'Torback hills' below the Roman road on the northern boundary.

Scottish Liddesdale – comprising the catchment area of Liddel Water and the northern Debatable Land – was separately administered by the Keeper of Liddesdale. He was expected to occupy or at least command the lonely fortress of the Hermitage. He had to be a man of great wealth, with lands to defend and a willingness to repress any trouble with lethal efficiency, if necessary in person. Official 'letters of fire and sword' entitled him to kill without judicial proceedings.

The Debatable Land had now been placed under modern administration. From that moment on, it seemed to slide back into an earlier, more chaotic era as though warlords from the Dark Age had come riding out of their burial mounds to rule over long-forgotten kingdoms.

✻

Given the requirements of the job, it is no wonder that the most prominent Keepers of Liddesdale were two of the most violent adventurers of the Elizabethan age: the fifth Earl of Bothwell and the Duke of Buccleuch (pronounced 'Bucloo'). The Earls of Bothwell had been lords of Liddesdale almost without interruption since 1491. From the dank bastion of the Hermitage, they controlled that Khyber Pass of the Borders which leads up through Liddesdale and down into lowland Scotland. For more than a hundred years, they battled the tribes of Armstrongs, Croziers, Elliots, Forsters and Nixons. Sometimes, the wounds had barely healed when those same versatile warriors banded together under the leadership of their oppressor to launch lucrative raids on the surrounding lands.

When Mary Stuart rode to the Hermitage in 1569 (p. 54), the Keeper of Liddesdale was James Hepburn, the fourth Earl of Bothwell. His nephew, Francis Stewart, assumed the title in 1585. 'Little Jock' Elliot, who had nearly killed the fourth Earl, was still going strong and now had several sons to help him. They served the fifth Earl as a private army. With the tacit connivance of James VI, Bothwell launched deniable raids into England, some of which were deemed by the English to constitute military invasions. There were fears that 'a warre might arise betwixt the realmes'. It was largely because of Bothwell and the 'Lyddesdales' (the men of Liddesdale) that the state of the Borders in the 1580s remained 'verie ticklie and dangerous'.

The records of this violent period of 'peace' between the two nations are full of microscopic mysteries and unsolved crimes. The system of redress and days of truce broke down almost completely and the intricacies of clan feuds, land-grabbing expeditions, reiving raids, invasions and counter-invasions can be as hard to follow as the moss-troopers' secret paths. How, for instance, did Lance 'Bonnyboots' Armstrong come into possession of the extraordinary sum of £4,000 sterling? In those isolated valleys, even two centuries later, money was of little practical use, but some of the reiving families had 'koyners' who turned stolen metal into coin of the realm, and this cottage industry would have provided their occasional employer, the fifth Earl of Bothwell, with a handy source of income.

Bothwell's reign was benign compared to that of his successor. Walter Scott, the Laird of Buccleuch, whose mother had married the fifth Earl, became Keeper of Liddesdale in 1591. His descendant, the current duke, is the biggest private landowner in the United Kingdom. In 1591, the estate was already enormous and grew larger under his rule. Before and after his appointment, Buccleuch was one of the few reivers who purposely killed his victims. Along with hunting and horse racing, murder was his favourite sport. The adjective which has stuck to his name – along with 'dashing', 'colourful' and 'generous' – is 'bold', because he appears as 'the bold Buccleuch' in the ballad of

Kinmont Willie (p. 155). Another ballad dubs him 'the gude auld Lord'. (Balladeers and travelling minstrels had to eat.) The activities of the real Buccleuch are a useful gauge of the historical accuracy of the ballads:

> But since nae war's between the lands,
> And there is peace, and peace should be;
> I'll neither harm English lad or lass,
> And yet the Kinmont freed shall be!

One Sunday in the spring of 1597, according to the 'bill' or complaint of the English border officials, the thirty-two-year-old Buccleuch galloped into Tynedale with his men.

> Sparing neither age nor sex, he cruelly murdered and slew thirty-five of her Majesty's subjects, of which number some he cut in part with his own hand, some he burnt with fire, some he drowned in rivers, and wilfully and for destruction sake burnt and spoiled. He drove away the poor inhabitants by the terror of his hostility, and taking the goods of the country, divided them amongst his soldiers by way of reward for their service. This cruel and odious act being accomplished with this circumstance, that it was done upon the holy Sabbath.

The Tynedale massacre was just the latest of Buccleuch's sprees, the effect of which was quite unlike that of the traditional reiving raids. The people of Tynedale not only fled from their burning homes, they also abandoned the summer shielings,* 'which is theire chefest profitt' and will not 'venture themselves without such guard against his continued cruelty'. As the appointed dispenser of justice, Buccleuch, in contrast to the common reivers, rode in broad daylight with trumpets blaring, though some of his 'bold' justice was administered more secretly. Somewhere between Langholm and Ewes, off the road to Edinburgh, there was a 'dubb' or deep hole in the bog into which 'my Lord Buckpleugh did wapp the outlaws'.

This repeated rewilding of the Debatable Land served the purposes

---

* 'Shieling': 'An upland or outfield pasture-ground to which sheep and cattle were driven from farms on the lower ground for the summer season and where their herds and attendants lived in temporary bothies' (*Scottish National Dictionary*).

of both governments just as well as the enclosure and cultivation of its pastures. Encouraged by the wardens to behave like savages, the reivers were increasingly seen as Highlanders of the south. They were no longer just troublemakers but 'wicked' and primitive barbarians. A Scottish statute of 1587 lumped the 'disordered subjects' of the Borders together with those of the Highlands and Islands who 'delight in all mischiefs, and most unnaturally and cruelly ravage, slay, plunder and destroy their own neighbours and native country people'. When Bothwell was relieved of his duties as Keeper of Liddesdale, it was considered appropriate to put him in charge of the Isles of Lewis and Skye. In the mental geography of administrators, the Borders had never been so remote. Later, as British dominion extended overseas, the reivers would be likened to 'Ostrogoths', 'Kaffirs' and 'Hottentots', 'a set of wild men, who . . . kept the southern part of Scotland and the northern part of England in a perpetual civil war'.

✳

Taking a long-term view of the matter, these troublesome clans were not the enemies but the servants of the two crowns. They were the unwitting advance guard of a single British nation which divided, 'manured' and civilized the Debatable Land, eventually erasing even the memory of its significance. As communications improved and small territories could no longer exist in isolation, it was inevitable that the Debatable Land would disappear and that peace would destroy what war had preserved. This was a result of historical processes in which individual personalities ultimately played a negligible role, though they may occasionally have risen up like shattered trees in a flood of the Liddel.

Until the last decade of the sixteenth century, when trouble spread to the towns and the rampaging of the wardens came to be seen as a diplomatic embarrassment, neither government had considered traditional Border reiving in itself to constitute a national emergency. Both governments could tolerate a certain amount of civil disorder, especially in a region which contributed little to the Treasury.

The reivers themselves appeared to have played only a peripheral role in the events of their time. This is one of the roots of their popularity: they seem to belong to an ageless, enchanted realm detached from all the complexities of historical chronology. In the records of their exploits, there are few reminders of the outside world: the French involvement in the division of the Debatable Land, fears of Spanish spies and Irish rebels crossing into England, or the periods of intensified misrule called 'busy weeks' when a monarch died or left the country. It was a rare event when a reiving inhabitant of the Debatable Land entered the stage of national history. Even then, like so many other incidents of Border history, the facts had to be twisted and travestied before they could be incorporated into the narrative of the two nations.

In December 1569, the Armstrong known as Hector ('Eckie') of Harelaw, whose tower overlooked the Liddel in the eastern Debatable Land, offered asylum to Thomas Percy, the seventh Earl of Northumberland. Percy was one of the nobles of northern England who had plotted to depose Elizabeth I and to place her prisoner, Mary Queen of Scots, at the head of a Catholic state. The so-called Rising of the North was swiftly crushed and the leaders, including Thomas Percy, fled to the borderlands. On Christmas Eve, the 'rebel earls' were reported by English spies to be 'lurking and hiding themselves in the woods and deserts of Lyddesdale'. Shortly afterwards, they were forced 'to fly to one of the Armstrongs upon the Debeateable' (*sic*).

Only in that undeclared and lawless country could they hope to be safe. For a few days, Percy enjoyed the reiver's hospitality. The site of Hector's tower or bastle was last recorded in the nineteenth century, when the foundation stones were removed by a carter. The site was then engulfed by a pine plantation. Cycling by in the early winter of 2015, I noticed a mechanical harvester felling the trees. The following Sunday, I walked up the freshly exposed bank and saw the long-obliterated view.

From Hector's windows, Thomas Percy would have been able to keep watch on a five-mile stretch of the Liddel valley. Over in England, the slopes behind Haythwaite and Catlowdy are stacked up like terraces: soldiers approaching on the roads from Bewcastle and Carlisle would have been easy to spot as they crossed the ridge of Kingfield Hass or rode down towards the river from the junction now marked by the white facade of the Bridge Inn. As he scanned that silent winter scene, Percy could not have known that the danger lay within. A large sum of money had been paid to his host by the Scottish regents, who had no desire to serve a Catholic queen. Percy was seized and handed over to the Scottish authorities, who sold him on to England. Three years later, he was beheaded at York.

Meanwhile (so the traditional story goes), having broken the reivers' code of honour, Hector of Harelaw became an object of repulsion far and wide. He fell into poverty and died, 'despised and neglected'. So infamous was his treachery that his name entered the language: 'to take Hector's cloak' meant to betray the confidence of a friend.

This is one of the fanciful tales which were supposed to supply the moral that seemed to be missing from events. There is no sign that any reiving family ever took sides in a religious conflict or felt a sense of loyalty to a high-born Englishman from another part of the country. Hector of Harelaw was not unique: the first person to betray Thomas Percy was a member of the Elliot family, and an Armstrong who lived a few miles up the valley had already shown him the kind of hospitality a noble gentleman could expect in the borderlands.

No 'code of honour' had been in evidence when the fugitive earls reached Liddesdale. They had stayed with John Armstrong of the Side (near the present-day Newcastleton) in 'a cottage not to be compared to a dog kennel in England'. During their stay, the horse of Percy's wife had been stolen along with those of her maid servants as well as ten other horses: when the Percys and their retinue passed from Upper Liddesdale into the Debatable Land, they did so on foot. Percy's confederate, the Earl of Westmorland, had been forced to exchange his suit of armour and sword for those of his host, who must have relished the spectacle of an English lord dressed up as a Border reiver.

The tale that 'the tratour Eckie of Hairlaw' was shunned and despised even by 'his own nearest kinsmen' appears to have begun as a fantasy of the poem-writing commissioner, Richard Maitland. Fourteen years after Percy's arrest, a list of all the Border riders included 'Hector Armestronge of the Harlawe and his frendes and allyes'. By then, he was known as 'Ould Hector'. Both his son ('Yonge Hector') and his daughter had married Grahams. The sinister nickname ascribed to Ould Hector – 'Hector of the Griefs and Cuts' – comes from an inaccurate paraphrase of a misread manuscript: in a list of the inhabitants of the Debatable Land, 'Hector of the Harlaw' is followed, in a separate entry, by 'The griefs and cuts of Harlaw' (mis-transcribing 'the thiefs and out[law]s'). All the documentary evidence suggests that 'Hector of ye Harlawe', whose tower is shown on a map of 1590, lived to a ripe old age in his home above the Liddel, surrounded by his numerous progeny, honoured by 'friends and allies' and enjoying the fruits of his innumerable crimes.

20

Scrope

The hovel worse than a 'dog kennel' in which the fugitives had stayed would have been the grubby, makeshift farmhouse which could be abandoned for the fireproof pele tower when a raid was expected. The permanent homes of wealthy reivers such as 'Ould Hector' were not entirely uncongenial. As the Debatable Land became more productive, its 'lairds' sat on chairs and settles instead of cold stone seats. Feather mattresses replaced the scented bedding of rushes, thyme and heather. In 1598, an English visitor to a border 'knight' – probably the Laird of Buccleuch – witnessed, without knowing it, a transformation in living conditions:

> Many servants brought in the meat, with blue caps on their heads, the table being more than half furnished with great platters of porridge, each having a little sodden meat. When the table was served, the servants sat down with us; but the upper mess instead of porridge, had a pullet with some prunes in the broth, and I observed no art of cookery or house-hold stuff, but rude neglect of both.

Domestic luxury was never uppermost in a reiver's mind. Proverbially, they deemed it 'better to hear the chirp of the bird than the cheep of the mouse'. But to wardens who had known the pleasures of a modern city, life in the Borders could be purgatory. Peregrine Bertie, the sad and exasperated warden of the East March, wrote to Robert Cecil in December 1600: 'Yf I were further from the tempestuousnes of Cheviot hills, and were once retired from this accursed country, whence the sunn is so removed, I would not change my homlyest hermitage for the highest pallace ther.' He envied Cecil 'the sun of the South' and prayed 'that one rayon of such brightnes may deliver me from the darknes heere, which I protest is no less to me than Hell!'

Recruitment was a constant problem, as it is today: professional posts in North Cumbria often lie vacant for months and tend to attract applicants whose principal motivation lies in fell walking and other rugged pursuits. Some wardens refused to serve; others manufactured their own sunshine: the deputy warden of the Middle March, according to Robert Carey's report in 1595, was 'so given over to drunkenness, that if he cannot get company, he will sit in a chair in his chamber and drink himself drunk before he rises!' The drunkard's father, Sir John Forster, had been warden since 1560 but was now quite immobile and demented. 'These be our chief officers that rule our country. I refer it to your honour's discretion whether there be not high time for redress.'

As usual, the catalysts of political change were bad weather, bad harvests, hunger and plague, which reached Carlisle in 1597 and killed one-third of the population of under two thousand. To stiffen the mouldering framework of the Marches, it would have taken a man of vision and authority – a man quite unlike Thomas Scrope, tenth Baron Scrope of Bolton, who served as warden of the West March throughout the hungry 1590s.

Scrope had neither the cunning nor the military experience of his father Henry. After taking up the post at the age of twenty-six in August 1593, Young Scrope sent a nervous report from Carlisle on the state of the Borders to the Privy Council in Westminster: 'The frontier here is very broken at present – with the liberty long enjoyed by the evil men, changes at the Scottish court, indifference of the opposite warden [Buccleuch] to justice – and will be worse as the nights grow long.' He ended his letter, rather oddly, with a promise to send a map of the Debatable Land as soon as he could find one.

Through the eyes of Thomas Scrope, the world as it appeared to an Elizabethan border official can be seen as clearly as the starry night sky over Liddesdale. It is strange to hear the English warden, this late in the day, still talking of that abolished land in the West Marches. He might have been a colonial officer recently posted to a distant province which had been abandoned in haste by his predecessor. Not only was the Debatable Land still a recognizable entity, it was still, incredibly, *terra incognita* to the Englishman who should have known it better than any other officer of the crown.

Elizabeth I and her Privy Council wanted to know exactly where Scotland met England in the West Marches. Eventually, in April 1597, Scrope managed to find a 'mapp or card' on which 'the English Bate-able grounds' were shaded in the 'murrow colour' (purplish-red) and the Scottish in 'read culler'. The document itself has disappeared but Scrope's description makes the conclusion inescapable: his map was forty-five years out of date. He was working with a copy of Henry Bullock's map of 1552 in its earliest state, *before* the final partition was marked on it.

The border as Scrope imagined it is not the actual border but, bizarrely, that of 'the Scots' offer', running from the north-western tip of the Debatable Land at Hawburnfoot to a point on the river Esk almost one and a half miles south of the Scots' Dike. Scrope knew that there was an earthen dyke, but not where it was. In his conception, the dividing line would have been almost at right angles to the real one, and the local political situation would have been the reverse of what it was, with the Grahams in Scotland and the Armstrongs in England.

This astonishing ignorance in the Queen's representative, which any native could easily have dispelled, might account for Scrope's jitteriness. In his house within the castle walls, where the candlelight played on the parchment blotches of purple and red, he could see no farther than his own muddy reflection in the black panes. Even in daylight, he was operating in the dark. While his counterpart Buccleuch knew every lonning and moss-trooper's path between the Solway and the Tyne, Scrope was sending his soldiers out into a vague and subjectively vast zone to the north of Carlisle with only the foggiest notion of where they were heading.

Such geographical vagueness was not unusual. A traveller today either follows directions or translates the lines on a map into motion. Almost everyone shares the same perception of time and space. The medieval borderlands were a world of several coincident spheres, each with its own population. In contrast to Scrope's guesswork and Henry Bullock's cartographic niceties, the mental geography of a moss-trooper varied with the length of day, the seasonal changes in terrain and the tell-tale sounds of rivers and birdsong. The beacons on the roofs of pele towers sometimes endowed the landscape with the orderliness of a map, but when the fires had died down on a moonless night, there were no lights to pick out the river valleys or the summits of the hills. The view of the Debatable Land from the edge of Skurrlywarble Wood was entirely dark.

✲

Even Carlisle was crazed with hedges and dunghills. The only stone buildings in that city of wattle and daub were the cathedral, the castle and the citadel at Botchergate. Sixteenth-century Carlisle was the small, decaying capital of an almost roadless frontier zone. Trade beyond Cumberland was practically non-existent. Its rivers were unnavigable and it was frequently cut off from its hinterland by 'greate waters and flouds', and even more by fear of the lands to the north, whether Scottish or English. For reasons of security, citizens of Carlisle were forbidden to employ apprentices born beyond Blackford, which is less than four miles north of the city centre.

The border forts were crumbling like old teeth. A wall of Berwick Castle had collapsed and part of the jail at Hexham 'was newlie comde to the grounde'. By 1604, the fortress at Bewcastle was 'in great ruine and decaye in such sorte that there is not anye roome therof wherein a man maye sytt drye'. Without fresh money from London, Carlisle Castle would soon be of no more use than one of the ruined milecastles on the Roman Wall. Even if the castle could be patched, the personnel were beyond repair: in 1596, the only man in Carlisle who knew how to fire a cannon was a butcher by trade and 'not worth his pay'. An urgent request was made in February for a proper cannoneer who could instruct others in the science of gunnery, 'wherof they have noe smale need at Carlisle'.

On the night of 13 April 1596, a Cumbrian rain was falling on the city. This meteorological phenomenon has no specific name and the local weather forecast never does justice to it. 'Light rain in the morning will give way to more prolonged showers in the afternoon.' The phrase 'give way to' is not quite accurate. The light rain will continue to fall while, from another section of the celestial orchestra, heavy drizzle joins in to the accompaniment of a thudding downpour, until the coincidence of precipitations creates a deafening deluge of unpredictable duration from which the earth will emerge, not refreshed, but beaten up and rearranged. This rain-within-rain is described by Hugh Walpole in his Cumbrian novel, *Rogue Herries*, as 'the especial and peculiar property of the district'; it falls with 'a fanatical obstinacy . . . in sheets of steely straightness, and through it is the rhythm of the beating hammer'.

A few walls from Scrope's residence in the castle, a dangerous prisoner was being held. A month before, Scrope's deputy, Thomas Salkeld, had arrested the arch-reiver and denizen of the Debatable Land, Kinmont Willie, after a truce-day meeting on the border at Day Holm, two miles upstream from the confluence of Kershopeburn and Liddel Water. Salkeld had left the holm with two hundred riders and was returning to Carlisle on the English side of the Liddel when he spotted Kinmont Willie and the Scottish deputy, who had attended the meeting, riding along on the Scottish bank. After giving chase, Salkeld and his men crossed the Liddel, surrounded the reiver and took him back to Carlisle.

This reckless arrest has never been explained. Kinmont Willie was a known murderer and, more importantly, had led a reiver army of a thousand horsemen into England. But arresting a man on a day of truce was a crime against March law and was bound to cause trouble. An explanation may lie in the geography of the chase. The road on the Scottish side of the Liddel is visible from England only between Kershopefoot and Penton Bridge. As far as the bridge, it would have been easy to track the progress of Kinmont Willie, just as some passengers of the 127 bus wait indoors on rainy days until they see the white dot inching its way across the hillside in Scotland. The capture of Kinmont Willie must have taken place along this stretch of the river, where the Liddel was still fordable. The main crossing point was Rutterford, four miles from Kershopefoot, on the edge of the Debatable Land. Perhaps Salkeld believed that by capturing the reiver inside the Debatable Land, he was absolved of the crime of truce-breaking.

Instead of releasing Kinmont Willie, Scrope had decided to hold him in Carlisle Castle, hoping that some lasting pledge of good behaviour would be received. He thought incessantly of his opposite number, the Scottish warden, Buccleuch, whose letters and messages always contained 'a note of pryde in him selfe and of his skorne towardes me . . . a backwardness to justice, except that kind that he desired, which was solely for the profit of his own friends'. One of those 'friends' was Kinmont Willie, and perhaps his incarceration would give Scrope some influence over Buccleuch . . .

So far, no pledges had been forthcoming. Scrope knew from his spies that Buccleuch had organized a day of horse racing at Langholm, where the principal reivers would be present, but he knew nothing of all the dealings that had been taking place in and around the Debatable Land, at Tower of Sark, at Carwinley and at Archerbeck, where 'speeches' had been made about 'her Majesties castle of Carlel and the deliverie from thence of Kinmonth'.

That night, the watch at Carlisle Castle – excepting the two who lay dead at the gate – were either drunk, fast asleep or, as Scrope later reported, 'were gotten under some covert to defende them selves from the violence of the wether'. At some point, a hammering which was not that of the rain became audible. Venturing from their hidey-hole onto the battlements, the guards saw either forty, eighty, two hundred or five hundred horsemen (accounts vary) issuing from the castle and cantering away in the direction of the river. Since Carlisle Castle usually contained no more than thirty horsemen, the fact was as obvious as it could be to a befuddled guard: the riders had come from *outside* the castle and were now returning to the darkness beyond the Eden bridges. At the head of the galloping throng – 'With spur on heel, and splent on spauld,* / And gleuves of green, and feathers blue' – were Kinmont Willie and the bold Buccleuch.

✻

Here, the disjunction of reality and border legend is at its most blatant. The Ballad of Kinmont Willie is such a well-crafted work of literature that it has been used a thousand times to tell the tale of rough-and-ready but righteous reivers restoring natural justice with a smile and a song.

> O have ye na heard o the fause Sakelde?
> O have ye na heard o the keen† Lord Scroop?

---

* 'With plate armour on his shoulder.'

† 'Keen' = 'avaricious, driving a hard bargain, looking sharply after his own interests' (*Scottish National Dictionary*).

How they hae taen bauld Kinmont Willie,
On Hairibee* to hang him up?

. . .

Now word is gane to the bauld Keeper,
In Branksome Ha† where that he lay,
That Lord Scroope has taen the Kinmont Willie
Between the hours of night and day.

. . .

'*And have they taen him Kinmont Willie,*
Against the truce of Border tide,
And forgotten that the bauld Bacleuch
Is keeper here on the Scottish side?

. . .

'*I would set that castell in a low,*
And sloken it with English blood;‡
There's nevir a man in Cumberland
Should ken where Carlisle castell stood.

. . .

And as we crossed the Bateable Land,
When to the English side we held,
The first o men that we met wi,
Whae sould it be but fause Sakelde!

'*Where be ye gaun, ye hunters keen?*
Quo fause Sakelde; '*Come tell to me!*'
'*We go to hunt an English stag,*
Has trespassed on the Scots countrie.'

The ballad's swaggering nationalism has no parallel in contemporary records of the reivers. The diminutive 'Willie' is an impish paragon of resistance to cruel and pompous tyrants, while the bold Buccleuch is a swashbuckling defender of Scottish pride. The tone of indignation is false: there was never any question of hanging Kinmont Willie, and although his arrest was a breach of March law, Buccleuch himself was in this regard a very dirty pot to Scrope's black kettle.

---

* Harraby Hill, south-east of Carlisle, the traditional place of execution.

† Branxholm Hall or Castle, near Hawick, seat of the Scotts of Buccleuch.

‡ 'Low' = flame or blaze; 'sloken' = quench.

For tenant farmers of the borderlands, the tyrants most to be feared were men like Kinmont Willie and Buccleuch. This is not the authentic voice of the 'little people' standing up to corrupt superiors and English aggressors. The raid on Carlisle Castle was a thoroughly Anglo-Scottish enterprise. The way had been prepared by the English Grahams – one of whom was the wife of Kinmont Willie – and by Thomas Carleton, Scrope's former deputy, a known traitor. This is, as George MacDonald Fraser said, 'a bombastic piece of Scottish propaganda at its worst' – or, considering its literary qualities, its best. It is, in fact, strikingly reminiscent of the broadsheets and ballads that were sold in cities. Nationalism of this kind was predominantly urban, as it was four centuries later in the Scottish Referendum. The 'burgess of Edinburgh', Robert Birrell, recorded the event in his diary in terms which suggest that the news of Kinmont Willie's escape had already been digested for a literate audience by professional writers.* This would explain why the lost original adapted by Walter Scott had the raiding party reaching Carlisle Castle by crossing the Esk rather than the Eden – a mistake that no borderer would have made.

✿

The dent to national pride was exclusively the concern of monarchs and their councillors. Queen Elizabeth was furious at being made a laughing stock by 'a night laroun'† who had broken into one of her castles and stolen a state prisoner. James's affable but aggravating attempts to mollify her were not immediately successful. He agreed that Buccleuch had behaved badly and suggested to the Queen's ambassador that the reiver would have done better to smuggle Kinmont out 'by secret passage through some window or such like practice'.

The Queen wrote to her ambassador in Edinburgh: 'I wonder how base mynded that Kinge thinks me that with patience I can disgest this

---

* 'The same 6 of Apryll 1596, the laird of Buccleugh past to the castell of Carleill w^t 70 men, and tuik out Will. Kynmonth out of the said castell: the said Will. lyand in ironis w^{t}in the irone zett [gate]. Yis he did with shouting and crying, and sound of trumpet, puttand the said toune and countrie in sic ane fray [uproar], that the lyk of sic ane wassaledge [daring deed] wes nevir since the memorie of man, no in Wallace dayis [not even in the days of William Wallace].'

† A 'laroun' was a thief. The usual transcription is 'largin', which has no meaning.

dishonourable [a blank in the transcription]. Let him therefor kno that I will have satisfaction or els.' The offer of a trial infuriated her all the more: why should such a wretch be granted the dignity of judicial proceedings when 'the breach in the door and wall of the castle can be seen by anyone who is not blind or that has but one eye'? She had to settle eventually for the brief captivity of Buccleuch at Berwick, where, though he was reported to be 'growing werie of the towne, and so more daungerous to be kepte', he 'behaved him selfe verie well and orderlie'.

As for Scrope, he was beside himself with rage and embarrassment – for himself rather than for his country. His epic petulance was not something that would have lent itself to a jolly ballad: that summer, three months after Kinmont Willie's escape, Scrope's vengeance swept through Liddesdale and the Debatable Land in a series of raids, the most vicious of which took place in August 1596 on the banks of the Liddel near Newcastleton.

It might have been a scene from the early period of colonial conquest. Soldiers burned down every dwelling along a four-mile stretch of the river. They tied the prisoners 'two and two together on a leash like dogs', while the women and children 'were stripped of their clothes and sarks, leaving them naked and exposed to the injury of wind and weather, whereby nine or ten infants perished within the following eight days'.

The Scottish complaints were inconsistent and exaggerated, but there was no question that Scrope had overstepped the mark. Elizabeth's chief minister, Robert Cecil, warned Scrope that such force should be applied only in extremis and reminded him to use more diplomatic language in his reports: King James of Scotland might soon be king of both countries. Scrope insisted that his raid had been a legal reprisal permitted by ancient border law, which called it a 'pune'.* Moreover, the women left naked in their native bogs with their terrorized children, were, in comparison with Buccleuch's outrages, 'as pictures and shadowes to bodies and lyfe' – an unconsciously

---

* 'Pune' actually referred to the lawful recovery or 'reprisal' of stolen property. Scrope was twisting the term into a synonym of 'revenge attack'. He misdefined 'pune' as 'armed justice, differinge from peaceable justice onely in forme, beinge in matter and substance one and the same'.

appropriate image. The raid, in any case, had been conducted in 'the greatest heat of somer', and where was the harm in spending a night or two naked on bare moorland after four years of bad harvests and a day of slaughter and destruction, with the wind blowing in off the estuary which modern Cumbrians ruefully refer to as the Costa del Solway?

The son of an equally ruthless but far more effective father, Scrope found himself strangely alone. His was the cry of the functionary overwhelmed by his own very public incompetence: 'What else could I have done?' While Buccleuch and the inexterminable tribe of reivers continued to burn, rob and murder, Scrope begged the Privy Council to send more men: 'The dishonour to her Majesty by the insolent pride of Buccleuch ... is intolerable, and I fear, to the shame of manhood, I shall sit without revenge, unless you assist me with some forces.'

21

Tarras Moss

It is impossible to know how much deeper into anarchy the Borders might have sunk if Scrope had not asked his brother-in-law, Robert Carey, to become his deputy. Despite the family connection, Carey was one of the 'new men' of the later Elizabethan age – men whose power was rooted in intelligence, enterprise and experience rather than inherited wealth. When Carey came to Carlisle and lodged in the castle with his wife, he was almost penniless, having contracted debts in London, but he had that rarest of qualities in Border officials: the ability to make himself liked.

Carey seems to have been the first warden to understand that killing people and torching their houses was counter-productive. Later, as warden of the English Middle March, he dealt with some persistent Scottish poachers by smashing the carts in which they hauled away the deer and then inviting them to his home: 'I made them welcome, and gave them the best entertainment that I could . . . and so we continued good neighbours ever after.' Amazingly, he found the reformed Buccleuch an easy man to work with, 'the onelye man that hath runn a dyrect course with me for the mayntenaunce of justice'. He even won over the homicidal Scottish warden of the East March, Robert Kerr of Cessford, who rivalled Buccleuch in cruelty. To the surprise of Robert Cecil, Secretary of State, who put him in charge of the Middle March in 1596, Carey refused the offer of a hundred horsemen. Forty would suffice, 'and they to be my own servants, and resident with me in my own house'. To Carey, it was a matter of pride – and professional calculation – to cost the Treasury as little as possible.

Carey's enlightened approach to personnel management helped

him to win one of the most telling victories over the reiver war-lords. Though several years would pass before the Borders and the Debatable Land were free from the outlaws' reign of terror, and though it would take the Union of the Crowns to loosen the grip of the self-serving wardens, Carey's coordinated offensive on Tarras Moss in the summer of 1601 showed that reivers could be defeated and reduced to a manageable rabble of 'inbred thieves'.

❀

The Scottish warden of the West March, Sir John Carmichael, had recently made himself unpopular by refusing to turn a blind eye to the Armstrongs' raids. He was also unusual in working closely with his opposite number, Scrope. For the reivers, Carmichael was a man not to be trusted, precisely because he was trustworthy. On 16 June 1600, he was riding back to Langholm from Annan when he was ambushed by eighteen riders – two Englishmen and sixteen Scots, one of whom was 'Lang Sandy', the Armstrong whose statue now stands near the bus stop in Rowanburn. Carmichael raced away but was shot in the back and stripped of his possessions. His corpse was carted off to Lochmaben. The tale that he was killed because one of his men had taunted an Armstrong and filled his scabbard with egg yolk – which prevents the sword from being drawn – has no foundation. Carmichael was murdered because he was an honest policeman.

The acting warden of the English West March, Richard Lowther, realized that this assassination was not an isolated incident but the start of a new war: 'I cannot keep this March, for now the thieves will ride.' The Armstrongs and their allies at once launched a series of raids, mostly in Scotland but reaching as far south as Stanwix on the edge of Carlisle. The Bishop of Carlisle was preaching there when eighty riders descended on the suburb, stole every horse they could find and wounded the bishop's sister-in-law.

Meanwhile, in the Middle March, Carey had had a relatively peaceful time of it, but now that the weather had improved, the Arm-strong army, numbering about one hundred and fifty, was extending its operations to the east, on both sides of the border:

> England and Scotland is all one to them, and they fear no officers of either side. They are so well provided with stolen horses, and the strengths they

lie in so fortified with bog and wood, that they know a small force cannot hurt them. They have begun to spoil in this March . . . and are like to do more before winter be done.

Carey had been covering hundreds of miles on horseback, discussing strategy with his Scottish counterparts. He had met King James on a diplomatic mission. The King had enjoyed Carey's company and now gave him permission to operate in both countries: 'He was well pleased I should do my worst to [the outlaws], if I took them in England, and if I sought them in Scotland he would not mislike it, but had commanded all assistance to be given me.' This was to be the key to lasting control of the Borders. James was inviting Carey to behave as though the two nations were already united.

None of this was apparent to the marauding Armstrongs, nor to those crop-destroying 'caterpillers', the Grahams, as Scrope called them. They seem to have been oblivious to the changing international scene. They knew only that the Laird of Buccleuch had become inconveniently uncorrupt and could no longer be relied upon to ignore their raids. Sim Armstrong of Whithaugh (near Newcastleton), who had been held as a pledge at York Castle after the murder of warden Carmichael, had escaped and returned to the West March, where he was now proclaiming that 'all fugitives, Scots or English, who join them, shall be aided and protected . . . so that all honest men will rue the time they came home'.

The winter, as usual, passed off quietly enough. It was not until early May the following year (1601) that the trouble began. A small town near the boundary of the West and Middle Marches was set on fire and hostages were taken. Carey retaliated in kind, rescuing the prisoners, burning the raiders' houses and, crucially, taking their best horses: 'I have power enough, and will weary them with their own weapons.'

Then news reached Carey from Hartwisell (now Haltwhistle), the Northumbrian market town below the Roman Wall near the borders of Cumberland. Hartwisell was a stronghold of the Ridleys, who were sworn enemies of the Armstrongs. They were used to defending their town against raiders from the west. Chains would be stretched across the bridges, forcing invaders to use the heavily defended fords. Nicholas Ridley, the Bishop of London who was martyred in 1555, grew up at the nearby Unthank Hall and remembered the thrills of a boyhood in the heart of reiving country:

> In Tynedale, where I was born, not far from the Scottish borders, I have known my countrymen watch night and day in their harness, such as they had, that is, in their jacks, and their spears in their hands ... especially when they had any privy warning of the coming of the Scots. And so doing, although at every such bickering* some of them spent their lives, yet by such means, like pretty men, they defended their country.

Two years before, those 'pretty men' had tried to have the Armstrongs massacred at their football game in Bewcastle (p. 129). This time, one of the Ridleys managed to lodge a spear in the body of Sim Armstrong, who came from Cat Hill (Cadgill) on the western boundary of the Debatable Land. Sim died of his wound and, as though this had been the point of the first attack, the Armstrongs vowed revenge, promising that, 'before the next winter was ended they would leave the whole country waste [and] there should be none to resist them'.

A few nights later, the Armstrongs came again. They burst into town with burning torches, plundering the houses and 'running up and down the streets with lights in their hands to set more houses on fire'. Taking aim from the window of a stone house, a Ridley shot dead 'one of the sons of the chiefest outlaw'. Enraged but undeterred, the Armstrongs for the second time made 'bloody vows of deep revenge' and the entire country beyond Liddesdale waited for the storm to break.

❀

It is not just a lucky chance that Robert Carey wrote his memoirs. He loved a well-turned plot and a lively adventure in which an inferior but more intelligent force was pitted against brute strength. In 1588, he had ridden to Portsmouth and jumped aboard a frigate which had taken him to within spitting distance of the Spanish Armada anchored off Calais. In 1601, after the burning of Haltwhistle, he found himself

---

* 'Bickering': 'skirmishing, exchange of missiles' (*A Dictionary of the Older Scottish Tongue*). 'Pretty' has the sense of 'brave' or 'worthy'.

on a broad and windy stage, confronted by a many-headed enemy which had defied two nations for eighty years. He had only forty horsemen and an audience of thousands begging him to save them from the outlaws:

> [They] did assure me, that unless I did take some course with them by the end of that summer, there was none of the inhabitants durst or would stay in their dwellings the next winter, but they would fly the country, and leave their houses and lands to the fury of the outlaws.

Carey sought the advice of the gentlemen of Cumberland and Northumberland, who urged him to accept the government's offer of a hundred horsemen, insisting that 'there was no second means'. 'Then I told them my intention': he would take his forty riders into the wastes of Liddesdale and lie entrenched as close as possible to the outlaws whilst remaining just inside England. The idea proved unpopular with the old and cautious, but several young gentlemen promised to bring horses, and when a list of the volunteers was drawn up (including the servants who had been volunteered by their masters), Carey found himself at the head of a respectable force of 'about two hundred good men and horse'. They agreed to meet in mid-June at the closest point of England to the Armstrong power base in upper Liddesdale. This would have been the grassy holm at the confluence of Liddel Water and Kershopeburn, just downstream from the Riverview Holiday Park for the over-fifties at Mangerton, where the ruins of an Armstrong pele tower can still be seen.

A tedious task was turned into a pleasant outing. Carey had several log cabins built, encircled by 'a pretty fort' on the banks of the river. These lodges may not have been as luxurious as the top-of-the-range 'Reiver Liddesdale' cabins of the holiday park, but they were equipped with beds and mattresses, and food and fodder were supplied by a doorstep delivery service: 'The country people were well paid for anything they brought us, so that we had a good market everyday before our fort, to buy what we lacked.'

Not only was this an excellent means of reassuring the local population, it also obviated the need to leave the 'fort' and maintained a steady supply of information. The gentlemen and their servants settled in to enjoy the fishing while Carey planned the next phase of his operation.

✳

On seeing the cavalry arrive, the outlaws had fled their homes and withdrawn 'with all their goods' into the moors of Tarras Moss. The moss was surrounded, as it is today, by bogs and areas of thick scrub. It is still an impressive sight, extending for miles on either side of the single-track road from Newcastleton to Langholm where often the only creatures to be seen, apart from butterflies and birds, are a herd of wild goats. Carey called it a 'large and great forest', and it is some-times pictured as a secure and leafy refuge. But the trees have not changed their habits. A 'forest' was only occasionally wooded and, in Scotland, more often mountainous and bare. It was usually a wide, open area where deer could be hunted. On Tarras Moss, there were patches of alder, birch, hazel and willow along the glens, but on the whole, unlike the banks of the Liddel, it was not a pleasant place in which to spend the summer.*

A sneering message was brought down from the moss-bound Arm-strongs: they hoped that Carey would remain there as long as the weather allowed and make the best of the Liddesdale wastes. Come winter, he would have no rest. His offensive was nothing but 'the first puffe of a haggasse'. Haggis was served piping hot, and when the sheep's stomach was punctured, it let out a jet of steam and a suitably intestinal noise. This throw-back to the days when soldiers opened hostilities with a barrage of insults might have come from a Border ballad were it not for the absence of any reference to nationality in the Armstrongs' blus-ter. (The haggis became a national emblem only after the publication of Robert Burns's ode to the 'Great Chieftain o' the Puddin-race' in 1786. At the time, it was primarily a dish of northern England.)

The fact that Carey recorded the haggis insult in his memoirs shows that he had none of Scrope's disastrous sensitivity to provoca-tion. As a crafty commander, he delighted in a boastful enemy. A

---

* In the 1790s, Walter Scott noticed that 'there are now no trees in Liddesdale, except on the banks of the rivers, where they are protected from the sheep'. The great sheep flocks and consolidated farms of the Buccleuchs had already begun to transform the landscape in the 1590s.

'muffled man'* – either a local scout or an Armstrong turncoat – was chosen to lead one hundred and fifty horsemen into Scotland. After riding north for twenty miles, they turned and headed back towards the border by a different route. On the edge of Tarras Moss, still undetected by the reivers, they split into three groups and covered the three escape routes to the north. The most important of these would have been the dilapidated but still usable Roman road, last shown on a map of 1821, which left the fort of Broomholm in the direction of Melrose. While the three detachments blocked the exits, the Armstrongs posted scouts on the hilltops looking south towards England.

At four o'clock on 4 July, at the first blush of dawn, Carey attacked, as expected, from the south. King James must have sent reinforcements since the battalion now numbered one thousand soldiers and three hundred 'horses', which, in view of the terrain, would have been moss-troopers' ponies. The Armstrongs abandoned their animals and possessions and fled into the bogs of outer Liddesdale, only to discover the triple ambush. Most of them escaped, but three of the ringleaders were captured and brought back, unharmed, to the cabins by the river, along with the stolen sheep and cattle, which were returned to their owners.

Two hundred years later, when Walter Scott rode into Liddesdale in search of ballads and folklore, he was told the tale of 'Carey's Raid' – a romance of olden days when those rollicking Robin Hoods of the Borders had shown a pompous southerner what northern men were made of.

> They tell, that, while he was besieging the outlaws in the Tarras they contrived, by ways known only to themselves, to send a party into England, who plundered the warden's lands. On their return, they sent Carey one of his own cows, telling him, that, fearing he might fall short of provision during his visit to Scotland, they had taken the precaution of sending him some English beef.

The 'uncommodious' house to which Carey had removed his wife, children and servants lay more than fifty miles to the east, at

---

* 'In border raiding parlance: one who betrays his neighbour by leading a marauding party over secret paths to his stronghold, and who muffles his face that he may be spared recognition and retribution.' (*Scottish National Dictionary*)

Widdrington near the Northumbrian coast. There is no record of an outlaws' raid on Widdrington. A face-saving anecdote must have been spun into a flattering tale and recounted by generations of borderers whose enjoyment of the story was unimpaired by knowledge of the facts. Something of that humour born of humiliation can still be heard in the merry boasting of Liddesdale raconteurs, though even at the annual Newcastleton Traditional Music Festival, it would be hard to find a minstrel who knew the true tale of Carey's Raid.

22

'A Factious and Naughty People'

The weather changes quickly on the high moors of Liddesdale. When the clouds are spilling over the Border fells or surging up the valley, a green hillside shining in the sun can suddenly turn black. In that volatile landscape, the rout of a band of reivers camped out on Tarras Moss seems inconsequential from whichever side the tale is told. It was far from being the last skirmish between reivers and government troops. In 1649, the author of a guide to Newcastle upon Tyne and its hinterland recalled the time when there were wardens of the East, West and Middle Marches 'who had power by martial law to repress all enormities and outrages'. To this day, he wrote, the 'country that William the Conqueror did not subdue' observes its own laws and customs: 'Highlanders' come down from the dales to steal horses and cattle with such cunning that another thief must be employed to steal the animals back. They 'subject themselves to no justice' 'but bang it out bravely, one and his kindred against the other'. Even so, every year, many of those wild men are 'brought . . . into the gaol of Newcastle, and at the assizes are condemned and hanged, sometimes twenty or thirty'.

The enduring image of the Tarras Moss battle is not the fictitious English cow or the log cabins by the Liddel but the spectacle of a thousand Scottish and English soldiers under one leader swarming over the moor below Tinnis Hill. An English warden with the backing of a Scottish king rode against a rebel clan which recognized neither one country nor the other. 'Administrative centralization' may not be words to stir the blood like 'the false Salkeld' or 'the keen Lord Scroop', but this was the true nemesis of the reivers.

On 11 July 1603, two years after the siege of Tarras Moss and two months after the death of Queen Elizabeth, the Union of the Crowns was proclaimed by King James, henceforth to be titled king of 'Great Britain'. The two nations had become a kingdom with 'but one common limit or rather guard of the Ocean sea, making the whole a little world within itself', with one language and one religion. Only now, with the abolition of its last remaining land border, could that kingdom be properly described, as it had been in Shakespeare's *Richard II* – a play recently staged in London by supporters of James VI – as a 'little world', a 'fortress built by nature for herself', a 'precious stone, set in the silver sea, / Which serves it in the office of a wall, / Or as a moat defensive to a house'.

The border counties became the Middle Shires – 'the Navell or Umbilick of both Kingdomes' – and the office of warden was abolished, if only in name. Border strongholds were to be dismantled (a difficult order, only partly carried out). All feuds would cease and the only horses permitted, apart from those of gentlemen, would be 'mean nags' for tilling fields. The borderers were to 'put away all armour and weapons, as well offensive as defensive, as jacks, spears, lances, swords, daggers, steelcaps, hagbuts, pistols, plate sleeves, and such like'. Sleuth hounds or 'slough dogs' – a speciality of the Borders – were to be kept at certain places, including Sarkfoot and Moat, for pursuing offenders through the otherwise impassable bogs and mosses.*

Four years later, when James addressed Parliament, the 'one nation' dream was still blossoming in his mind as it withered in reality. The sun of righteousness had risen and warmed the fertile lands between the Cheviots and the Solway:

> Where there was nothing before ... but bloodshed, oppressions, complaints and outcries, they now live every man peaceably under his owne figgetree† ... The Marches beyond and on this side Twede, are as fruitfull and as peaceable as most parts of England.

---

* The borderers' sleuth hounds were considered one of the wonders of Scotland by the historical compiler, John Monnipennie. In 1594, he explained that the people who 'live in sleuth and idleness' neglect their own possessions, 'then have they recourse to the Dog, for reparation of their sleuth'. ('Sleuth' actually comes from the Old Norse '*slóth*', meaning 'track' or 'trail'.)

† Cf. Micah 4:4: 'But they shall sit every man under his vine and under his fig tree; and none shall make them afraid: for the mouth of the Lord of hosts hath spoken it.' (King James Bible)

The symbolic heart of the Middle Shires, the Debatable Land, which had long been 'a little world within itself', was to be taken from the 'rebels, thieves, plunderers, outlaws and other evildoers and disturbers of our peace'. The English portion was bestowed on the Earl of Cumberland and the Scottish portion on James Maxwell and Robert Douglas, who were expected to police the territory. The two land grants precisely describe the limits of 'the debatable landis', many of whose secret places were mentioned here in writing for the first time. Somehow, in all the tussles of a hundred years, that ragged remnant of ancient law and custom had retained its shape and identity.

March law, which had ensured the region's peculiar unity and independence, was replaced by the law of the land or rather, since administrators were becoming more self-consciously Scottish or English than ever, by the laws of both lands: the Border Commission set up to pacify the Borders was in practice two quite separate commissions. The old system of trods, trysts, bills and bauchling was civilized and moderate by comparison. In James's Great Britain, minor theft was punishable by death, and, as the reivers were about to discover, state justice could operate with terrifying speed.

The borderers who disturbed the pious dream of unity had been living for many years in a country in the middle of Britain which was neither Scottish nor English. Those 'mysguyded menn' were now to be eradicated. 'All theeves, murderers, oppressouris and vagabondis', declared James in 1604, must be 'quyte rooted out', and 'severe and indifferent justice [must] be ministered upon all offenders'. Thomas Armstrong, who had shot the Scottish warden Carmichael, had been hanged in 1601 after having his right hand cut off. His chained body was displayed on Burgh Muir on the southern edge of Edinburgh. In 1606, the case was reopened and several other presumed murderers of Carmichael, including 'Lang Sandy', were hanged in Edinburgh. Many more were executed for other offences.

Technically, the purge was not a massacre since all those who were strangled to death received a trial. The trial, however, came *after* the execution. The practice came to be known as 'Jeddart justice', from the court at Jedburgh. This efficient, modern system was considered by James VI an infinitely better means of furthering God's plan than the

laws and customs of 'the late Marches', which were now 'utterlie frustrated and expyred'.

✻

The other preferred solution to Border anarchy had been considered
as early as 1527, when the Scottish Privy Council had suggested
rounding up the Armstrongs, Nixons and other thieves and traitors of
both countries and shipping them off to 'Ireland or other far parts,
from which they might never return home again'. In 1604, shortly after
the latest banishment from Scotland of 'all idle persons', including
fairground charlatans, 'buffoons and strolling bards, and any calling
themselves Egyptians', James VI instructed the Border commissioners
to expel 'all in whom there can be expected no hope of amendment
. . . to some other place, where the change of aire will make in them
an exchange of their manners'.

The Grahams, who had gone on the rampage in the 'busy week'
following the death of Queen Elizabeth and who were still murdering
and extorting 'blackmail' from their neighbours, were made to sign a
document in which they begged the King to 'banish us (as a tumultuouse Collony) into some other partes of your kingdomes', where they
would 'spend the residue of our miserable and sorrowful dayes in
lamenting and sorroweing for our offences committed against your
highness'.

Though it proved difficult to find reliable escorts, one hundred
and fifty Grahams were finally shipped to the ports of Flushing and
Brill in the Netherlands, which the English had occupied since the
Dutch rebellion against the Spanish. They sailed from Newcastle on
7 July 1605. Some died, but others escaped, and just over a month
later, Grahams were reported to be hiding in Eskdale and even walking openly in the streets of Edinburgh.

It was then decided that they should be deported to Ireland. Sir
Ralph Sidley, an English landowner in Roscommon, agreed to take
them as tenants. Donations were extracted from the gentlemen of
Cumberland and Westmorland: this would provide the settlers with
livestock and, it was hoped, encourage them to leave peacefully. The
Graham chiefs asked for the money to be paid to them directly. For
obvious reasons, the request was refused. In the late summer of 1606,
fifty families were taken to the port of Workington on the Cumbrian

coast. Pregnant women and children were left behind: they would follow the menfolk in the spring, when the colony had been established.

The Trail of Tears of the Graham clan in 1606 has been described as one of the great neglected tragedies of Anglo-Scottish history. The clan was uprooted from the fields and marshes it had occupied for ninety years. As tenant farmers in Roscommon, the Grahams suffered, not only from their own incompetence – the most capable of them having fled or died – but also from the scourge of homesickness. In August 1607, Sir Arthur Chichester, Lord Deputy of Ireland, informed the Privy Council that the plan to enrol some of the Grahams in the army might not prove workable: 'their minds are so much at their homes from whence they came, without hope of return, that they will not like the poor soldier's life and fare, but will steal away into England, do what they can to the contrary'.

The Irish from whom the land had been taken were supposed to serve the Grahams as a labour force, but none of the Grahams spoke Gaelic and the deportees were naturally treated with suspicion. A pathetic petition signed by William Graham of Meedop, who, ten years before, had assisted Buccleuch in his rescue of Kinmont Willie, stated that they had found their assigned lands to be waste, devoid of wood and water, that they were now starving, and that Sir Ralph Sidley had kept all the donations for himself and was currently nowhere to be found. (He had had to leave for Dublin and London on official business.) 'Some of them had travelled a day's journey in search of Sir Ralph Sidley, but without success.'

Evicted from the lands which their great-grandfathers had misappropriated, the reiving Grahams were exonerated in the eyes of later generations by the cruelty of their treatment. In the wretchedness of exile, their wheedling and foot-dragging, their endless broken promises and manglings of the truth were, for once, not entirely unjustified. One of their descendants, John Graham of Grasmere, was so convinced by their pitiful cries that he wrote a book, *Condition of the Border at the Union: Destruction of the Graham Clan* (1907), in which he claimed that the name of his 'race' had been blackened by the Earl of Cumberland because he wanted to get his hands on the Graham estate.

The Earl, in fact, had found the English Debatable Land a poisoned chalice. As a professional buccaneer, he preferred to snatch his wealth from Portuguese and Spanish ships, and the Grahams were a worse prospect than any band of pirates: 'My thoughts must turn from intercepting of carracks [merchant galleons] to sowing of corn, from rigging ship to breeding sheep, and from honour to clownish cogitations.'

> Even from their cradles bred and brought up in theft, spoil and blood ... Neither have they any other trade, nor any other means (many of them) to live but by stealing, which they account not shame, but rather a grace and credit unto them ... I fear they are not on the sudden so easily to be reformed.

In Roscommon, Sir Ralph Sidley carefully administered, rather than 'pocketed', the funds that were destined to establish the Grahams. The owner of a vast territory spoiled by war and neglect, he had no reason to leave his tenants to starve, but he found them as idle as horse thieves. They let the summer and autumn pass without preparing for the spring and appeared to spend 'both the time and anything they had or might get, in drinking, and upon horses and dogs for hunting and pleasure'. Others who had to deal with them thought them 'a factious and naughty people'.* The Grahams who were sent to join the army were 'so turbulent and busy† that one of them is able to dispose a whole garrison to become so'.

✿

In this dark night of the Graham clan, a retrospective light shines on the little country they had left behind. If the deported Grahams were so hapless in Ireland, neither building houses nor purchasing the necessary corn and livestock, how is it that their half of the Debatable Land had become such a model of productive pasture and reclaimed wasteland? In 1608, while the fields of Roscommon lay fallow, only a tiny proportion of the English Debatable Land was still 'mossy ground' or 'marshland'. Half the remainder was pasture, the other half was 'known ground',‡ consisting of meadow and arable.

---

* 'Factious' = seditious; 'naughty' (or 'noughtie') = worthless or wicked.

† 'Busy' = troublesome.

‡ 'Known ground(s)' (unrecorded in dictionaries) apparently referred to any land that

The crofts, paddocks, cornfields, grassland and managed woods of the former Debatable Land proved the surprising economic benefits of the reiving system. A list drawn up in 1602 recorded the names of four hundred and forty-two male adults living on lands controlled by the Graham clan. Almost one-third of these were Grahams, of whom twenty-four were 'goodmen' (headmen), responsible for a number of tenants, servants and other dependants. Most of these two hundred and ninety-six inferior people had a different surname: Batie, Bell, Byers, Calvert, Dixon, Dunne, Halliday, Little, Pattison, Storey and seventy-seven other names, all still present in the area today. These are the people – mostly Scottish immigrants – who had drained and improved the fields of the Debatable Land under the lairdship of the Grahams and whose names only rarely appear in the records of reiving raids. They formed a large underclass in this bottom-heavy hierarchy. Though they were exploited by the Grahams, they were protected from the more catastrophic plundering of other tyrants. As Thomas Musgrave explained in 1583, 'the poore are oppressed' but 'are glade to sell their levinges [livelihoods] to them that oppres them'.

The expulsion of the Grahams was not a lowland equivalent of the Highland Clearances. It was a specific attack on the 'lairds', whose authority would be replaced by that of the state. The list of families to be transported to Ireland is almost exclusively a list of Grahams. Only eighteen of the one hundred and twelve had a different sur-name.

The feudal regime of the Grahams explains the obscure rebellion which took place on the quayside at Workington on the Cumbrian coast. Several of the deportees, including some subservient members of the Graham clan, were visibly more wretched than the others. They were observed to belong to 'the poorer and least dangerous sort'. Just as the ship was about to sail, their masters being for once restrained and powerless until they reached Ireland, they seized their chance and 'at the instant [of transportation], fled and hid themselves . . . rather out of weariness of the bondage they lived under their masters the chief Greames . . . than any other cause'.

---

could be used, whether for grazing or planting crops. E.g., in 1761: 'the arable, lay-meadow, pasture, and feeding commons . . . and all other the known grounds [*sic*] and lands, lying . . . within the parish'.

✿

Though the purging of the English and Scottish Middle Shires was directed by the 'King of Great Britain', pacification measures on the Scottish side took a very different form. Claiming to be 'loth to take away the lives of his subjects when any other means will serve', James nonetheless granted immunity to anyone who would cull the reivers. In 1607, a year after the execution of several Armstrongs, they and the neighbouring Irwins (including 'Curst Georgie') were still ensconced in every corner of the Scottish Debatable Land, at Harelaw, Hollows, Kinmont and Rowanburn. Bent on self-destruction or unable to mend their ways, they had 'impeded and stayed' the men who were sent to conduct a fresh survey of the 'debetable landis'. By 'thair insolent caryage and behaviour', and by 'oppressioun and bangstrie'*, they were preventing the new owners of the land, Maxwell and Douglas, from enjoying their property, thus making the King's gift 'ineffectuall'.

The men who were given the job of 'purifying' and policing the Scottish Marches believed that deportation and trials were a waste of time. Mass hangings took place at Jedburgh and Dumfries. Meanwhile, outlaws continued to break out of prisons and to sneak back from abroad.† By good fortune, the 'bold Buccleuch', who had been fighting the Spanish in the Netherlands, returned to Scotland in 1608. James and the Privy Council thought him just the man for the job.

A possible objection was that Buccleuch would be butchering men who had fought for him in the past. This turned out not to be a problem. Buccleuch's blitzkrieg on the borderers is known from the 'letter of approval and indemnity' issued to him by King James once the massacre was over. Buccleuch was not to be punished for his excellent service 'in hanging with a halter and drowning all the said malefactors taken and apprehended, in slaying and killing the fugitives . . . and in

---

* 'Bangstrie': 'violent or bullying behaviour' (*A Dictionary of the Older Scottish Tongue*).

† The Grahams who crept back to Scotland are said to have reversed their name and called themselves Maharg. The name 'Maharg' is Gaelic and unrelated to 'Graham' – a spelling which was almost never used at the time. The commonest forms, which still reflect the pronunciation of the name, were 'Grame', 'Graym', 'Greme' and 'Greyme'.

combustion, fire-raising, casting down, demolishing and destroying of their houses and their buildings'.

> In consequence of the lack of prisons, and to prevent the importun-
> ate intercession of certain good persons, the most part of these
> desperate men, at once and immediately on their apprehension,
> were necessarily hanged, and punished with death by pit and gal-
> lows off-hand on the very spot at which they were apprehended,
> dispensing with the ordinary forms of justice, as they were pub-
> licly known.

In other words, by ignoring the law of the land and every plea for mercy, Buccleuch had, with sword and rope, solved the problem of overcrowded prisons, thereby 'furthering and stablishing the peace and quietness of the kingdom'. As one of the Buccleuch family's nineteenth-century hagiographers puts it, 'that letter . . . is a very important testimony in favour of Buccleuch', and the slaughter of those 'desperate and wicked men' provided a fitting end to 'the stirring career of the Lord Buccleuch'.

❖   ❖   ❖

In this way, the 'batable land', which had been a model of peaceful cooperation until the invasion of Armstrongs and Grahams in the 1510s, became the scene of one of the worst purges in British history. Sir William Cranston, deputy lieutenant of the Scottish Marches, pursued the work of 'purification' with torture and execution and was praised by King James for hacking off 'the rottin and cankered mem-beris and flesche being in those pairtis of oure kingdome'. A sombre image of its former self at the heart of James's new nation, the Debat-able Land seemed to mark the end of its history by becoming the centre of events.

Despite its official abolition in 1551, it had remained impressed on the landscape for another half century. Ten years before the Union of the Crowns, Robert Carey had ridden to the Graham tower at Neth-erby to arrest the murderer of a churchman. A boy had been seen galloping away on his horse to raise the alarm, and Carey's fellow officer had said, 'Do you see that boy that rideth away so fast? He will be in Scotland within this half hour' — which can only mean that several miles of Debatable Land were still considered to separate England from Scotland. Even after the Union, official raids had been concentrated in the Debatable Land, and its special, separate status had been reconfirmed by the survey and the land grants of 1604.

By 1629, most of the people who had known the Debatable Land in its wildest days were dead – James VI, the Duke of Buccleuch, Lord Scrope and (presumably) Kinmont Willie. Horse-thieving continued, but it was a local nuisance rather than a threat to national stability. That year, three English gentlemen were travelling through Cumberland on their way to Scotland. Leaving Carlisle, they passed through 'wet moorish mossy ground', but after crossing the river Lyne, they came into a fertile plain where the fields were filled with corn stacks. Here, they were told, was 'the debateable land': 'The debateable land is three miles long and 3 broad, Soleme moss is on debatable land beyond Esk in Arthuret parish'.

Not a single one of the early medieval chapels remained, but at Arthuret itself, a new church had been built by national subscription as part of a campaign to bring the civilizing influence of religion to the borderers, with ministers 'to inform the lawless people of their duty, and to watch over their manners'. The builders had absconded with the money without completing the tower, and the poor people of the parish could still not say the Lord's Prayer, but it was only a matter of time before the true, Protestant religion prevailed over what the new owner of Netherby called their 'lewd vices'.

The English travellers in 1629 were looking at a scene rich in history: 'By this church [Arthuret] is the Howe end where the thieves in old time met and harboured.' At Netherby, they saw 'the houses of the Graemes that were'. There was 'one little stone tower garretted and slated or thatched', and 'some of the form of a little tower not garretted'. But this, they later discovered, was normal accommodation for a Scottish laird. Surprisingly, the former stronghold of the Grahams was occupied by a clan chief, known as 'the Good Man of Netherby in the Wood'.*

Sir Richard Graham, member of parliament for Carlisle, had just bought back the English Debatable Land from a relieved Earl of Cumberland. Richard was the second son of the reiver Fergus Graham

---

* 'Good man' (or 'gudeman'): the head of a household; also applied to the laird.

of Plomp (now Plumpe, on the river Sark near Gretna). 'Fargus the Plumpes' or 'Fargie of the Plump', as he was also known, had been one of the conspirators in the release of Kinmont Willie from Carlisle Castle. His first son had been deported to the Netherlands, but young Richard had lain low for a time and then set off for London on foot, where he found employment as the groom of King James's lover, the Duke of Buckingham, 'having some spark of wit, and skill in moss-trooping and horse racing'.

While Richard was ingratiating himself with powerful gentlemen, another young reiver had been learning to exploit his reiving expertise. After a youth of sheep-stealing, Archibald Armstrong, who was born in or on the edge of the Debatable Land, became King James's favourite jester, specializing in mock jousts. He retained his position in the court of Charles I. On a royal visit to Spain, Archie taunted the Infanta with the defeat of the Armada. Despite antagonizing the Archbishop of Canterbury, he 'jested himself into a fair estate' and became a landowner and a ruthless money-lender. Apart from Sir Richard Graham's official correspondence, the only notable text known to have been written by a former reiver is Archie Armstrong's pamphlet, *Archy's Dream*, in which the Archbishop of Canterbury is consigned to Hell.

> Changes of Times surely cannot be small,
> When Jesters rise and Archbishops fall.

Perhaps it was the ultimate fate of the reivers to provide entertainment, just as they now play a leading role in Cumbrian and Borders tourism. The antics of Richard Graham and Archie Armstrong are reminders of the sheer callous fun of reiving in its glory days, when humble farmers played practical jokes on the high and mighty, burned down their houses and mills, galloped over the mosses under a harvest moon and stole anything that moved. 'By my soul', an old reiver returning from a raid is said to have exclaimed when passing an unusually large haystack, 'Had ye but four feet, ye should not stand lang there!'

❈

After 1629, there are no more substantial records of the Debatable Land as a recognizable entity. The last sign that its boundaries lived on in local memory dates from nearly two centuries after its partition. One day in 1740, the rector of Kirkandrews set out to trace the limits of his parish. He reached the river Sark, where the boundary of the former Debatable Land coincides with the border between England and Scotland. In talking to his parishioners, he discovered that parts of the national border had been misplaced. Tradition was so tenacious that the local people could have drawn a map more accurate than that of any cartographer: 'From the foot of Sark, up Sark to the Scotch Dike, [the border] frequently crosses Sark and follows old water courses, which are known by the inhabitants of both sides.'

This is one of the inconspicuous gems which occasionally wash up on the storm-battered beach of Border history. To the people of the border, the frontier followed the river – but the river as it had run in the distant past, when the Debatable Land was still a separate country. In their eyes, the landscape lived in four dimensions, the shadows of its earlier selves coexisting with the actual scene like the familiar ghosts of ancestors seated at the fireside.

This meant that some parts of England and Scotland were stranded in the opposite country. In a future dis-United Kingdom, when the Sark decides again, as it sometimes does, to move its bed, it might provide English and Scottish property lawyers with some lucrative complications. Even now, there may be some English fields along the Sark which, historically, belong to Scotland, and vice versa.*

Though something of its a-national spirit survives, almost no one living here today knows where the Debatable Land began and ended or even what it was. Some local visitors to the house, when I identified the land across the Liddel as a country that was once neither Scotland nor England, have found it quite plausible that their ancestors didn't give a hoot about nationality; others said, simply, 'Sounds like a good idea!' As for historians, few consider the disappearance of the Debatable Land significant. Most are unaware of its exceptional nature and lump it together with the rest of the border badlands. On a background of national politics, it seems an exotic but irrelevant vestige of

---

* There is a modern legal precedent in the Debatable Land for taking an older rather than the present course of a river as the border. Liddel Water once flowed at the foot of the cliff on which Liddel Moat was built. The engineers of the North British Railway pushed the river two hundred and fifty feet to the west, leaving one acre of Scotland on the English side.

local tradition, the domain of ethnology rather than history, doomed to disappear along with the pele towers and the reivers. Having no equivalent in British history, the Debatable Land is easily ignored – a country independent of the two kingdoms, sustained but not created by official treaties, and dating from a time when neither England nor Scotland nor the idea of them existed.

23

Silence

In 2013, for the first time in more than three hundred years, the borderlands felt the tug and pressure of the two great nations on either side. It was as though something previously believed to be immovable had shifted and could no longer be taken for granted. At church, in the village hall, on the roads and lonnings and on the cross-border 127 bus, there were quiet, anxious conversations which contrasted with the strident voices on the radio.

Far away in southern England, there was only the faintest perception of what was coming, and the polls suggested in any case that a referendum on the question of Scottish independence, to be held in September 2014, would result in a clear defeat for the Scottish nationalists. But in Scotland – in Glasgow and Edinburgh and parts of Perthshire – I had seen entire streets festooned with Scottish flags. Some windows were entirely blotted out by the cross of St Andrew.

A special kind of history was evolving on both sides in which every battle and belief was tattooed with an indelible dividing line. The Debatable Land belonged to a different history, curiously in keeping with the spirit in which its present inhabitants faced the gathering storm. A few Border families had had their 'bravehearts' and unionists, but to most borderers, as to their twenty-first-century Liddesdale descendants, 'independence' in the current sense would still have meant subservience to a state.

With the two nations fighting an increasingly bitter political battle, these expeditions into the land that was once neither Scottish nor English should have become a picturesque irrelevance, yet they

took on an incongruous urgency. The boundaries of the Debatable
Land might soon be resurrected as a frontier, and it seemed more
important than ever to discover the age and origins of the country
between the two kingdoms.

All I knew, however, was that, despite the persistence of its boundaries, and apart from two temporary Roman camps, the Debatable
Land had been uninhabited from the end of the Bronze Age to the age
of Grahams and Armstrongs (p. 109). Two place names – Wobrethills
and Brettalach – might refer to an aboriginal British population, but
the assortment of material evidence was ridiculously meagre: a rein-
guide, a jug, a buried hoard and two drowned cows.

In the face of this silence, there was nothing more to be said.
At that distance in time, the historical vista was as impenetrable
as the moors and mosses when a Liddesdale drow has descended.
That vast gap in the archaeological record was a discovery in itself,
but there were no human voices to explain the emptiness, only the
river of the 'loud dale', proclaiming the ancient boundary with its
noise.

                          ❋   ❋   ❋

One morning in early summer when it was just warm enough to write
out of doors, I was sitting on a bank above the Liddel making the final
changes to a book on the surveying skills of the ancient Celts. The
sheet in front of me was a reproduction of the only ancient map on
which the approximate location of the future borderlands can be sur-
mised. Ptolemy's map of Britain, created in Alexandria in the second
century AD, consists of one hundred and sixteen place names dotted
about a hopelessly distorted outline of the British Isles. The section
which appears to cover what are now the Borders shows a small
scattering of towns, rivers and estuaries.

In a fantasy film, the map could be fed into a computer and forced
to yield its secrets with the magic word, 'Enhance!' But even a fantasy
computer would struggle to make sense of Ptolemy's map: many
of the places have never been identified and the names that can be
attached to real sites appear to be wildly misplaced.

Over in the Debatable Land, I heard a rumble above the rushing
of the river. A flock of sheep had just seen their hay being delivered

by the farmer and were galloping towards the feast. At that moment, I realized that if the map did by some remote chance contain any usable information about this far-flung corner of the Roman Empire, there was a means of finding it out.

PART FOUR

24

Graticules

Somewhere in the Great Library of Alexandria, in about AD 150, a local scholar named Klaudios Ptolemaios (or Ptolemy) sat amongst a huge and miscellaneous collection of scrolls and tablets from all corners of the earth. Thanks to the library's aggressive acquisitions policy – confiscating and copying any documents found on ships putting in at Alexandria – there were sailors' logbooks, travellers' diaries, 'itineraries' which gave estimates of distances and sometimes directions where no roads existed, and first-hand reports from merchants who had prospected the routes and resources of distant lands long before the arrival of the Roman army. There were even some 'precise maps', painted on wooden boards or etched on metal plates.

Ptolemy's ambition was to create a map of the entire known world 'by using the researches of those who have visited the places, or the positions of those places on the more accurate charts'. The maps of particular regions on wood or metal were naturally of great value, but, as Ptolemy explained in the introduction to his eight-volume *Geography*, these were painted landscapes rather than mathematical descriptions. The information he prized above all took the form of coordinates which had been obtained using the latest scientific techniques. Only astronomical measurements, he believed, could produce a reliable map.

His main source was a world map composed but never completed by a Greek mathematician, Marinus of Tyre, who had probably died by the time Ptolemy started work. Marinus had assigned coordinates of latitude and longitude to every place, defining its exact position on the earth. This is the method which Ptolemy adopted. In effect, he digitized the information.

Each section of his 'map' listed and located the *poleis* ('towns') of each region, with the names of the tribes to whom they belonged, as well as river mouths, estuaries, headlands and islands. This, for example, is part of the section which details the towns and tribes of southern Caledonia (lowland Scotland):

... To the east of the Selgovae and farther north live the Damnonii, whose towns are:

Colanica	20° 45'	59°
Vindogara	21° 40'	60°
Coria	21° 30'	59° 20'
Alauna	22° 45'	59° 50'

A painted map would have disappeared centuries ago, but in the superficially tedious form of lists of numbers, Ptolemy's world map was able to traverse the centuries. The text of his *Geography* was rediscovered in the late thirteenth century, and when its eight thousand coordinates of towns, rivers, islands, bays and headlands were plotted on parchment, the ancient world appeared as fresh as though Ptolemy himself had just unfurled his great scroll on the floor of the Library of Alexandria.

Contemplating this masterpiece today, when the astronomical measurements prized by Ptolemy are so refined that the global position of a blade of grass can be determined in an instant, the inadequacies of the map are obvious. As Ptolemy knew all too well, the quality of the information varied. Some travellers had recorded their geographical observations in 'a crude manner', 'perhaps because it was not yet understood how useful the more mathematical mode of investigation is'. Both he and Marinus had continually revised their maps as new information arrived, but for remote regions, unvisited by people with 'scientific training', only the older, unsophisticated varieties of map were available.

How much accurate information could one expect to obtain, for example, from those foggy isles whose shores were sometimes visible from the north coast of Gaul? The conquest of Britannia had not begun until AD 43, and it was only in AD 84 that a ship of the Roman fleet had circumnavigated the island now called Great Britain. The names on the British section of Ptolemy's world map suggest that he had been forced to work with antiquated data. The 'Legio II Augusta', located below Isca (Exeter), had operated there in the AD 50s. Several towns had their original British rather than Roman names. The island of Great Britain itself was labelled with its older name, 'Albion'. Modern, astronomical readings were available for only nine places in the British Isles.

Even if the information had been accurate, there was another problem to solve. The coordinates of latitude and longitude have to be plotted on a grid or 'graticule', from the Latin *craticula*, meaning a finely woven lattice. Unless the dimensions of the graticule are known, the coordinates are practically worthless and the resulting map is about as useful as a blank chess board or a treasure map scaled to the paces of an unknown species.

Ptolemy derived his graticule, in part, from what he took to be the distances separating lines of latitude. The farther north, the shorter the distances. Accordingly, for each part of his world map, he specified a different grid: '2 by 3' for Gaul, 'approximately 11 by 20' for the British Isles, and so on. These were simply educated guesses. The main point was to enable readers to draw their own copies of the map. The more names there were to fit on the map, the larger the 'boxes' of the graticule.

✿

This digital map kit is one of the great wonders and disappointments of the ancient world. When the British coordinates are plotted on Ptolemy's specified grid of 11 by 20, the tantalizing wealth of geographical data grows dull like a glinting stone removed from a clear pool. Assembled according to Ptolemy's instructions, the map is ludicrously inaccurate (fig. 7). Some places appear on the wrong coast, Scotland has swung ninety degrees to the east on a giant hinge located somewhere along the future Anglo-Scottish border, and the region of the Debatable Land seems to have vanished into the pit of ignorance.

The queer contortions of Ptolemy's map are assumed to reflect the ancients' hazy view of the world. The Romans certainly harboured some bewilderingly erroneous conceptions of European geography, but Rome was not the only scientific civilization in Western Europe. After studying the art and technology of the ancient Celts of Gaul and

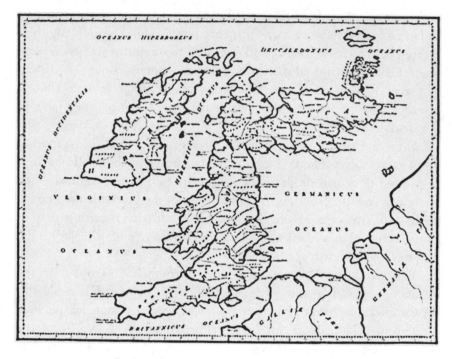

Ptolemy's coordinates for the British Isles
as plotted in Joan Blaeu's atlas of Scotland (1654).

Britannia, I was full of admiration for the precision of their science,
and so I wondered: what if the original data obtained in Britain had
been accurate? Perhaps it had become muddled only when Ptolemy
pieced it all together and fitted it to his grid . . .

I chose two places whose ancient locations are known – Londinium (London) and Camulodunum (Colchester). Then I stretched the
grid in both directions, horizontally and vertically, until both places
were correctly positioned relative to each other. This produced a
graticule of 4 by 3 instead of Ptolemy's 11 by 20. Logically, if the data
had been accurate, all the other known places would now appear on
the map in their correct positions – which would mean, of course, that
the *unknown* places could also be identified.

I made the necessary adjustments, using the 'resize' function in
Microsoft's 'Paint' program, and with that simple operation, the
mechanism which had seemed damaged beyond repair began to tick

like a well-regulated clock. Not only London and Colchester but also all the other known towns appeared in their proper locations.

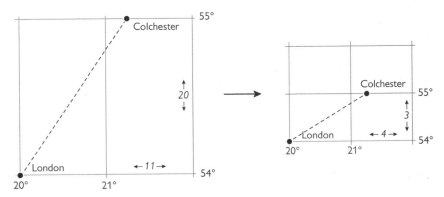

Correcting Ptolemy's map. Left: London (54° 00', 20° 00') and Colchester (55° 00', 21° 15'), using Ptolemy's suggested graticule of 11 by 20. Right: on a graticule of 4 by 3, the two places are correctly positioned. Applied to the rest of the map of southern England (fig. 10), this graticule reveals a remarkably accurate map of the entire area.

A few hours later on the same day, in accordance with the staring-us-in-the-face-all-along phenomenon, I noticed that the solution had been spelled out on the pages I was correcting by the river. I had discovered that, unlike the Romans, who attached no particular significance to one ratio or another, the tribes of Gaul and southern Britain had organized their urban settlements according to certain basic ratios. The ratio used in Britain had been 4:3 – the same ratio which had just opened the way back to the ancient borderlands.

Despite their practical uses, mathematical ratios have an aura of esoteric mystery – especially when applied to Celts and Druids. But here, in the restored map of southern England, was a radiant confirmation, with as many particular proofs as there are towns on Ptolemy's map. The ratio of 4 and 3 produces a perfect 'Pythagorean' 3–4–5 triangle. It now appeared that this simple formula had been used with spectacular success in the mapping of southern Britannia.

Discoveries like this often turn up at the last minute like chaotic, luggage-laden travellers. My publishers were hard at work on the final details of the book on the ancient Celts, and the four-hundred-page balloon was already sufficiently inflated. It would have been inconsiderate, to say the least, to come rushing up with another load for the creaking basket. The book would have to be launched as it was. But another journey was beginning. In the distant past, I could see a well-charted landscape of rivers and towns and, by implication, roads that might lead back to the borderlands, and although the details of that journey had yet to be worked out, the Debatable Land in its earliest days no longer seemed entirely beyond reach.

✿   ✿   ✿

Three years before, we had travelled up from the south of England to the borderlands. This time, the journey would take place on paper and two thousand years in the past. The task now was to check that the navigational equipment was reliable, which meant working out how the map had been produced.*

With its tin and gold mines, Britain had long been a target for merchants. In the sixth century BC, a trader or explorer from the Greek port of Massilia had walked the length of Britain. Either by Luguvalium (Carlisle) or a more easterly route, Pytheas of Marseille had passed through the borderlands with no more trouble than King James's favourite cow (p. 90). Since then, sailors from Gaul and Spain had called at ports on both sides of the Irish Sea and travelled far inland in search of minerals and exotic merchandise. This would explain why Ptolemy's map includes eleven 'towns' in Ireland, which no Roman army ever visited.

Some of the charts and *periploi* (written descriptions of sea routes) used by maritime merchants would have provided Ptolemy with the coastal information he needed for his map. Most of the coastal features can be identified, but they were plotted far less accurately than the towns. The reason is that distances at sea were calculated by the time it took to sail from one port or headland to the next. Easy sailing contracted the apparent distances; adverse conditions had the opposite effect.

On land, with measuring instruments placed on a stable surface, more accurate information can be obtained. This was the second key to understanding the map. The coastal coordinates have to be treated as an entirely separate set of data. With his passion for completeness,

---

* For the essential details: pp. 292–3 and figs 7–12.

Ptolemy tried to fit the two discrepant sets of data together. To assemble the map of Ireland, for instance, believing the maritime data and the land data to be compatible in their original forms, he squeezed the coastal locations to give the impression that the eleven towns stretched from coast to coast. In reality, they cover little more than half the island.

I now knew that this apparently defective land map of ancient Britain and Ireland had been based on information of an extraordinarily high quality. The coherence of the information had made the process of 'hacking into' the map unexpectedly straightforward: first, the map had to be resized to conform to the original graticule; second, the land data had to be separated from the coastal data. The third and final key presented itself quite naturally, though it took some time to realize that I was looking at the only contemporary cartographic evidence of the Roman conquest of Britain: the map of the towns of Britain is not a single map but an atlas, comprising five distinct maps, each with its own graticule (figs 8 and 9). Here again, any attempt to reconstruct the original source as though it had been a coherent whole was doomed to failure.

Ptolemy's re-plotted coordinates confirmed the system described in the book on the ancient Celts, but they also showed that the basic principle had been applied more widely than I had thought. In analysing the organization of roads and settlements in pre-Roman Britain, I had found that the ratio of 4 and 3 operated only in the southern half of England, as far north as Mediolanum (Whitchurch in Shropshire). I had tentatively identified this as a sphere of Druidic influence beyond which no such pattern was detectable. This was confirmed by Ptolemy's atlas, in which the 4:3 graticule operates only up to Mediolanum.

North of Mediolanum, it seemed at first as rough and ready as one would expect an ancient map to be. Even in those days, 'the North' was considered less sophisticated, and I assumed that the lack of evidence was a sign of backwardness. Writing the book in a land where sheep outnumber human beings, I had come to think of Oxford and London as palaces of learning shining on a far horizon, and I was not predisposed to discover in the region of Lancashire, Yorkshire and Cumbria the intellectual treasure of a maligned civilization.

✻

The unsuspected glories of map-making at the dawn of British history are a wonderful and disconcerting sight. The map of southern England seems to be unique in the history of cartography, though it may have been typical of ancient Celtic mapping. It functions like a direction finder on a viewing platform or like a giant signpost: each finger on the signpost points in the right direction, while its length gives a rough idea of distance. The distances are approximate but the directions are accurate to within two degrees from certain nodal points – in particular, London.

This is, to all appearances, a land map designed to be used in Londinium (fig. 10). Though its practical uses would have been limited, it would have suited the purposes of an ancient Briton who, like a Muslim praying to Mecca, wanted to know the exact direction in which a certain place lay but for whom distance and journey time were unimportant. The item acquired by the Library of Alexandria might have resembled one of the portable Roman sundials which occasionally come to light. The original map was certainly more accurate than Ptolemy's sample since the bearings could not have been so precisely calculated without knowledge of the correct distances.

The map of northern England, by contrast, is so much like a modern map that, without the medieval copies of Ptolemy's *Geography*, it could be mistaken for a modern forgery. It uses a graticule of 3 by 2. Distances as well as directions are shown with a precision unmatched until the Renaissance. Its only obviously exotic feature is its orientation, which is based, conveniently, on the sun rather than the North Pole (a sensible rather than superstitious convention since, at that time, there was no star at the pole).

These are by far the most accurate maps to have survived from the ancient world. For the purposes of the original surveyors, they were effectively faultless: expressed anachronistically in degrees, the bearings appear impossibly precise, but each angle is the product of a simple whole-number ratio (3 and 5 for Colchester, 5 and 9 for Winchester, etc.). This is the proof which Hugh Davies lacked in 1998 when he argued, controversially, that the Roman road system must have been based on maps produced by triangulation. It also answers a long-standing question: how did Marinus of Tyre know that the exact distance between London and Chichester was fifty-nine Roman miles?

It was comparatively easy to measure distances by road, but this, remarkably, is the distance in a straight line.

In Ptolemy's mind, the lack of British coordinates based on astronomical readings was a severe shortcoming. As we now know, he was right to think that only measurements of the sun's shadow and the length of day could precisely define a location on the earthly sphere. The problem was that, although the theory was correct, the technology (especially chronometers), like most latest technologies, was full of bugs and glitches.

The result can be seen in Ptolemy's map of Gaul. This long-established Roman province, with its road network and universities, should have been one of the best-mapped parts of the empire. In theory, the map of Gaul was more sophisticated, but in reality, it would have been unusable: Reims appears as a suburb of Paris, Paris is shown to the south rather than north of Nantes, and several parts of the map are almost upside-down. Its main cartographic value is as a record of erroneous readings. In Britain, older but more reliable methods of determining geographical position had remained in use. These methods, like those used for medieval portolan charts, were perfectly adequate for relatively small parts of the globe such as northern England.

The division of England into separate maps, each with its own conventions, is a graphic guide to the early Roman conquest of Britain. The towns on the map of southern England had all been conquered by about AD 60. Those on the northern England map were conquered only later, in the AD 70s. Perhaps, at the end of each campaign, the information obtained by Roman officers from natives or merchants was sent back to Rome, from where it eventually reached Alexandria. The new frontier was then consolidated in preparation for the next advance.

These borders which temporarily marked the northern limit of the Roman Empire have long been suspected but never traced in detail. They may already have existed as tribal boundaries. Use of the 3:2 rather than 4:3 system probably reflects a cultural divide. Most of the map of northern England covers the territory of the tribe or tribal federation of the Brigantes. 'Brigantia', previously thought to have stretched to the borders of what is now Scotland, must have ended much farther south at Epiacum. This name is currently applied to the

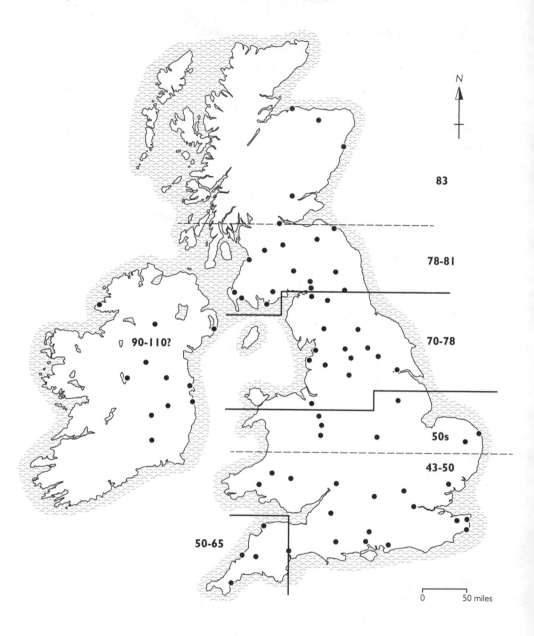

N

83

78-81

90-110?

70-78

50s

43-50

50-65

0   50 miles

Places recorded on the separate maps of Ptolemy's British atlas, with the
approximate foundation dates (AD) of the Roman forts and towns.
For more detail, see figs 8–12.

Roman fort of Whitley Castle, advertised as 'the best preserved fort in the Roman Empire', but the restored map of Ptolemy shows beyond doubt that it belongs to the lonely fort at Low Borrowbridge.

North of Low Borrowbridge, the road and the railway climb to the pass of Shap which many first-time travellers from the south, impressed by the obvious geographical frontier, mistake for the Anglo-Scottish border. In the AD 70s, the Roman legions pushed on beyond Shap, up the western side of the Pennines, to Whitley Castle and Carlisle, leaving the eastern side for a later campaign. These two towns of the Selgovae tribe accordingly appear on the map of northern England. The forts on the eastern side were established only later, in the AD 80s, which is why they appear on the later, Caledonian map.

The Pennines are still a barrier, especially when the Hartside Pass is snowbound and landslips have closed the railway. To find this geographical reality in the digital hieroglyphics of a second-century atlas was a strangely thrilling experience. There on the edge of the map of northern England, Carlisle looked like an outpost, as it had done in 2010. Beyond, lay other places with enigmatic names. Only one of them – Bremenium – had ever been identified. But if the map of Caledonia followed a similar logic, there was every hope that, after Carlisle, the skies of the borderlands would remain clear.

25

The Kingdom of Selgovia

It took several weeks to reach this point in the atlas and I still had no idea what was waiting in the borderlands. The maps were certainly accurate enough to allow previously unidentifiable places to be identified.* Since Ptolemy noted the tribes to which each town belonged, this had already led to a significant modification of the tribal map of Britain. I knew, too, that many of the towns shown on the maps had certain features in common. All of them stood at junctions of the Roman road network, almost one-third were inland ports and many, not surprisingly, lay in regions known to have been mined for precious minerals. It seemed likely that the Solway Firth and the inland port of Netherby/Castra Exploratorum would have been of particular interest to merchants and military commanders. But first there was the problem of the Caledonian map to be solved.

The peculiar rotation of Scotland to the east is easier to correct than to explain. The original map may have shown west at the top and Ptolemy reproduced the map as he found it, assuming north to be at the top. The other possibility is that this is an early example of southern meteorological prejudice. The Roman geographer Strabo had asserted that human life was impossible anywhere north of Hibernia (Ireland), and so Ptolemy 'corrected' the map which implausibly showed several tribes and towns in the supposedly frozen north by turning it ninety degrees to the right. In either case, the map simply has to be re-rotated ninety degrees anti-clockwise. Though the Caledonian map is less accurate than the northern England map – probably

---

* The process of identifying unknown places on the map, which can also be used to test its accuracy, is described in fig. 11.

because it covers a much larger area – it can be read without much difficulty on a graticule of 4 by 1. The smaller number of Roman forts in Scotland makes identification relatively unproblematic since there are fewer candidates for each site (fig. 12).

The fort of Bremenium in the bottom-right corner of the restored map is known from the second-century Antonine Itinerary to be the fort of High Rochester which lies on the Roman road, Dere Street, just below Carter Bar on the Anglo-Scottish border. The place labelled 'Alauna' would have stood on or near Hadrian's Wall. The most likely candidate is Corbridge – either the Roman fort or the neighbouring civilian settlement. Both these Northumbrian places are attributed by Ptolemy to the Votadini tribe, while the two Cumbrian forts to the west are attributed to the Selgovae.

In this sparse configuration of points, two other towns lie close together. Their names are Colanica and Curia. These are Celtic words, thought to be generic terms meaning 'tribal centre' or 'meeting place'. Neither town has been identified until now.

Despite their proximity, each town is attributed to a different tribe – Colanica to the Damnonii of southern Scotland, Curia to the Votadini of northern England. This must account for the inclusion of two places so close together. Nowhere else on the British atlas are two towns shown in such proximity. The original map-maker evidently thought it important to indicate this tribal frontier. A merchant travelling from one to the other would have wanted to know with which tribe he would be dealing.

The accuracy of the restored map makes it possible to identify these neighbouring places with complete certainty. Thanks to the data gathered in Britain and digitized by Ptolemy, the cryptic coordinates of Colanica and Curia are as legible as the road signs on the A7 which crosses the border between Longtown and Langholm. Curia of the Votadini was the 'ancient Citie' whose 'strange and great ruins' lie under the fields of Netherby by the Esk, while Colanica of the Damnonii was the British town and Roman fort eight miles up-stream at Broomholm, on the grassy platform at the end of the Roman road which forms the northern boundary of the Debatable Land.

✿

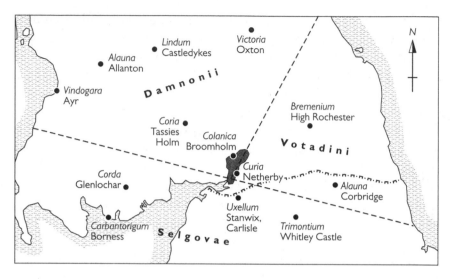

Towns of the Damnonii, Selgovae and Votadini (straddling Hadrian's Wall)
and approximate tribal territories. The shaded area is the Debatable Land.
For more detail, see figs 12 and 13.

It seemed (and was) an extraordinary stroke of luck to discover on a
map of the second century AD the exact markers of the northern and
southern boundaries of the Debatable Land. For some reason, this
obscure corner of Outer Britannia was one of the most precisely
mapped parts of the Roman Empire. It was strange to think that, in
the second century and in 1552, when Henry Bullock created his
'platt' of the Debatable Land, this small region, which, even now, is
missing from most guidebooks, was depicted on the most accurate
maps of the time.

But was it really so astonishing to see the Debatable Land rise from
the night of ages? In the land on the other side of the Liddel, two tribes,
each controlling a vast area, had faced one another across a frontier.
Apart from the rivers themselves and the Cheviot watershed, this is the
earliest sign of the future Anglo-Scottish border and one of the oldest
clues to any political division in pre-Roman Britain. The emptiness
revealed by the archaeological record was not misleading. The medieval documents had been right to call that oddly resilient realm 'ancient'.
Neither Scottish nor English in the Middle Ages, in the late Iron Age
it had been neither Damnonian nor Votadinian.

Ptolemy's maligned atlas of ancient Britain also reveals a crucial difference between the frontier which still exists and its Celtic ancestor. The inter-tribal zone was not just a buffer between two states. A short distance to the south, the map shows a town or fort called Uxellum, attributed to the Selgovae tribe. This is Uxellodunum, where Hadrian's Wall reaches Carlisle on the bluff above the river Eden.

It is easy to think of the tribes of ancient Britain as either proto-English or proto-Scottish, but the territory of the Selgovae belongs to a different era. Ptolemy's map proves that the Selgovae inhabited both sides of the Solway Firth, which now divides England from Scotland. Their kingdom was a Mediterranean of the north: it stretched from the highest Pennines in the east to the middle of the Galloway peninsula in the west. The broad arm of the Solway looks like the permanent marker of an ancient division, but two thousand years ago, when a Selgovian stood where King Edward I gazed at Scotland for the last time, he would have been looking at his own country, and when he walked out over the sands at low tide, he would have crossed the water without leaving the motherland.

*

The kingdom of the Selgovae would have met those of the Damnonii and the Votadini in the region of the Debatable Land. Though the Selgovae possessed the Cumbrian Plain and both shores of the Solway, the vital inland port at Netherby belonged to the Votadini, while the Damnonii controlled the northern end of the Esk corridor at Broomholm, where roads converged from north, west and east, tapping the rich mining and agricultural areas of lowland Scotland. This tripartite division centred on a march is typical of the ancient Celts. A very similar situation existed in Gaul, where the great tribal federations of the Aedui, the Arverni and the Bituriges formed a broad frontier zone, later called the Marche, which is still recognizable as a linguistic and cultural watershed. The arrangement is rare if not non-existent in the modern world, despite its obvious geopolitical value.

With shared boundaries in the flatlands on the edges of the Debatable Land, all three nations had access to the trade routes of the Irish Sea. This inter-tribal zone still looks like a no man's land. The landscape has been transformed by roads and railways, wind farms and pylons, but the physical and even the human geography is unaltered. At Longtown, the farmers of Cumbria and Dumfriesshire meet at Britain's biggest sheep market. In 2001, the area's centrality was demonstrated by an infected sheep sold at Longtown Mart, from where foot-and-mouth disease spread rapidly to the rest of the country.

The proto-Debatable Land may have arisen as a buffer zone in the aftermath of a destructive war, or it may have been created by consensus or divided inheritance when the region was settled by Celtic tribes. These tripartite divisions cushioned by a broad frontier could be as sturdy as the arch of a bridge sustained by the force of compression. Each tribe had an interest in preserving the mutually beneficial arrangement. The closest examples today are antagonistic rather than cooperative. The buffer zone in Cyprus, which separates Greek and Turkish Cypriots, is administered by a third party, the United Nations. Large parts of the 'Dead Zone' have been abandoned to nature and are useless to the people on either side. To judge by the long absence of any settlement, the Celtic solution, which was still being applied by the Anglo-Scottish borderers five hundred years ago, was to make the buffer zone 'batable' rather than debatable. The livestock of opposing tribes or nations maintained the unoccupied zone as pasture and prevented it from turning into wasteland.

The oldest known trysting place in the borderlands was still in use when the Debatable Land was partitioned in 1552. The Lochmaben Stone at the foot of the Sark, on the south-western tip of the Debatable Land, where English and Scottish officials discussed international matters, bears the name of a local Celtic god, Maponus (p. 98). It has often been suggested that the sacred stone was once a meeting place of Celtic tribes. This now looks more than likely. The monolith on the ocean's edge, where the river-borne rubbish of two nations gathers in the mud before being carried out to the Irish Sea, stands in the area where the three Celtic nations of the future borderlands came together.

The worn stone of Maponus now has nothing to tell us, and the trail revealed by the second-century map ends like the ghostly footprints on the stairs of Netherby Hall. The history of these tribal and national divisions can be traced only in the centuries-long emptiness of the Debatable Land. Perhaps the sanctity of the buffer zone was preserved by a religious veto, later materialized in the chapels which stood on its borders. The only other clue is a name traced faintly on the map of 1552, which identifies the land by the Esk at the end of the Scots' Dike as 'Dymisdale'. A document of the same period calls it 'Dimmisdaill, as the common people say'. The name disappeared from maps and local memory long ago. Three other Dymisdales or 'Doomsdales' in Britain are associated with justice and execution; the Dymisdale of Inverness, for example, was the way that led to Gallows Hill. Did the ancient Celts and their Dark Age successors picture that sacred enclave, which lay deserted and silent after sundown, as the other world, inhabited only by the spirits of the dead?

The zone's political significance is easier to grasp. Its nearest equivalent in the Roman Empire is the tribal frontier zone 'of doubtful ownership' between the Rhine and the Danube. This Debatable Land of Germania had a similar history. It was eventually invaded by 'worthless vagabonds' from Gaul who, like the Armstrongs and Grahams, involuntarily acted as the spearhead of a greater power. Its integrity destroyed, it was swallowed by the Roman Empire, primarily so that its inhabitants could be taxed. In both cases, borders established for the purposes of trade and cooperation became barriers to be exploited for financial and political ends.

❊   ❊   ❊

As the day of the Scottish Referendum drew near, I often looked at the map of the kingdom of Selgovia. The Solway Firth, where one country seems to pull away from the other, was not an ancient border after all. It had been no more a boundary to the people of the Iron Age than it was to the oystercatchers and the barnacle geese. After the Romans, it had belonged to the kingdom of Strathclyde, which straddled the future border. Only much later was this kingdom which embraced both sides of the Solway divided. That division, which now seems such an essential feature of British history, had lasted only five hundred years, and for much of that time, England and Scotland had been officially at peace. The frontier zone shared by three powerful tribes had continued to serve its purpose, and when the two modern nations had united, its spirit had lived on. Now, there was a real possibility that they would be separated again.

The Celtic tribes of the borderlands proved that independent nations could form a stable partnership. Ptolemy's map and the history of the Debatable Land could be used to support rational arguments on either side of the independence debate. But the tone of the debate was aggressive and the references to Anglo-Scottish history were becoming increasingly dubious. The Border ballads were read as evidence of fierce national pride. Even some academic historians seemed to guide the hand of history towards a 'Yes' vote. One scholar claimed in a study of the Scottish Middle March that cross-border marriages had been a myth invented by the English: 'Reports of them were partly the result of English scaremongering.' The absence of marriage contracts was held to prove that interbreeding had not been prevalent – though it is hard to imagine illiterate reivers postponing their wedding feasts so that the proper documents could be obtained from the relevant authority.

The view which prevailed in this part of the borderlands was more in keeping with recorded history. What was traditional and ancient in the Debatable Land was not division but agreement. In metropolitan Scotland, the borderers' reluctance to see their cross-border community disrupted was characterized as 'rural', as though people who stand in the rain without umbrellas and who recognize the seasons within seasons must be out of touch with important realities.

On a last visit to the Lochmaben Stone, a few feet from the national border, I turned down the lane which leads to the sea in the part of Gretna called Old Graitney. In a field bordered by houses, a farmer was trying to separate two bucking cows. As I cycled past, he was nearly knocked off his feet by the cows and shouted, 'Gie ower!' ('Stop it!') The words are identical in the two dialects of English spoken in the region – Southern Scots and Cumbrian – and it was as hard to tell whether the man was English or Scottish as it might have been to know on which side of the Solway a Selgovian farmer had been born.

26

'Arthur'

At the time, the map appeared to have nothing more to say about the borderlands. Instead, I used it as a source of themes for longer bike rides. The point of a theme is that it can take you to places you might never have visited and it makes the memory of the ride more vivid. In this case, there was the added incentive of using a map of second-century Britain to plan a cycling route.

We explored the kingdoms of the Selgovae, the Damnonii and the Votadini, impressed by their vastness and the natural wealth of their lands. Wherever possible, we followed the Roman roads which had connected the places on the map. In Ayrshire, Dumfriesshire and the Galloway peninsula, there were sites whose importance to Roman traders and the native British had only now become apparent, and although these rides were recreational, they began to feel like a necessary experiment. There was no sign that the map could bring back to life that dark age of the Debatable Land, but it was already offering answers to questions which had been raised by the earlier expeditions.

For example, since practically every place on the map stood at a road junction, this confirmed the idea that Broomholm had been served, not only by the Roman road which was 'plain to be seen' on Canonbie Moor in 1757, but also by the 'dry march' from the west which marked the boundary of the Debatable Land (p. 90). This meant that Colanica/Broomholm had been a major crossroads in Roman Scotland, and it showed that almost the entire northern boundary of the Debatable Land had been traced by a Roman road. (Coincidentally, an archaeological survey of Broomholm in the summer of 2016 showed that the site was 'more substantial than originally thought': 'Most people regard the fort as being off on a limb . . . Now, it's looking as if it was quite large and important.'*)

The other main theme of these longer rides seemed at first to have only a tenuous connection with the map. It concerned a heroic figure of such questionable reality that he may never have existed. If he did exist, no one knows whether he came from the West Country, Wales, the north of England or Scotland.

Most of the places which bear the name of Arthur are in Wales and the south-west, but there are also thirty-seven 'Arthur' places scattered over the Scottish lowlands and the north of England. Several of them are less than a day's ride from home: the closest are a wooded ridge on the road to Bewcastle called Arthurseat and a farm near Carwinley Burn once named Arthur's Cross after a stone placed at the intersection of three parishes.† Arthuret itself, despite its legendary connection with Myrddin or Merlin, may be only accidentally Arthurian.‡

Even if a hero of that name had lived in late Roman or Dark Age Britain, it is doubtful that any historical truth would have survived. The comparatively recent figures of Johnnie Armstrong and Kinmont Willie had quickly mutated into figments of legend, their exploits confused with the antics of Robin Hood or associated incongruously with Scottish national sentiment. If a real Arthur had existed, how many other layers of confusion must have built up over the centuries? On Hadrian's Wall, King Arthur's Well, the crag of Arthur's Chair and tales of Arthur's sleeping knights were no more enlightening than the wordless monoliths of the Debatable Land's boundaries.

Yet there was one common feature which emerged when I plotted all these places on a map with a view to planning the bike rides. The distribution of 'Arthur' place names in Wales and the West Country closely matches the distribution of stones inscribed in the Ogham

---

* *Eskdale & Liddesdale Advertiser*, 14 September 2016. Full report pending.

† Arthur's Cross Farm was last shown on a map in 1823. The 'stone which none might lift' was probably the plinth of a cross. It was removed some time after 1847. According to the farming family, it now survives only as a field name on High Plains Farm.

‡ See p. 93. The list excludes place names referring to later 'Arthurs' or to members of Clan Arthur or MacArthur. Fig. 14 includes four other places associated with early (rather than chivalric) Arthurian legend.

alphabet, which in turn reflects the Irish settlement of Wales in the late fourth and early fifth centuries. They also tend to be found in relatively inaccessible areas. The 'Arthurs' of the North are quite different and form a distinct group. Though fewer in number, they are more widely spread and, for some reason, they tend to occur on or near Roman roads.

I had not seen this peculiarity mentioned and assumed it to be of no real historical significance. Its main interest lay in the fact that the proximity of northern 'Arthur' places to long-distance roads made it easy to include them in a cycling route. 'Arthur' himself could safely be placed between inverted commas and escorted from the scene of serious history.

✿   ✿   ✿

In 2014, serious history was being written all over the borderlands. The words 'Yes' and 'No' (to Scottish independence) were prominent even in sparsely populated areas. They appeared on telegraph poles and pylons, on sheds and barns, on farm machinery and on the walls of ruined cottages. Riding through Ayrshire, I saw a white cow wearing a waistcoat marked 'No' and several sheep tattooed with a 'Yes'.

In living memory, the national border had never been so important, and it was only now that it became obvious how many British people had no idea where it ran. Sometimes, it seemed as though James VI and my mother had been the only people who knew that the border cut Great Britain approximately in half. A local driver who used to take tourists to Hadrian's Wall and other local sites told me that he was constantly badgered with questions: 'Is *this* the border?' 'Are we in Scotland yet?' Some of our visitors from the south thought that they must have arrived in Scotland when the train had crossed Shap, until they remembered that they had yet to reach Carlisle. But then others thought that Carlisle was in Scotland. Many more visitors, including some who have academic qualifications in history, assumed that Hadrian's Wall marked the border.

This reminded me of the man who had urged Elizabeth I to build another Roman Wall, believing that the 'Romaynes' had built theirs to defend themselves 'from the dayly and daungereous incurtyons of the valyaunte barberous Scottyshe nation'. The half-Scottish member of parliament for Penrith and the Border exacerbated the confusion with his 'Hands Across the Border' campaign, which invited English people to form a human chain along Hadrian's Wall 'bearing torches in a bid to convince Scots to vote "No" in September'. A bogus 'Reverend' who published a Scottish nationalist blog imagined '100,000 English people lined up on a wall' as 'target practice', but observed that, unfortunately, parts of Hadrian's Wall lie 'sixty-odd miles from the Scottish border'.

On the English side of the Debatable Land, in the parish churches of Arthuret, Kirkandrews and Nicholforest, the talk was all of the referendum. Nicholforest Church, which hides in the woods near Liddel Water far from anything that might be called a village, is one of the rare churches which still use the King James Bible and the *Book of Common Prayer*. It is unusual, too, in the unpredictability of its services. Because of the size and remoteness of the border parishes, there are not enough vicars to go around and the officiating priest can change from one Sunday to the next.

The sounds of Jacobean English and hymns rarely heard since Victoria fill the church with an air of olden days. The setting evokes an even more distant age, when small congregations worshipped secretly at forest shrines, praying to save the guttering flame from extinction. 'Vicars . . . we're a dying breed!' were the first words I heard at Nicholforest. They came from the rear of the church, where a door leads out into the graveyard. The vicar, who had been delayed by snow and chronic back pain, sounded almost cheerful.

One Sunday, a minister I had not seen before was officiating. He spoke with a distinct Scottish accent: for a moment I imagined a clerical fifth-columnist sent by the Church of Scotland to infiltrate the Anglican community. The organist explained to me that this was a 'runner' – a peripatetic minister who takes the place of an absent vicar. The noun in its ecclesiastical sense is unknown to the *Oxford English Dictionary*, the closest definition being 'a wanderer, a rover; specifically, an itinerant seller of supposed medicines and remedies'. I had come across the word in the report of a Puritan bishop who visited Nicholforest and other border parishes in 1599: 'In divers places of the Borders the churches have walls without covering, and they have none to celebrate divine service save certain beggarly runners which come out of Scotland.'

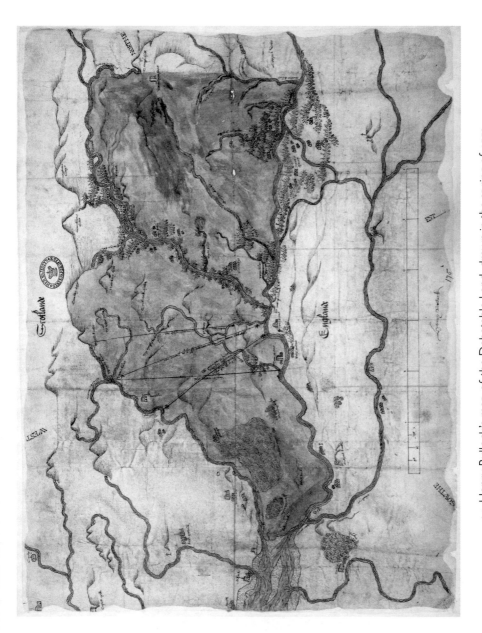

14. Henry Bullock's map of the Debatable Land, drawn in the spring of 1552.

15. 'Mile-Castle near Caw-Fields', on a reivers' route from Liddesdale to Tynedale. From The Roman Wall by the Rev. John Collingwood Bruce (1851).

16. The Scots' Dike (in England) or March Bank (in Scotland), built to mark the partition of the Debatable Land in 1552.

17. Thomas Scrope, tenth Baron Scrope of Bolton, and his mother Margaret Howard,
shortly before his appointment as Warden of the English West March in 1593
at the age of twenty-six. Anonymous portrait.

18. Scrope's deputy, Robert Carey, first Earl of Monmouth.
Anonymous portrait, c. 1591.

19. Richard Beavis, 'The Rescue of Kinmont Willie', 1872. No contemporary portraits survive of 'Kinmont Willie' and 'the Bold Buccleuch', who rescued him from Carlisle Castle in 1596. The horses and the armour belong to a slightly later period.

20. Kirkandrews church and graveyard, looking towards the Grahams' pele tower and the Scots' Dike, March 2016.

21. Hills Tower, Lochfoot, four miles south-west of Dumfries: a tower house or bastle with gatehouse and barmkin built c. 1530 for the Maxwell family, many of whom served as wardens of the Scottish West March. The more comfortable house on the left was added in 1721. Photographed from the south-west in 1911.

22. A farm track on the line of the lost Roman road leading north from the Debatable Land into Tarras Moss, September 2013.

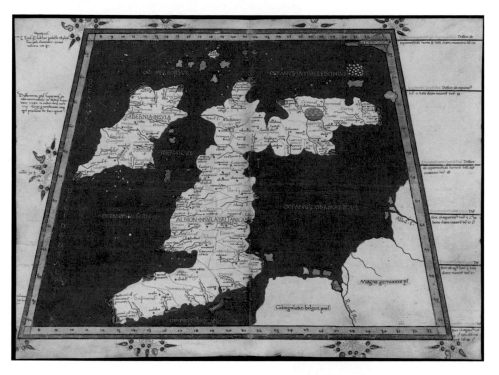

23. The British Isles according to Ptolemy's coordinates (C. AD 150), plotted by
Jacob d'Angelo in *Cosmographia Claudii Ptolomaei Alexandrini* (1467).

24. A Roman cavalryman trampling a British barbarian, first century AD. In Hexham Abbey, probably removed from the Roman fort at Corbridge. A similar tombstone was discovered in 1787 in the wall of Stanwix church (Carlisle).

25. The 'Border Reiver' statue (2003) on Kingstown Road, Carlisle.

There was nothing 'beggarly' about the Scottish Anglican. He delivered his sermon in a stern but affable and sometimes ironical voice which reminded me of ministers I had heard in Scotland on family holidays. He leant on the edge of the pulpit, scanning the flock, and began in an admonitory tone: 'Now, we're all *Christians* here . . . *aren't* we?' I recognized the allusion to the tale of a traveller lost in Liddesdale who, seeking help in vain, had cried out, 'Are there nae Christians here?', only to be answered, 'Na, na, we's all Armstrongs and Elliots.'

The sermon ranged widely over the minister's bookshelves – the books unread ('the *Complete Works* of Robert Burns for instance'), and the books long forgotten. Much of the sermon was devoted to John Wesley's *Primitive Physick, or An Easy and Natural Method of Curing Most Diseases*. This led back by a carefully meandering route to the New Testament reading, which had been the Raising of Lazarus. It was an odd sermon for the church of a predominantly agricultural community, where the most popular service is the annual blessing of sheep. At the end of the sermon, as he gathered up his notes, the minister appeared to have an afterthought: 'There's one thing I could never understand. *Why* did Jesus bring Lazarus back from the dead, knowing full well that poor old Lazarus would only have to jump through the hoop a second time?'

There were long silences between the prayers which followed. The minister prayed for the sick and the dead, 'and also for the souls of those whose names have become illegible on the gravestones outside'. Then came a longer silence while the congregation took communion. I was in the habit of reading the Order for the Burial of the Dead or another liturgical text from the time of the reivers. But that Sunday, thinking of Arthurian excursions, I was pondering a litany even older than the Book of Common Prayer.

The list of the twelve battles of Arthur is the only detailed record of events in Dark Age Britain. It forms part of a *Historia Brittonum* ('History of the Britons'), which was cobbled together from various sources in 828 or 829. The scribe was not a historian in the modern sense. He rummaged through chronicles and fragments of folklore, 'heaping together all [he] could find' in order to create a heroic narrative. One of those ancient texts was a list of nine battle sites at which twelve battles had been fought by 'British kings' under a great com-

mander described as a 'leader of battles' (a direct translation of the
Celtic 'Cadwalader').

The original, lost Brittonic text would have been written several
centuries before. It had probably been a poem, with the names of the
battles providing the rhymes. The scribe updated the old chronicle
and rewrote it for a contemporary, ninth-century audience which
was facing the threat of heathen Saxon invaders. In this modernized
version, the Saxons were the villains and the hero was a semi-myth-
ical British hero called Arthur, who may or may not have appeared
in the original poem. (This was the prototype of the Arthur who,
much later, became the central figure of the medieval chivalric fantasies involving Merlin, Guinevere and the Knights of the Round
Table.)

> Then Arthur fought against them in those days with British kings, though
> he himself was the leader of battles.
>
> The first battle was at the mouth of the river called Glein.
>
> The second and third and fourth and fifth battles were on another river,
> which is called Dubglas and is in the Linnuis region.
>
> The sixth battle was on the river which is named Bassas.
>
> The seventh was the battle in the Celidonian forest, which is to say the
> Battle of Celidon Wood.
>
> The eighth was the battle at Guinnion fort, in which Arthur carried the
> image of the Holy Perpetual Virgin Mary on his shoulders and the pagans
> were put to flight that day and great slaughter was upon them by the pow-
> er of Our Lord Jesus Christ and of Holy Mary His Mother.
>
> The ninth battle was in the city of the Legion.
>
> The tenth battle was fought on the shore of the river which is named
> Tribruit.
>
> The eleventh battle was on the hill which is called Agned. (Variant:
> which we call the battle of Bregion [or Bregomion].)
>
> The twelfth was the battle of Badon Hill, in which, in one day and a
> single charge by Arthur, nine hundred and sixty men fell, and he alone
> and no one else cast them down, and in all those battles he emerged the
> victor. (Alternative: The Battle of Camlann, in which Arthur and Medraut
> fell.)

Since early Brittonic texts usually contained factual rather than
legendary material, even if there never was a real Arthur, this record

of a military campaign at the dawn of British history is potentially priceless. This would be the earliest detailed account of historical events in Britain from a British point of view. Unfortunately, only two of the places can be identified; the others are either ambiguous or completely obscure. One scholar has angrily dismissed it as a poet's fabrication, but most agree that the list of battles refers to real places and that, if they could be identified, 'Arthur' and his world might return to the light of recorded history.

Having memorized the list imperfectly, I was trying to recall what came after the river called Dubglas in the region of Linnuis. '*Linnuis*' is the Old Welsh form of the Roman name for the region of Lindum, which is now the city of Lincoln. The problem is that no river Dubglas (or Douglas) runs anywhere near Lincoln. Then I remembered that Ptolemy's map of Britain shows two places called Lindum. One is Lincoln; the other can now be identified as the Roman fort of Castle-dykes near Lanark.

This had been one of the little gems thrown up by the restored map. The Scottish Earls of Lindsay, who owned a large part of Lanarkshire and whose family goes back at least to the Norman Conquest, have never been able to explain the origin of their name. The Lindsays had no connection with the part of Lincolnshire once known as Lindesey and there was no district of that name either in Normandy or Scotland. The identification of Lindum as Castle-dykes solved the mystery: the territory of the Lindsays was indeed the region of Lindum or Linnuis. Perhaps this northern Lindum would also be the key to the four battles on the elusive river Dub-glas . . .

*

After the post-communion cup of coffee, I cycled home with a tail-wind and unfolded the map of the Upper Clyde Valley. Three miles south of the fort of Lindum, the Clyde is joined by one of its main tributaries. Printed along the winding blue line on the map was the long-lost coincidence of river and region . . . The name of the river is Douglas Water or, as early Britons said, '*Dubh-glas*' ('black water').

> The second and third and fourth and fifth battles were on another river,
> which is called Dubglas and is in the Linnuis region.

Now, when I looked back at the second-century map, figures seemed to be moving across it. An invasion force landing on the west coast, in the bay which Ptolemy calls Vindogara, might, like the later Viking invaders, have followed the river valleys to Lindum and the Dubglas.

Suddenly, the map lit up with another lost connection. The Roman road between the Irish Sea and Lindum runs alongside a river which flows into the sea at Irvine. The river is now called the Irvine, but, 'strictly speaking, its parent stream, on account of its length and the volume of water it carries', is the river Glen.* Of the three British rivers called Glen, this is the only one that could be said to have a mouth or an estuary ('*ostium*').

> The first battle was at the mouth of the river named Glein.

There was no longer any doubt that these places had existed. Not only that, but they also appeared to have been listed in a logical, geographical order. This was a campaign which had actually taken place. The date of the campaign and the identity of the 'leader of battles' were still a mystery, but pieces of that Dark Age puzzle were beginning to fall into place like the tumblers of a lock.

The twelve battles of Arthur are usually thought to have taken place in the sixth century. The fact that the key had been supplied by a map of the second century seemed to be no more than a fortunate coincidence. I made a note of the discovery and filed it away. It had no obvious connection with the history of the Borders and the Debatable Land, and I was not keen to make it public. By then, my book on the ancient Celts had been published. One of its themes was the seductive power of insignificant coincidences. I had illustrated the point with a jokey reference to the defunct 'Camelot' amusement park near Wigan in Lancashire. This had generated garish articles in two national newspapers and a corresponding chorus of tweets and retweets: a 'historian' with my name and face was claiming to have discovered the fabled court of King Arthur just off the M6 motorway.

The newspapers reported this as though Camelot, that Hogwarts

---

* Stewart Clark, 'Ayrshire Fishing Guide' (2011). Principal rivers were often renamed after one tributary or another. The Liddel, for example, was sometimes called the Kershope, from the name of its largest tributary.

of the Middle Ages, might conceivably have existed. If I published the discovery now, it would be tantamount to saying, 'I haven't found Camelot, but I am on the trail of King Arthur – and, by the way, he's Scottish!' I decided to attribute the discovery of the battle sites to an anonymous reader and pursued the investigation.

✻

It soon became clear that the map had more to say on the subject. It revealed one other battle site and confirmed the locations of two others, leaving only three unidentified sites. It also suggested a rational itinerary which might provide clues to the three remaining sites.

Those place names had not been conjured out of thin air by a Brittonic bard. The course of a forgotten war traced itself across the map, and the ghostly warriors of Arthurian legend began to look substantial, imbued with purpose and direction. The date of the battles was narrowed down to a period much closer to the map of Roman Britain than to the age of the Saxons. In fact, there was no sign at all of the Saxons whom the compiler of the *Historia Brittonum* supposed to have been the enemy: no Saxon invasion ever took place on the west coast of Scotland, and there are no Saxon settlements anywhere in the region.

If the battle list pre-dated the Saxons, who, then, had been the enemy? Piratical raids from the Irish Sea went on for centuries, but there was no full-scale invasion, and Vikings did not arrive in Irvine Bay until several decades after the *Historia Brittonum* was written. The text refers to a confederation of British kings fighting under a single leader. 'King', in Latin and in ancient Celtic, was the usual term for a tribal chief. This might suggest the Dark Age kingdoms which were established or restored at the end of Roman rule in the 400s, but the battles of this period seem to have pitted Briton against Briton and there is no trace of any pan-British alliance.

The historical chronometer has to be wound back to an even earlier age. The first two battle sites, and those to come, are Roman rather than British. Most – perhaps all – of the battles took place, not at Celtic hill forts, but at key military installations on the Roman road network. The original source seems to have had an unusually good grasp of the geography of a wide area: this is the most coherent sequence of place names in early British literature. Along with the alliance of kings under a single leader, this would imply a relatively stable political situation which was troubled for a time by an invasion sufficiently momentous to be commemorated in a poem.

One possibility, first raised in 1924, is that 'Arthur' was a Roman. A certain Lucius Artorius Castus commanded the Sixth Legion in Britain, which had its headquarters in York. An experienced and successful soldier, he had served in Syria and Judea, and later led two legions against the Armenians. The theory has been discredited by the tenuous speculations on which the chronologically deranged film *King Arthur* (2004) was based, yet the twelve battles do appear to have been fought between the Humber and the Firth of Clyde, which was precisely the area controlled by Artorius's Sixth Legion.

Perhaps the name 'Artorius' stuck in the popular mind. Later, Celticized as 'Art(h)ur' or 'Arto-rix' ('bear king'), the Roman name might have been attached to a home-grown British hero. But if Arthur's army was a combined force of Romans and Britons, this would have been a strange campaign to celebrate in a Brittonic poem. Most of the battles would have been defeats, with the invaders pushing ever southwards through the lowlands, the borderlands and the Pennines until they reached the heart of Roman power at the 'City of the Legion'.

The 'Roman Arthur' theory has proved compelling because it fits the traditional fable of the nation's origins: the daggy, tartan-clad warriors of ancient Britain who skulked in smoky huts like people of the Stone Age, living on porridge, roots and beer, were given the gift of civilization by the Roman army. This view, which most Romans would have shared, has been repeatedly demolished by archaeology. The Celts had towns and roads, high-speed transport and well-managed farms. They used metal-working techniques which have yet to be reinvented. Several ancient texts refer to their meritocratic education system. Yet these sophisticated ancestors are still viewed with the same colonialist prejudice with which the metropolitan Scots and English of the Middle Ages regarded the barbarians of the borderlands.

The map of second-century Britain turns this tale on its head. This was not a Roman-led campaign of resistance to foreign invaders. The course of the war makes sense only if this was, as the battle list says, a British force united against a common enemy. That enemy was neither Saxon nor Celtic. The kings of Britain banded together – as Celtic 'kings' or chieftains often did in times of national emergency – in order to reconquer from the Roman usurpers the lands that had once been theirs.

*

A few weeks after finding the first battle sites on Ptolemy's map, we set off from home, crossed the border into the Debatable Land and headed north. By then, I knew that the itinerary revealed by the map agreed with recorded history. The Roman chronicler Cassius Dio had described a major invasion of Britannia which took place in the early 180s.* This invasion is consistent with the sequence of battles, and it was on a scale that might well have secured it a place in legend. According to Cassius Dio, it was 'the biggest war' fought anywhere in the Roman Empire during the reign of Emperor Commodus (AD 177–92). For the Romans, the invasion was a near catastrophe, but for the allied tribes, it would have been a formative event in the birth of a united British nation of the north.[†]

---

* There is only one other candidate. The great 'barbarian conspiracy' of 367 – which was more coincidence than conspiracy – involved various tribes from Caledonia, as well as Franks and Saxons from across the North Sea, but the main attack was concentrated in the far south-east, on the coasts facing Gaul; the crucial victory over the invaders took place at London, and the northern incursions were a series of raids rather than a wide-ranging war.

[†] The probable course of the invasion is shown in figs 14 and 15.

27

The Great Caledonian Invasion

Despite appearances, this is the end to the story of the Debatable Land: the discovery of its lost beginnings and the recognition of its lasting place in British history. The future of another United Kingdom was soon to be decided, and although physical geography in the twenty-first century seemed to have become detached from political history, there was a powerful sign of long-term forces at work in the fact that the paths of that epic campaign of the second century led back to the borderlands.

✳

In about AD 163, the Antonine Wall was abandoned and Hadrian's Wall, eighty miles to the south, once again became the main line of defence. To control the troublesome northern tribes, several forts between the two walls retained garrisons. The borderlands then became a Roman buffer zone or *limes*, with command centres at Castledykes (Lindum) and Newstead protecting the main roads to north and south.

In the early 180s, ominous tidings reached the south. The unconquered tribes of Caledonia had 'crossed the wall which separated them from the Roman legions': 'they proceeded to do much mischief and cut down a *strategos* [a general or military governor] together with his troops'. The account by Cassius Dio is corroborated by signs of destruction or rebuilding at various forts in northern England and the Scottish lowlands (fig. 14).

Fear of invasion spread far beyond the frontier. In southern Britannia, a massive building programme was launched. Between the mid-180s and the mid-190s, many towns, both large and small, which until then had been open and undefended, began to surround themselves with earthworks. Nowhere else in the Roman Empire was there such a rush to protect the urban population. The crossing of the wall (whether Hadrian's or the Antonine) and the killing of a Roman general and his troops were alarming enough to induce a sense of panic, and there is palpable evidence of the relief that was felt at the end of the emergency in the coins which were struck in 184 and 185 to celebrate a victory in Britannia.

✻

More than a thousand years separate the Border reivers from the confederate army of British kings, but the geography of the region is largely unchanged and the pastoral, cattle-raiding society of the Celts would have been recognizable to a medieval warden. The Caledonian warriors were 'very fond of plundering', says Cassius Dio. 'Consequently, they choose their boldest men as rulers.' They ride 'small, swift horses' and 'can endure hunger and cold and any kind of hardship'.

Cassius Dio probably owed his information to a Roman Robert Carey who had seen his enemy disappear into the trackless mosses:

> They plunge into the swamps and exist there for many days with only their heads above water, and in the forests they support themselves upon bark and roots, and for all emergencies they prepare a certain kind of food, the eating of a small portion of which, the size of a bean, prevents them from feeling either hunger or thirst.

These hardy tribes of the northlands, equipped with nimble ponies and the Iron Age equivalent of the energy bar, either marched south from the Antonine Wall or sailed down the coast from the Firth of Clyde. After an opposed landing at the mouth of the Glen in Irvine Bay – which was once the largest port in western Scotland – another four battles were fought along the Douglas in the region of Lindum (Castledykes). Here, the road connecting the Antonine Wall with Hadrian's Wall met the road which crossed Britain from the Irish Sea to the North Sea. For several days, weeks or even months, this vital crossroads of the northern British network became the theatre of war. After the fifth battle, the invaders finally broke through into the Southern Uplands where the roads led south into the heart of Roman

Britain, towards the place which the battle poem calls 'the City of the Legion'.

The sixth battle, on the river 'Bassas' – somewhere on the route from Castledykes to the border – was probably at the fort of Tassies Height (Coria, on Ptolemy's map) along the shallow river Annan, which flows to the Solway Firth. The seventh was in a place we now know well: Celidon Wood, where the bard called Myrddin took refuge after the Battle of Arfderydd in the parish of Arthuret (p. 93).*

Remnants of that wood still exist along the steep banks of the Liddel where most of North Cumbria's ancient woodland grows, preserved from browsing deer and wood-cutting humans by its inaccessibility. On a modern map, the patches of old broad-leaf forest on the Debatable Land boundary from Netherby and Carwinley to Penton Wood look like the shredded cloak of someone fleeing through the thickets towards the Kielder Forest. They are still a refuge for several threatened species of plant and animal.

This would therefore be the earliest known of the many battles that were fought around the Debatable Land or, as it was then, the buffer zone of the Damnonii, the Selgovae and the Votadini. A victory in this crucial area would have opened the way to the south. If ever 'Arthur' saw the twin knolls of Arthuret, it would have been after his seventh battle. The wood which covers the knolls is known locally, but not on maps, as Crow Wood. The people of Longtown who played in Crow Wood as children like to think of it as the grave of King Arthur. On a foggy day, when the lower slopes are draped with shining white sheets of plastic mulch, the site has an almost ceremonial air.

✲

Invasions tend to follow the same routes from one century to the next. Like the Jacobite army in 1745, the Caledonian invaders headed for Carlisle, where an inscription of the AD 180s, unearthed on the site of Bonnie Prince Charlie's headquarters in English Street, gives thanks

---

* Not to be confused with the legendary Caledonian Forest – a confusion anticipated by the writer: 'the Celidonian forest, which is to say the Battle of Celidon Wood'. On Ptolemy's conflation of Celtic '*drumo*' ('ridge') and Greek '*drumos*' ('oak wood'), see p. 296. The position of the '*Kaledonios Drumos*' on Ptolemy's map suggests the mountainous region which begins at the Highland Boundary Fault: fig. 7.

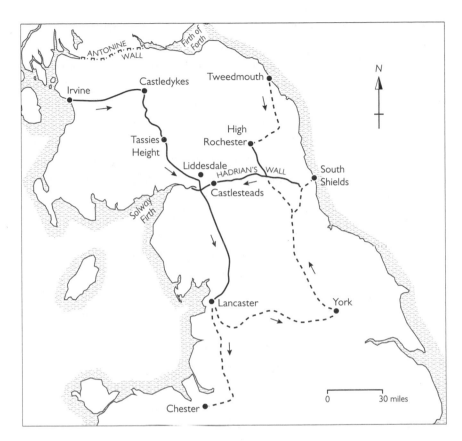

The Great Caledonian Invasion. The uninterrupted lines show
the probable route; the broken lines show the possible route.
For more detail, see figs 14 and 15.

to the deified emperor Hercules-Commodus for ensuring the safety
of the garrison when it was attacked by a barbarian horde. The inscription does not explicitly commemorate a victory: the 'barbarians' may
simply have passed through that notoriously pregnable city. The
battle list shows that they had a more distant goal: beyond Shap and
the forbidding and beautiful gorge of the river Lune, where the drystone walls and teetering sheep give an exact measure of the fells'
steepness, lay the fort of Guinnion.

'Guinnion' is a later form of 'Vinnovium', which is shown on
Ptolemy's map of northern England. Previously assumed to be Bin-
chester on the other side of England, it can now be identified as

Lancaster, where vestiges of a Roman fort have been found on Castle Hill. The geographical logic of the battle list is obvious: Lancaster lies on Roman roads to Chester and to York, and, like several of the battle sites, it was an inland port. A century before, Agricola had advanced up the west coast with the fleet on the Irish Sea supporting the ground forces. The British kings might have used a similar strategy. The first eight battles – from Irvine Bay to Lancaster – suggest a mass attack on the western seaboard, while the later battle sites are consistent with a parallel or subsequent invasion from the east.

After the victory at Guinnion, which the author of the *Historia Brittonum* attributes anachronistically to the power of the Virgin Mary, the hypothetical route divides. The ninth battle took place 'in the city of the Legion'. This must be either Chester (labelled 'Legio XX' on Ptolemy's map) – which was no more than a 'rearward works establishment' in the 180s – or, more likely, York (labelled 'Legio VI'), which by then was the main base of Roman power in the north. For the British kings, the legionary fortress at York would have been the more significant target. The final battles were fought north of the Humber, and so 'the Legion' would naturally have referred to the Sixth, which operated all over the north, from Manchester to the Antonine Wall, and which, at that time, was stationed in York under the command of Lucius Artorius Castus.

A spectacular Roman road runs through the Aire Gap and over the moors to the city of York. By following this route, the Britons would have remained on familiar, upland territory. Along that road of terraced climbs and hair-raising descents, two forts, Ribchester and Ilkley – both shown on Ptolemy's map – were rebuilt in the late second century and may have been wrecked in the invasion.

The tenth battle, at 'Tribruit', is a mystery but the search can be narrowed to a tidal estuary on the North Sea coast – probably Tweedmouth near the eastern end of the future Anglo-Scottish border or South Shields at the terminus of Hadrian's Wall. The site of the eleventh battle is less mysterious: Bregion or Bregomion is the fort of Bremenium, which stood at a junction on Dere Street. Its location is confirmed by Ptolemy's map: it lies off the main Newcastle road below the border pass of Carter Bar, beyond the rotting hulk of a reconstructed Iron Age house and a sign marked 'No Access to Military Vehicles or Troops'.

Bremenium was one of the forts in the frontier zone north of Hadrian's Wall which retained a Roman garrison after the abandonment of the Antonine Wall. Its ruins are as evocative of Border reivers as of Romans. In the sixteenth century, a bastle was built out of the crumbled walls as a defence against the rampaging Elliots of Liddesdale. But some of the stones were left in situ and several burial mounds and monumental tombs have been found nearby. The cemetery at Bremenium remained in use from the early second to the early fourth centuries and was apparently reserved for officers. Perhaps it was there that the general mentioned by Cassius Dio was 'cut down together with his troops'.

✿

By the time the British rebel army reached Bremenium, it would have covered more than four hundred miles. It had ravaged northern Britannia, caused panic in the south and was being talked about in Rome. The British kings and 'Arthur' now found themselves on the principal frontier of the Roman province and the only permanently defended border in the far north of the empire.

Arthurian scholars have long suspected that the twelfth and last battle in the *Historia Brittonum* list was borrowed from another source. The famous Battle of Mount Badon was fought in an entirely different time and place: in the south of England, in the sixth century and against the Saxons. As a British victory, it provided the ninth-century historian with a gratifying conclusion, but, as we know, second-century Britain was not reconquered from the Romans by a barbarian horde. Another 'last battle' is recorded in the tenth-century *Welsh Annals*: the Battle of Camlann, at which Arthur died. Many scholars believe that this unhappy episode was the original ending. The itinerary suggested by Ptolemy's map supports this theory, as does the fact that 'Camlann' would have fitted the rhyme scheme of the battle list.

The location of Camlann is well established. Souvenirs of Hadrian's Wall manufactured in a pseudo-Celtic style were sold to Roman veterans of northern Britannia. Three items of cookware have been found on which the names of Wall forts are inscribed in the correct

sequence. They show that Camlann or Camboglanna was the fort
which stood between Carlisle and Birdoswald. Its modern name is
Castlesteads.

This is one of the key strategic positions on the western Wall.
Roads presumed to be Roman lead north-west towards Netherby and
east to the valley of the South Tyne and the fort at Whitley Castle.
The area was often occupied by invaders. Nearby, at Lanercost Priory,
the ailing King Edward I spent five months in bed on his way to fight
the Scots; in 1311, Robert the Bruce made the priory his army's headquarters. In the second century, the British army might have been
heading for Carlisle to re-join the western invasion route or to secure
a link between the west coast and the east. Beyond Carlisle, ships
would be waiting on the Solway to ferry the warriors back to Caledonia. The whole expedition would have followed the circular route of
an epic cattle raid.

When the translator of William Camden's *Britannia* visited Castlesteads fort in the late eighteenth century, he saw the 'foundations
of walls and streets', a profusion of iron nails stuck in mouldering
lumps, and 'good stone of all sizes for building, most of them black as
if the whole building had been burnt'. There were 'several foundations
of houses still standing there pretty high but hard to come at for the
bushes'.

War damage can be repaired, but it takes an enormous, continual
effort to prevent natural destruction. A few years after the Caledonian
invasion, a sandstone altar was erected at Camboglanna to commemorate the restoration of a temple to the Mother Goddesses of Every
Nation which had 'fallen in through age'. The site of the fort is now a
secret, subtle place compared to the more famous forts to the east.
Even on a bank holiday, the Hadrian's Wall tourist traffic barely
touches Castlesteads, and it ceases altogether when the lanes head off
across the treacherous expanse of Walton Moss.

At the top of a farm track, an undulating path leads through an
oak wood glowing with bluebells in spring to a sudden drop: a mere
filament on the map, the Cam Beck cuts like a ploughshare through
the clay and has devoured large portions of the hillside. Much of the
fort has been lost to the river. The blight of landscaping which
destroyed the Roman 'citie' at Netherby continued to eat away at the

remains of Camboglanna. The site of Arthur's last battle is now marked by the towering sandstone wall of a private garden.

✽

According to the *Welsh Annals*, the general known as Arthur died at Camlann, but the leader of a British uprising would not have been buried at a Roman fort. When the rebel army reached Camboglanna, it was heading west along the great Wall towards Carlisle and the Irish Sea, and towards the other fabled site of Arthur's death.

The names of five of these battles reappear in a slightly garbled form in a fantastic twelfth-century compilation, the *Historia Regum Britanniae* ('History of the Kings of Britain'). Its author, Geoffrey of Monmouth, borrowed, corrupted and mislocated but did not invent ex nihilo the place names of his Arthurian tales.* One of those names – the Insula Avallonis or Isle of Avalon – might have fitted the rhyme scheme of the battle poem, and some scholars believe that it belonged to an unknown version of the battles of Arthur. It was there, supposedly, that Arthur died or had his wounds tended after the battle of Camlann. The Celtic name comes from '*avallo*' or '*abalo*', meaning 'apple orchard'. Celtic 'apple' place names are common in Continental Europe but there is only one in Britain – the fort of Aballava or Avalana. The name is found on two of the Hadrian's Wall souvenirs next to Uxellodunum and Camboglanna.

Aballava stood at Burgh by Sands near the western end of the Wall and the Solway coast. The fort had been built about twenty years before the invasion, when the turf of Hadrian's Wall was being replaced with stone. As the site of a hero's death, it might satisfy a film director or a nationalist – the bloodied warrior gazing out, like Edward I, over the ever-changing sand banks and river channels at the hills of what would one day be Scotland. But even this aquatic frontier is an illusion: Ptolemy's map shows that both sides of the Solway lay in the territory of the same Celtic tribe. Neither Scotland nor England could claim this particular Arthur as their own.

✽

---

* The City of Legions, the river Duglas, the forest of Caledon, the province of Lindesia, the river Cambula.

With the defeat of the British kings, the first official purge of the borderlands began. The most extensive reprisals were led by the Emperor,
Septimius Severus. Like the wardens of the Marches, he found the
northern tribes intractable and elusive. Advancing into the bogs and
hidden valleys, he witnessed a tactic which was later used by the
people of Tynedale in the days of the reivers. As Cassius Dio reported:

> . . . he fought no battle and beheld no enemy in battle array. The enemy
> purposely put sheep and cattle in front of the soldiers for them to seize,
> in order that they might be lured on still further until they were worn
> out.

This is the earliest record of the skilful herding of livestock in the
British Isles. Even in the second and third centuries, a walker in the
fells might have thrilled to the sight of a distant flock spinning itself
out over a hillside at the chivvying of a shepherd and his dog.

That stubborn pastoral society, which was considered a cause of
trouble and anarchy by the Roman Empire and by the governments
of Scotland and England, was also the source of some of the oldest
British literature. Preserved by the lattice of its rhymes, the battle
list traced the limits of a distinct linguistic zone – the area in which
the Cumbric dialect of Brittonic was spoken. From 'Glan' to
'Camglann', through 'Dubglas' and 'Bassas', to 'Celidon', 'Guinnion',
'Legion' and 'Bregion', the battles of Arthur, like the legends of the
tribes of Gaul, might have framed an epic which celebrated a cultural identity. For the descendants of the Damnonii, the Selgovae,
the Votadini and the Brigantes, it might have recounted the birth of
a new British kingdom.

The setting of these battles corresponds to the Dark Age kingdom of Strathclyde-Cumbria at its greatest extent, or the greatest
extent of its territorial claims. Intriguingly, it also reflects the distribution of 'Arthur' place names in the north of Britain. Some of those
Arthurian sites would have seen the invaders heading south in the
180s: Arthur's Craigs above the Clyde; Arthur's Seat and Arthur's
Fountain at the head of the Annan; Arthur's Cross near Carwinley;
Arthur's Bower at Carlisle; King Arthur's Well and Arthur's Chair on
Hadrian's Wall.

Some time after the invasion, a Cumbric bard coaxed a simple
narrative from the years of war in the bloody borderlands, fitting a

period of history to a single human life. When a new enemy had emerged, and the Romans had been replaced by Saxons, the rhymes still told an epic tale of national resistance which served the purposes of other kingdoms and confederations. The battles could always be stitched into a colourful and coherent campaign, just as a certain form of nationalism unfurls rhetorical tapestries on which the heroes and martyrs of Scottish history run seamlessly through the centuries from Mons Graupius to Bannockburn and from Flodden Field to Culloden.

The region whose boundaries are traced by those ancient battles is now almost equally divided between Scotland and England. The frontiers have changed, but attempts are still being made to claim 'Arthur' for one administrative area or another. National pride is not the most resilient of emotions. Threatened by the arbitrariness of borders, the ambitions of political leaders and the size and diversity of its domain, it must attach itself to something stable. Perhaps only legend can defend it from change and allow its believers to call a halt to the infidelities of history and to say that, here, the frontier stood and should stand again.

28

Polling Stations

Less than a fortnight before the day of voting, an opinion poll showed for the first time a majority in favour of Scottish independence. The southern English seemed to discover at the last minute that the land of tartan and haggis was not a picturesque appendage but a nation with a will of its own.

Ambassadors had been sent north from Westminster to offer blandishments and to explain the economic arguments for remaining a part of the United Kingdom. They seemed to believe that this was above all a matter of public finance. Some of the English emissaries struggled to adapt to the foreign form of debate. On local radio, an angry discussion took place on the subject of agricultural subsidies. The Scottish representative of farming interests brought it to an abrupt end: 'Well, I don't care about arguments anyway. I'm a nationalist, and that's that!' Perhaps this was the spirit in which the twenty-four Scottish knights had stymied the twenty-four English knights when they walked along the borderline in 1245.

In and around the Debatable Land, there was a feeling of horror at the ineptitude of the 'No' campaign. Its leader, nominally a Scot, always looked like a man who had just stepped out of a taxi in Whitehall. English politicians seemed to be ventriloquized by Scottish satirists: they acquired a snooty, patronizing tone and mispronounced Scottish place names. English commentators referring to the independence debate endlessly repeated the words 'dour' and 'canny', as though the only two words of Scots in their vocabulary happened to be an adequate description of that wily, tight-fisted race of surly foreigners.

One day, some men arrived to cut the high branches under the electricity wires which run through the woodland. One of the men was Northern Irish, the others came from either side of the border. As usual, we stood for a moment looking over into Scotland. In previous years, there had been banter about customs posts and whisky smuggling. Now, the mood was more sombre. The question was simply, 'What do you think about it?' I observed that if a dis-United Kingdom left the European Union and an independent Scotland re-joined it, retaining the free movement of labour, then these remote stretches of the Liddel, where the reivers used to come and go, would be an ideal crossing point for illegal migrants. This was no longer considered a subject for mirth.

On a Friday morning, we walked to the unmarked bus stop. A mile to the north, the 127 bus ran along the southern slopes of the Debatable Land and, after picking up its last Scottish passengers, dropped down towards the border. On the bus, there was something I had never experienced before but which I imagine must be the mood that follows a declaration of war. A storm cloud had risen from the muddled history of the Borders and was solidifying into something permanent and unreal. The future of the United Kingdom was about to be decided by one-twelfth of its population, and the Debatable Land might be partitioned once again. No one knew exactly what the consequences would be, and although mass deportations were unlikely, the people of the Anglo-Scottish borders, like their sixteenth-century ancestors, felt the state's impending weight, its enormous power of interference.

This borderless community was unrecognized and, faced with the dictatorship of a popular vote in place of a parliamentary democracy, unrepresented. The 'No' camp had come to be associated with reason and the 'Yes' camp with passion. But passion itself had been redefined as loudness and intransigence. There was as much passion in the Borders, but it took a different form: this was fear at its most contagious, a collective fear which could see no source of guidance or solace.

*

On the day of the vote (18 September 2014), we cycled to every polling station in or on the edge of the Debatable Land. It was a thirty-three-mile round trip. The polling stations were far apart and, for some people who live in remote areas without the use of a car, inaccessible. I saw voters entering and leaving the village halls – a witness, I thought, of a historical event but in reality a ghost which lived in a house on the border, whose family was Scottish but whose Scottish name was nowhere in the register of voters.

The first voters we saw were two women standing outside Canonbie Public Hall. They were discussing local news while an English Springer spaniel waited patiently on a leash. Both women spoke in southern English accents. In cities to the north, they might have been more guarded, but there was never any doubt that in the Borders a majority would vote 'No' to secession. Even the referendum debate had failed to generate any noticeable Anglo-Scottish antagonism.

On the mile-long main street of Newcastleton, there were 'No' posters in many of the windows. We cycled on to Hermitage Castle and turned up the single-track road which leads to the pass between Liddesdale and Ewesdale. A mile up the valley, at the point where Mary Queen of Scots rode down to Hermitage Water, a farmer had festooned the front of his house with a two-storey-high Union Jack which seemed to mirror the vast arch of the castle.

This was the spirit of defiance which had come to be associated with the 'Yes' campaign. We saw it again in Langholm, where voting was taking place at the Buccleuch Hall. On the edge of town, road signs announce Langholm as the 'Birthplace of Hugh MacDiarmid', the Communist poet who twice stood as a candidate for the Scottish National Party, but on 18 September, travellers entering Langholm on the A7 were greeted by a gigantic municipal banner bearing the single word, 'No!'

Apart from the banner and an elderly man distributing nationalist leaflets in Buccleuch Square, it would have been hard to tell that a chapter of Border history was being written. In the north, statues had been decked with patriotic flags and scarves; in Rowanburn, the effigy of 'Lang Sandy' the reiver was unadorned and the only hint of nationalist fervour was a Welsh flag fluttering outside a cottage across the road. At Gilnockie Hall, voting took place under the painting of Johnnie Armstrong riding his horse across the Esk. On the edge of a wood in an almost uninhabited part of the Debatable Land, the Gilnockie polling station was as quiet as the nearby abandoned railway. A farmer was driving away; a face appeared at one of the windows, saw the bicycles and shrank out of sight. No one else came. After fifteen minutes, we headed back to Canonbie, crossed the river into England and, along with the rest of the country, waited for the result.

❊

In an age when elections are so minutely tracked and recorded that they might almost be held for the benefit of statisticians, there is no way of knowing how the people of the borderlands voted. Information from a particular polling station is never available (the ballot papers are mixed before counting), and, on this occasion, there were no exit polls. The figures for each electoral ward usually provide a comprehensive view of voting patterns, but the referendum was organized by region, not by ward.

The two regions adjacent to England are vast: Scottish Borders (1,831 square miles), which extends to within eight miles of Edinburgh, and Dumfries and Galloway (2,481 square miles), parts of which lie more than eighty miles from the border. Within those two regions, for every person who voted for independence, two voted against. Throughout Scotland, the 'No' vote was 55.3% and the 'Yes' vote 44.7%. The only other area with a lower 'Yes' vote was Orkney (32.8%). In the borderlands themselves, to judge by anecdotal evidence and a clear split over the whole country between urban and rural voters, the 'No' vote was certainly much higher.

In Liddesdale and the Debatable Land, there was little talk of the referendum in the months that followed. Few people wanted to discuss it: they were glad that it was over. But instead of evaporating, the fear became foreboding. The 'Hands Across the Border' cairn at Gretna was vandalized more than once and there was a feeling that, sooner or later, despite the vote, the two countries would be severed.

❊   ❊   ❊

More than a year later, not long after Christmas, a friend from Newcastleton came to repair some storm damage to the house. He pointed at the oil tank (oil is our main source of heating after firewood) and said, 'I hope you've ordered some more: it's half what it cost a year ago!' Oil prices had plummeted and were still falling. Since revenue from North Sea oil had been a mainstay of the nationalists' economic plan, this was hailed as a retrospective victory for the 'No' campaign, confirmation that an independent Scotland would have foundered in debt. In the event, it proved only that economics had not been the main concern for nationalists. Opinion polls showed practically no difference in support for Scottish independence.

The house has a third potential source of heating apart from oil and wood. The river occasionally delivers small lumps of coal to the shingle beach. Along a curved line below the hanging woodland, moles push up pebble-sized pieces of coal from a depth of about two feet. These black nuggets burn quite well in the wood stoves and could conceivably be mined. In the 1820s, adits were dug into the riverbank cliffs and there was a proposal to lay rails so that horses could take the coal up to the level ground where the railway was later built.

The seams of carboniferous limestone form part of the vast Canonbie coalfield which underlies much of the former Debatable Land on both sides of the border. Shallow pits were once worked all over the area, from Carwinley Burn to Peter's Crook and Liddelbank. Industrial mining began in the late eighteenth century. There were two pitheads – one at Rowanburn and one at Blinkbonny, joined by an inclined plane. The workable seams were exhausted by 1922, but mining companies have been hovering over the area ever since.

One day, some people who live on the edge of Canonbie noticed a piece of white paper nailed to a tree. The Buccleuch Estates had given permission to a multi-national mining company to extract coal-bed methane from the coalfield. Nineteen drilling sites were marked on the printed map. There might eventually be as many as a hundred, and there would certainly be pollution, noise, heavy traffic and lasting eyesores. The fragile tourist trade would be wrecked.

There was near-unanimous resistance and a protest group was formed, but many farmers and householders are tenants of the Buccleuch Estates and were afraid to voice their opposition. The modern descendants of the reivers are generally law-abiding, social-minded folk. The response of the Buccleuch Estates was a reminder that the image of the borderer as a troublemaker was largely a creation of the landed gentry and the representatives of state interests. The CEO replied to the 'vociferous minority' in the *Eskdale & Liddesdale Advertiser*. There was no hint of compromise or compassion, merely the wish to silence 'those vociferous voices who don't want to see any economic development in the area': 'I have little sympathy for that because it behoves us all to try to create economic development.'

The region of the Debatable Land is popular with fracking and wind-farm companies because of its small, scattered population and, despite the appearance of remoteness, its proximity to ports and major trade routes. A plan to send electricity pylons twice the normal height marching across the southern Debatable Land was recently dropped – for the time being – but the northern half, with its unique history and landscapes, may soon be devastated by the construction of multiple wind turbines in the Tinnisburn and Newcastleton Forests.

29

No Man's Land

The Debatable Land – even if enough people knew where and what it was – will never redeclare its independence. No Scottish or English region, nor the whole island of Great Britain, can be a world within itself. The English half of the Debatable Land is now a part of the City of Carlisle. Carlisle has a population of 75,306, but, since the local government reforms of the 1970s, 'Carlisle' encompasses a vast rural hinterland with a population of 32,218 and an area of more than four hundred square miles. As a former mayor pointed out to me with a mixture of pride and a sense of the ridiculous, this makes 'Carlisle' the largest city in England.

On Kingstown Road, which leads out of the city towards the Debatable Land, running parallel to the Roman road, a bronze reiver, ten feet tall, steel-bonneted and heavily armed, stands hunched and ready on a brick plinth in front of a health club. The statue was erected in 2003 by a local housing developer, Story, whose ancestors were reivers. It confronts the cars and trucks with the determined but slightly fearful expression of a borderer preparing for a warden's attack or, in view of its situation, a cyclist about to negotiate the traffic system up the road.

The statue might have been intended as a monument to civic pride, but reiving was never an urban phenomenon. The reivers came from the wild lands to the north and east of the city which are now officially designated, for agricultural purposes, 'Disadvantaged' or 'Severely Disadvantaged Areas'. In some municipal minds, the human population of those areas is still a nuisance.

The sense of inferiority which inspired some of the more belligerent nationalist campaigning in Scotland is also noticeable in the professional and administrative echelons of Carlisle. Rural Cumbria is seen as a potential asset, but only as part of that half-imagined, leafy suburb of metropolitan Britain which includes the over-visited Lake District and the Scottish Highlands. To anyone who knows the area or travels through it, the people themselves are a vital part of its attraction, but this is not an asset which stirs civic ambition. The appealingly named AD122 bus which serves small towns and isolated settlements along Hadrian's Wall runs only between March and September, when tourist money justifies its existence. Cumbria County Council now refuses to support it. The two Cumbrian towns (Carlisle and Alston) whose predecessors are shown on Ptolemy's map and on the Roman letter found beneath Tullie House Museum (p. 293) are connected by a bus service only two days a week and not during school holidays.

The idea that Carlisle is hampered by its hinterland is also evident in official attitudes to the environment. Planning committees have taken to heart the expression, 'a once-in-a-hundred-years event', with its consoling suggestion that no one who makes a disastrous decision today will live long enough to be held responsible. It was applied to the floods of 2005, 2009 and 2015, when not even the bold Buccleuch and his band would have tried to cross the river Eden. Water has become a greater economic threat than the reivers ever were. When Carlisle was cut off by floods in 2015, aerial views of the city showed it almost as it had been in the Middle Ages, with the cathedral, the castle and Ptolemy's Uxellum (Stanwix) high and dry and the Civic Centre under water.

❊

Even the ancient woodland along the Liddel came under threat. Some of the woods on the edge of the Debatable Land where Myrddin sought refuge and where 'Arthur' fought his seventh battle are officially designated 'ancient'. This gives them some protection against 'unnecessary' development. Other areas of woodland are effectively defenceless. But the plants and animals which live along the river have no more respect for official designations than the reivers did for the national border, and if the unprotected woodland under the administration of 'Carlisle' were to be developed, the rare and endangered flora and fauna would be confined to segregated enclaves in which no population could flourish.

For five years, we had cycled through the Debatable Land and its region in ever-widening circles. Meanwhile, parts of the woodland near the house had remained unexplored. Most ancient woodland has survived because it was managed continuously for centuries: otherwise, it would have turned into a tangle of shrubs and invasive plants of little value either to humans or to animals. We had coppiced several sections, removing the rhododendron, letting in the sunlight and allowing the enormous hazel stools which are older than the biggest trees to send up fresh shoots. As a result, countless woodland flowers had woken from a long slumber.

Less accessible parts of the woodland had remained untouched for a good reason. After weeks of steady rain, the boulder clay heaves itself up and slumps towards the river. Like heavy blankets slithering off a bed, thick layers of soil and stone move downhill overnight. Trees fall with a crack and a thud, offering their upper branches to mice and voles, terracing the muddy slope with their trunks and making room for the next generation.

With the threat of development downstream, I looked again at the old maps and title deeds. The house had changed hands often enough since the early nineteenth century that, besides the printed maps, there were also hand-drawn charts and plans coloured in crayon and paint. Some of them showed a path which had forded the burn and climbed up from the Liddel towards the disused railway. This must have been the track by which 'Romany' and his wife had reached the house in the 1910s: 'Down a steep bank we slid, across a trickle of a stream and up the other side we clambered.'

There was no longer any trace of a path. The largest-scale maps showed that it had reached the ford near the mouth of the burn by descending a bank between an English oak and a Scots pine. To judge by their girth, both trees had begun to grow not long after the division of the Debatable Land when the 'order of watches' was set. Some time in the last century, the bank had collapsed. A deep dell had formed at the foot of the oak, and the pine now clung to the cliff with twisted roots. It was here, at the confluence of the burn and the river, that the two horsemen who patrolled the lower Liddel had been relayed by the four riders who watched the remoter stretches to the north.

Otters had made a mud-slide on the opposite bank: their prints could be seen in the sand washed in by the river. Beyond lay an area of hanging woodland which the previous owner of the house had pointed out to us as an unsolved mystery: 'No one we've talked to knows who owns it. It might be no man's land!' Since the days of 'Romany', landslips had obliterated the path. Many years had passed since any human had walked through that muddy jungle, and without the need to watch every step I would not have noticed that the invisible path was still in use.

Clutches of black, glossy beads marked its course on either side of the ford. Even after the collapse of the bank had made the path impracticable for humans, roe deer had continued to use it. I scrambled up the slope, grabbing branches of hazel, until the way was blocked by tangled wire. Fallen birches had pushed a fence to the ground; its posts still jutted obliquely out of the mud. Their half-rotten state suggested that they were no more than thirty years old. Pausing to catch my breath, I looked down at the burn, which was now forty feet below, and at that moment I became aware of a stranger in the wood.

On the edge of a waterlogged sinkhole stood a tall and slender tree, its bark shining like old silver. I could make out a tracery of delicate twigs high up in its crown and tiny, crinkly leaves of a kind I had never seen. It would have taken a long time to identify it without the metal label, partially engulfed by the bark, on which a hand had scratched the word 'Pumilio'. In the confusion of native trees, a rare species of Antarctic beech had made its home and appeared to be thriving.

Over the years, tree guide in hand, I had discovered that the exotic specimens planted by Nicholas Ridley in the late 1980s observed a secret geographical logic. No written evidence of the plan existed, but the trees themselves were proof that Baron Ridley of Liddesdale had conceived the half-island on which his house stood, hemmed in by wooded ridges and the river, as a world in miniature. The Pumilio's Patagonian origin matched its position on the extreme southern edge of the property – which meant that the fallen fence running across the hillside beyond the burn must mark the original boundary.

On one of the old charts, a faint line had been drawn on the far side of the burn. Later, I found another example in the neighbourhood of this unusual type of boundary, which attributes both banks of a watercourse near its mouth to one property and the upstream banks to another. I charted the fence line and sent the redrawn maps to the Rural Land Registry in Carlisle. Several weeks later, after consultation with the relevant authorities, an official version of the map came back with the new property line labelled 'Unconfirmed Boundary'. Apparently, confirmation is a formality, but the expression seemed appropriate.

This part of the woodland at least would be safe from development. We decided to maintain it as a buffer zone and as a Debatable Land in which no man should 'set stob and staik'. The land is too dangerous to build upon in any case. Even walking there is risky. Dusk comes early in that part of the woods. The sun sinks below the cliffs when the fields on higher ground to the north and west are still in daylight. The hours pass quickly in the woods, and apart from a saw and a billhook, the most useful tool is a means of telling the time.

At that exact spot, two horsemen reached the end of their nightly watch and looked over into the Debatable Land. The sounds are unchanged – the guttural murmur of the burn, the rumble of the river, a rustle and a splash that might be a water vole or an otter. Five hundred years ago, it might have been a rider coming from no country but his own place of birth or returning to a stone tower with a stolen sheep and the contents of a farmhouse.

The slabs of tombstone limestone which form the riverbed at that point might still tempt a fugitive or an adventurer to cross the border, but when the river was high, carrying the brown peat of the Liddesdale hills, there would have been no cause for worry – only the natural devastation, the river stealing soil from the banks, erasing evidence of human endeavour and importing its own miscellaneous archive: the stones of a demolished building, a shard of metal that might once have been a weapon or a tool, or some other eroded object bringing unexpected news of the past.

30

The River

In June 2016, the river's 'loud dale' became a chasm. After a long dry spell during which it had provided a perfect practice ground of rills and pools for ducklings, the Liddel rose and the amphitheatre of woodland was once again a stadium of noise. On the evening of the 23rd, we went to sleep with a feeling of anticipated relief. The pound was rising; the markets were confident.

In the early morning, a strained quality in the voices of the radio presenters made it obvious, before the reading of the news, that the catastrophe had occurred. More than half the electorate had decided that England, Wales, Scotland and Northern Ireland should leave the European Union. The United Kingdom would after all become what a Scottish king had once called 'a little world within itself'.

Almost immediately, there was talk of a new referendum on Scottish independence. Every region in Scotland had voted to remain in the Union, and the Scottish First Minister vowed that Scotland would not be evicted from Europe by the reckless gamble of an English Prime Minister whose primary aim had been to resolve a dispute in his own party.

Not since I lived in the United States had I felt so historically, culturally and personally European. The proximity of the border suddenly had a cruel poignancy: I would be looking over to a country from which I might soon be expelled. Emails of condolence came from friends and acquaintances in France. I replied in what seemed at that moment, like the Scots I had learned from my father, one of my native tongues: '*La rivière qui entoure presque notre maison sera bientôt plus large que la Manche.*'

The oddest detail in that wakening to a state of national hallucination was the map on the computer screen which showed how each area had voted. All of Scotland was neatly severed along the border from the rest of Great Britain. In the regions of Scotland which are contiguous with England, 55.8% had voted to remain in the European Union; on the English side of the border, in Cumbria, 60.1% had voted to leave. I was on the point of completing a book – this book – in which the cross-border community was said to have overridden national differences and administrative divisions. Yet here was proof of the contrary. On a matter of historic importance, the two sides faced in opposite directions.

This seemed especially odd in an area which is heavily dependent on agricultural and other subsidies from Europe. At a recent local meeting, farmers – those who were working rather than retired – had been strongly in favour of remaining in Europe, but the meeting as a whole had been divided.

*

The chasm was as unreal as the fantasies of opportunist politicians who had lied about the workings and purposes of the European Union. Scottish voters had been sensitized to the benefits of European membership by the campaign for Scottish independence. On the English side, there was confusion and ignorance. The areas which had most to lose from leaving Europe and which had the lowest 'educational attainment' were the areas which voted most heavily to leave.

Lack of higher qualifications is not always seen as a serious disadvantage in Cumbria. Local newspapers publish articles in praise of young people who have decided to stay at home instead of going away to university. This appeared to have played a role in the Cumbrian vote. There was not much evidence of the xenophobia which was said to have inspired some voters in the south. In Carlisle and elsewhere, I had talked to people who had a sincere desire to learn the truth and to form a clear opinion but little idea of how to go about acquiring the necessary knowledge. One young woman explained, a week after the referendum, that, to her regret, she had not cast a vote because she had been unable to discover any solid facts that might have helped her to make up her mind. Information seemed to her a rare commodity to which only certain people had access.

In the absence of information, they had relied on their families, favouring especially the views of grandparents, who claimed to remember some powerful infancy of the nation when Britain had been 'great' and had 'stood on its own two feet'. But the respected wisdom of the elders was an exact regurgitation of slogans. The descendants of reivers had been told a fairy tale of men in suits who lived in a distant city, imposing the laws of another land and plotting the downfall of the little people. And so, setting out on a new adventure, and ready to suffer the economic consequences, they boldly voted for what might destroy them and their community. Meanwhile, that administrative fiction the border, which for so long had been an irrelevance to the people of the borderlands, was hardening into a political reality.

For the rest of that month, it rained, sometimes quite heavily, and by the time I completed this book a few days later, I knew that, once the river was calm again and falling, the shingle beach and the flower-covered banks would be quite transformed.

Appendix

Fig. 1: The Anglo-Scottish border and the Marches
(inset: The Debatable Land)

Fig. 2: Surnames of the West Marches and the Debatable Land

Fig. 3: Marriages in and around the Debatable Land and Liddesdale

Fig. 4: A key to Henry Bullock's 'platt' of the Debatable Land, 1552

Fig. 5: The partition of the Debatable Land on Bullock's 'platt'

Fig. 6: The colonization of the Debatable Land

Fig. 7: Ptolemy's map of Albion and Hibernia (Britain and Ireland),
with parts of Gaul and Germany

Figs 8 and 9: Ptolemy's atlas of the British Isles

Fig. 10: Ptolemy's map of Southern and South-Western England

Fig. 11: Ptolemy's map of Northern England

Fig. 12: Ptolemy's map of Caledonia

Fig. 13: An Iron Age buffer zone in the region of the Debatable Land

Fig. 14: The Great Caledonian Invasion (1)

Fig. 15: The Great Caledonian Invasion (2)

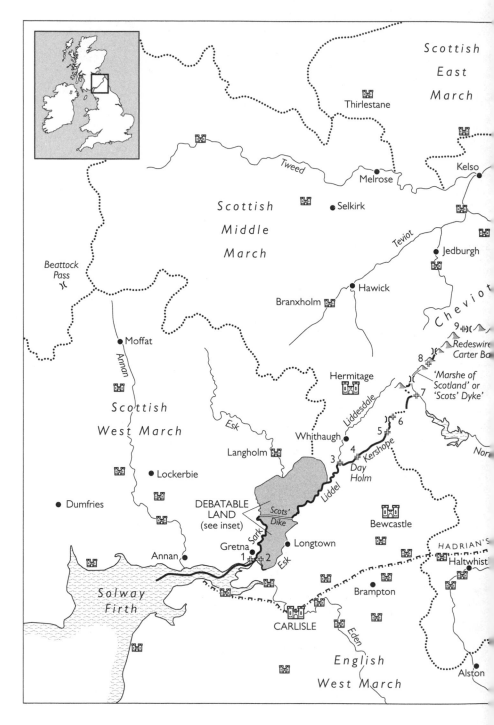

Fig. 1: The Anglo-Scottish border and the Marches
(inset: The Debatable Land)

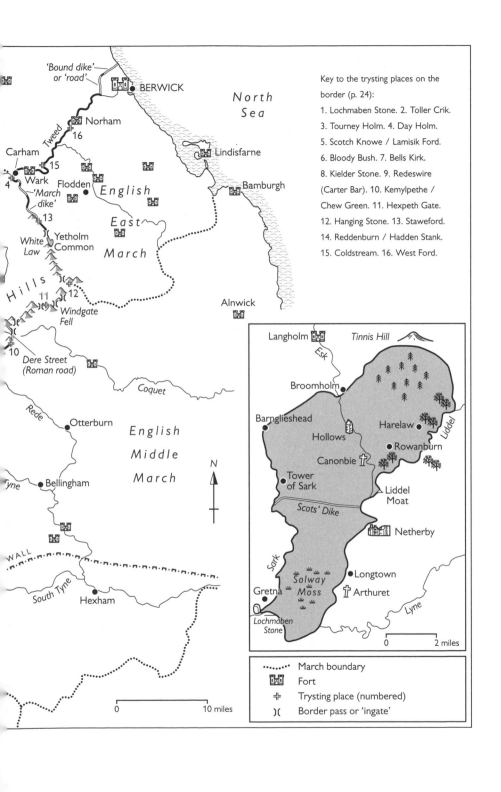

'Bound dike' or 'road'

BERWICK

North Sea

Norham
16

Tweed

Carham

15

Wark

4

'March dike'

Flodden

Lindisfarne

Bamburgh

English

East

13

White Law

Yetholm Common

March

Alnwick

Hills

11

12

Windgate Fell

10

Dere Street (Roman road)

Coquet

Rede

Otterburn

English

Middle

March

N

Tyne

Bellingham

WALL

South Tyne

Hexham

Key to the trysting places on the border (p. 24):
1. Lochmaben Stone. 2. Toller Crik.
3. Tourney Holm. 4. Day Holm.
5. Scotch Knowe / Lamisik Ford.
6. Bloody Bush. 7. Bells Kirk.
8. Kielder Stone. 9. Redeswire
(Carter Bar). 10. Kemylpethe /
Chew Green. 11. Hexpeth Gate.
12. Hanging Stone. 13. Staweford.
14. Reddenburn / Hadden Stank.
15. Coldstream. 16. West Ford.

Langholm

Tinnis Hill

Esk

Broomholm

Barnglieshead

Harelaw

Liddel

Hollows

Rowanburn

Canonbie

Tower of Sark

Liddel Moat

Scots' Dike

Netherby

Sark

Solway Moss

Longtown

Gretna

Arthuret

Lyne

Lochmaben Stone

0   2 miles

········   March boundary

Fort

Trysting place (numbered)

)(Border pass or 'ingate'

0   10 miles

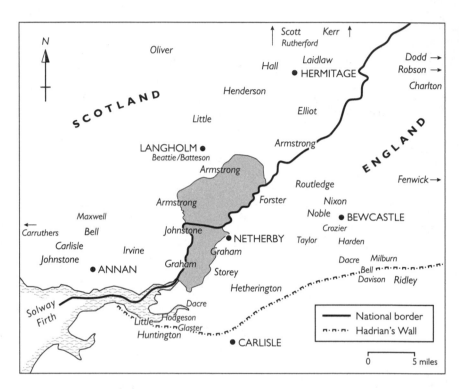

Fig. 2: Surnames of the West Marches and the Debatable Land

The distribution of clans or 'surnames' in the 1580s and 90s. From reports of the English and Scottish wardens.

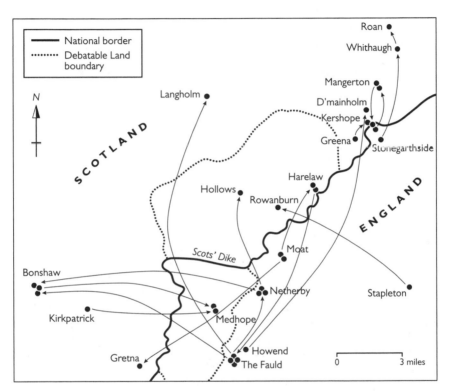

Fig. 3: Marriages in and around the Debatable Land and Liddesdale

Each arrow represents a bride's journey to her new home. The map shows all the 'alliances' – not just those that bridged the border – for which both places can be identified. From Thomas Musgrave's report to Lord Burghley (William Cecil) on 'the riders and ill doers both of England and Scotland', late 1583 (*Calendar of Border Papers*, I, 120–27).

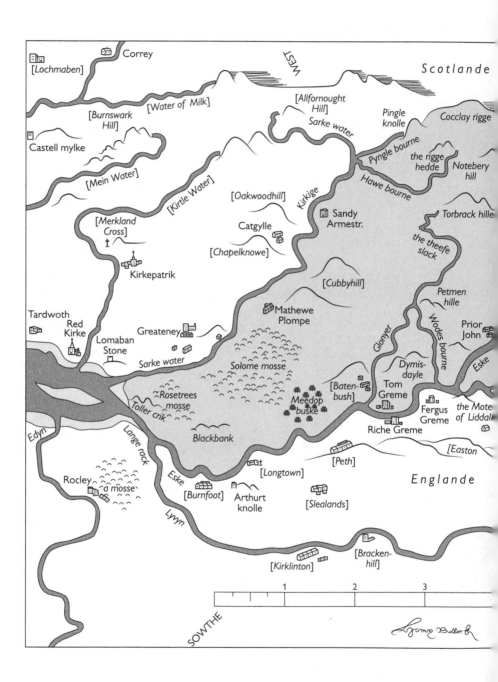

[Lochmaben] Correy

Scotlande

WEST

[Water of Milk]

[Burnswark Hill]

[Allfornought Hill]

Sarke water

Pingle knolle

Cocclay rigge

Castell mylke

Pyngle bourne

the rigge hedde

Notebery hill

[Mein Water]

[Kirtle Water]

[Oakwoodhill]

Kirkige

Hawe bourne

Torbrack hille

[Merkland Cross]

Catgylle

[Chapelknowe]

Sandy Armestr.

the theefe slack

Kirkepatrik

[Cubbyhill]

Petmen hille

Tardwoth

Red Kirke

Greateney

Mathewe Plompe

Glonyer

Dymisdayle

Wodes bourne

Prior John

Eske

Lomaban Stone

Sarke water

Solome mosse

[Batenbush]

Tom Greme

Fergus Greme

the Mote of Liddal

Rosetrees mosse

Meedop buske

Riche Greme

[Easton

Toller crik

Blackbank

[Peth]

Englande

Edyn

Lange rack

Eske

[Longtown]

Rocley

a mosse

[Burnfoot]

Arthurt knolle

[Slealands]

Lyvyn

[Brackenhill]

[Kirklinton]

1   2   3

SOWTHE

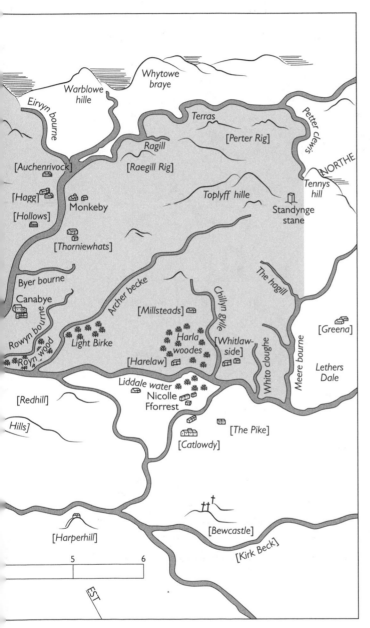

Warblowe
hille
Whytowe
braye
Eiryvn bourne
Terras
[Perter Rig]
Petter clewis
Ragill
[Raegill Rig]
[Auchenrivock]
NORTHE
Tennys
hill
[Hagg]
Monkeby
Toplyff hille
Standynge
stane
[Hollows]
[Thorniewhats]
Byer bourne
Archer becke
The hagill
Canabye
Rowyn bourne
[Millsteads]
Chillyn gylle
[Greena]
Light Birke
Harla
woodes
[Whitlaw-
side]
Royn wood
Whito cloughe
Meere bourne
Lethers
Dale
[Harelaw]
Liddale water
[Redhill]
Nicolle
Fforrest
Hills]
[The Pike]
[Catlowdy]
[Harperhill]
[Bewcastle]
[Kirk Beck]
5   6
EST

Fig. 4: A key to Henry Bullock's 'platt' of the Debatable Land, 1552

See plate 14. The names in square brackets are those of features depicted but not named on the map. The lines tracing the proposed divisions of the Debatable Land are reproduced separately (fig. 5).

On the map's orientation, see p. 137. The scale is impressively consistent within the shaded area (one of Bullock's miles is equivalent to about one-and-a-half modern miles). Beyond the Debatable Land, the scale varies and distances are slightly telescoped. The accuracy of the plotting makes it possible to identify most of the unnamed places, from Lochmaben (top left) to Bewcastle (bottom right). The lines indicating cardinal points of the compass are less accurate than the map itself, which correctly shows Liddel Moat as the centre of lines drawn between Tinnis Hill and Arthuret Knoll and between Tower of Sark and Harper Hill. These triangulation points are all visible from the summit of Tinnis Hill.

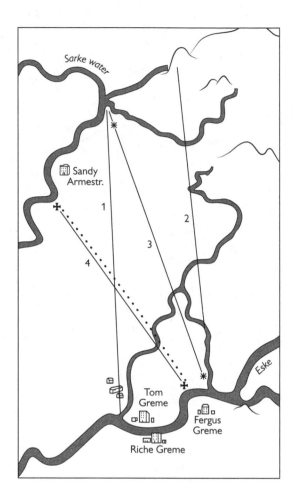

Fig. 5: The partition of the Debatable Land on Bullock's 'platt'

The four straight lines on Bullock's map show the Scottish proposal (1), the English proposal (2), the French ambassador's compromise (3) and 'the last and fynal Lyne of the particion concluded xxiiii Septembris 1552' (4). The dotted line represents the Scots' Dike or March Bank which marked the new Anglo-Scottish border (p. 137).

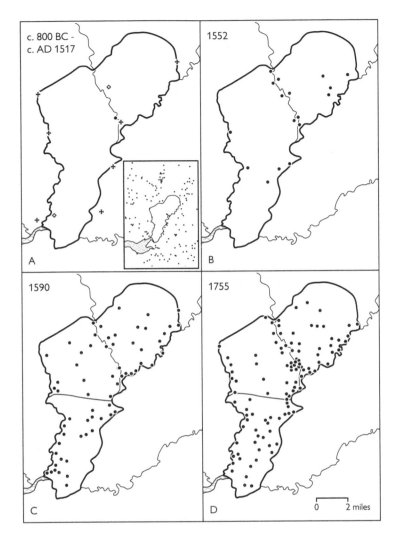

Fig. 6: The colonization of the Debatable Land

A. From the end of the Bronze Age to the first reiver settlements in the 1510s, the only permanent human habitation in the Debatable Land was in the religious enclave of Canonbie Holm (see pp. 87 and 277). The rectangles are the two temporary Roman camps; the crosses are the medieval perimeter chapels. Inset: settlements and traces of settlement in the surrounding area in the same period. (See p. 109.)

B. Farmsteads and pele towers in the Debatable Land on Henry Bullock's 'platt', immediately before the partition of 1552.

C. On the 'Platt of the opposite Border of Scotland to ye West Marches of England' produced for Lord Burghley (William Cecil) in December 1590.

D. On William Roy's Military Survey of Scotland (1752–5).

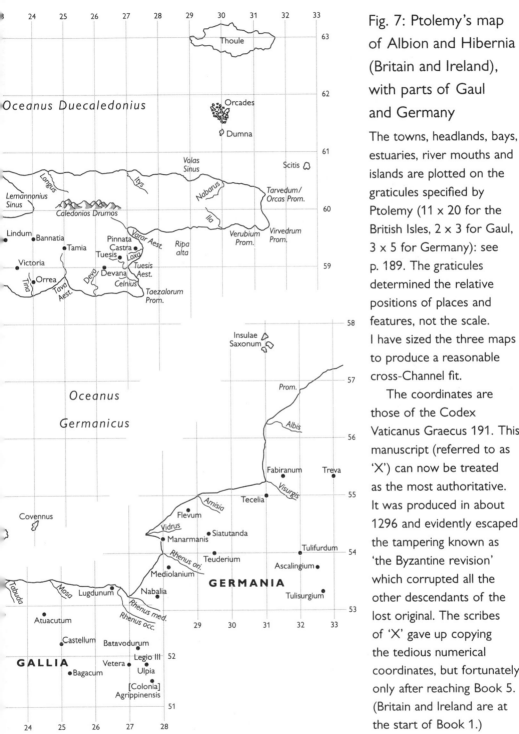

	24	25	26	27	28	29	30	31	32	33	

Thoule — 63

Oceanus Duecaledonius — *Orcades* — 62

Dumna

Volas Sinus — *Scitis* — 61

Longus *Ibys* *Nabarus* *Tarvedum/ Orcas Prom.* — 60

Lemannonius Sinus

Caledonios Drumos

Ila

Lindum *Bannatia* *Pinnata Castra* *Varar Aest.* *Ripa alta* *Verubium Prom.* *Virvedrum Prom.*

Tamia *Tuesis* *Loxa*

Victoria *Tuesis Aest.* — 59

Orrea *Deva* *Devana* *Celnius*

Tina *Tava Aest.* *Taezalorum Prom.*

— 58

Insulae Saxonum

— 57

Prom.

Oceanus

Albis — 56

Germanicus

Fabiranum *Treva*

Visurgis — 55

Amisia *Tecelia*

Covennus *Flevum*

Vidrus — 54

Manarmanis *Siatutanda*

Tulifurdum — 54

Rhenus ori. *Teuderium* *Ascalingium*

Mediolanium **GERMANIA**

Tabuda *Mosa* *Lugdunum* *Nabalia* *Tulisurgium*

Rhenus med. — 53

Rhenus occ. | 29 | 30 | 31 | 32 | 33 |

Atuacutum

Castellum *Batavodurum*

Legio III 52

GALLIA *Vetera* *Ulpia*

Bagacum *[Colonia] Agrippinensis*

— 51

| 24 | 25 | 26 | 27 | 28 |

Fig. 7: Ptolemy's map of Albion and Hibernia (Britain and Ireland), with parts of Gaul and Germany

The towns, headlands, bays, estuaries, river mouths and islands are plotted on the graticules specified by Ptolemy (11 x 20 for the British Isles, 2 x 3 for Gaul, 3 x 5 for Germany): see p. 189. The graticules determined the relative positions of places and features, not the scale. I have sized the three maps to produce a reasonable cross-Channel fit.

The coordinates are those of the Codex Vaticanus Graecus 191. This manuscript (referred to as 'X') can now be treated as the most authoritative. It was produced in about 1296 and evidently escaped the tampering known as 'the Byzantine revision' which corrupted all the other descendants of the lost original. The scribes of 'X' gave up copying the tedious numerical coordinates, but fortunately only after reaching Book 5. (Britain and Ireland are at the start of Book 1.)

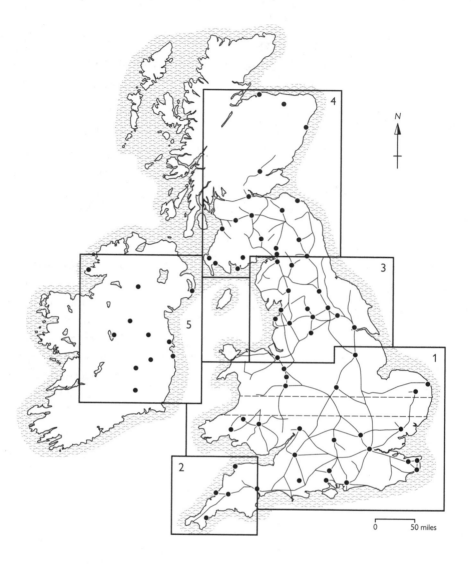

Figs 8 and 9: Ptolemy's atlas of the British Isles

The lines on fig. 8 represent Roman roads.

Ptolemy's map of the British Isles was assembled from several different maps, each of which observed its own conventions (p. 193). The coastal data was faulty, but, plotted on the correct graticule, the coordinates of *poleis* (towns) – including those of the three ports, Magnus, Novus and Setantiorum – are astonishingly accurate. The area between dotted lines is unrepresented in the data, perhaps because that section of the map of southern Britannia never reached the Library of Alexandria.

The incorrect latitude and longitude degrees are, in effect, arbitrary and

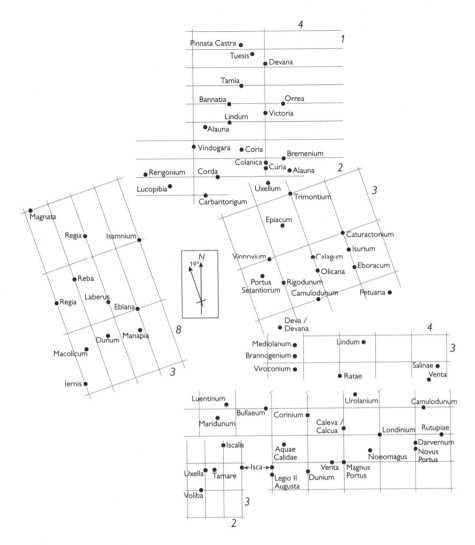

imposed by Ptolemy on the original maps. Any system showing vertical and horizontal positions would have served (e.g. A1, B2, etc.) or, since the triangulated positions on the 4 by 3 graticule turn out to have been calculated by whole-number ratios based on Londinium, 4:1, 5:3, etc., with a cardinal point and an indication of distance.

The approximate foundation dates of Roman forts and towns suggest that each map corresponds to a stage in the Roman conquest of Britain. Ireland was never invaded, but Roman finds indicate trade and, at Iernis (Stoneyford), civilian settlement: 1) AD 43–50 (lower section), AD 50s (upper section). 2) AD 50–65. 3) AD 70–78. 4) AD 78–81 (lower section), c. AD 83 (upper section). 5) c. AD 90–110.

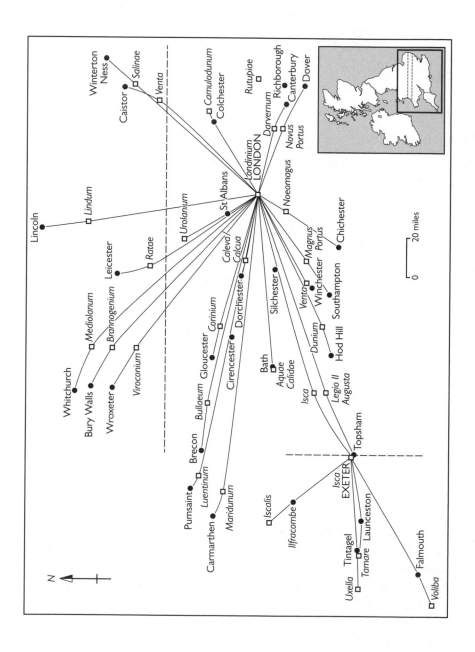

Fig. 10: Ptolemy's map of Southern and South-Western England

The squares are towns on Ptolemy's map; the circles are the places in their actual locations.

On the functioning of this unique map, see p. 194. Distances are approximate but bearings from Londinium are remarkably precise, with an average deviation of only 1.8° for the south-west and 1.7° for the rest of the map. In fact, since the survey was based, not on degrees, but on right-angled triangles with whole-number sides, most of the deviations are consistent with the inevitable margin of error. The blatant exception is Rutupiae (Richborough), which deviates from the true bearing by 13.5°. Its coordinates may belong to the faulty coastal data (p. 192) or, since this was the landing site of the invasion of AD 43, to military measurements using water clocks.

The coordinates of Corinnium (or Corinium) and Calcua (or Caleva) clearly define the positions of Gloucester and Dorchester-on-Thames. Bearings from these two places to the other towns are almost as accurate as they are from Londinium. The only evidence for the Roman name of Cirencester (probably a later, Anglo-Saxon name) is Ptolemy's misinterpreted map and the muddled Ravenna Cosmography of the seventh century (Coates). Cirencester itself became an important Roman town only about twenty years after the production of the map.

The map of the far south-west uses a different graticule and takes Isca (Exeter) rather than Londinium as its focal point.

A section or panel of the original map appears to be missing. Logically, it would have included several other major sites at road junctions: Kenchester, Towcester, Water Newton, etc. The original may have been engraved on metal plates or on stone tablets, like the Roman cadastral map of Orange (second century AD). To fill the gap, Ptolemy or Marinus of Tyre shifted the upper section of the map, which reflects a slightly later stage of the Roman conquest, to the south and west. The seven places in this section are mutually coherent and share the same directional accuracy relative to Londinium.

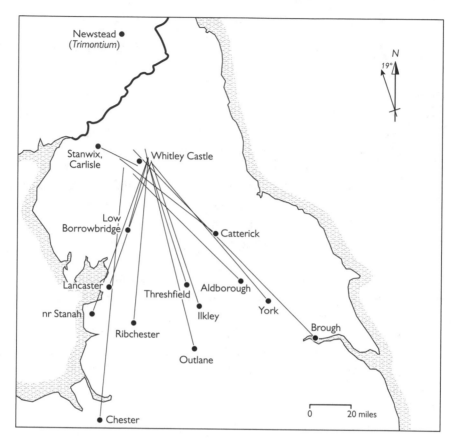

Fig. 11: Ptolemy's map of Northern England

On the graticule and orientation of the map, see pp. 194 and 293. In contrast to the previous map (fig. 10), distances are impressively exact. Bearings are slightly less accurate, with an average deviation of 2.5°, excluding the obviously misplaced Isurium (34.5°) and Caturactonium (19.4°). Caturactonium is one of the places for which Ptolemy had 'modern' data expressed in length of day, which would explain the inaccuracy (see p. 195). He may have known that Isurium stood on Dere Street between Caturactonium and Eboracum and so inserted it in what seemed the logical position. This exception proves the usual refinement of the mapping since a correct positioning of Caturactonium would have required only a small adjustment: 58° 10', 19° 50' instead of 58° 00', 20° 00'.

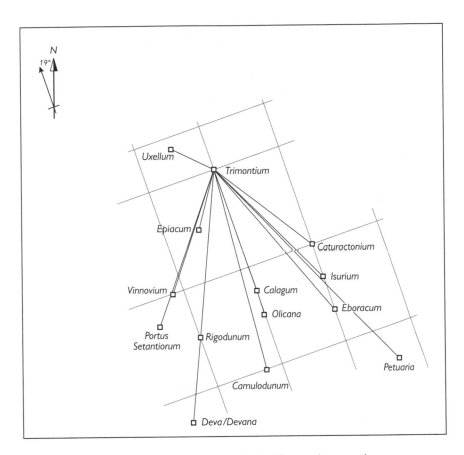

The convergent lines show the process of identifying unknown places:

1. On Ptolemy's map (right), lines were drawn from each town to the place labelled 'Trimontium'. 2. These lines were transferred – preserving the exact trajectories and relative distances – to a modern, rhumb-line map (left) on which the known places are correctly positioned. 3. The convergence of lines indicates an area in which the only significant Roman site is the fort of Whitley Castle near Alston (currently assumed to be Epiacum). Conclusion: this 'Trimontium', listed among the towns of the Selgovae, cannot possibly have been the fort of Newstead, which lies far to the north and well inside the territory of a different tribe.

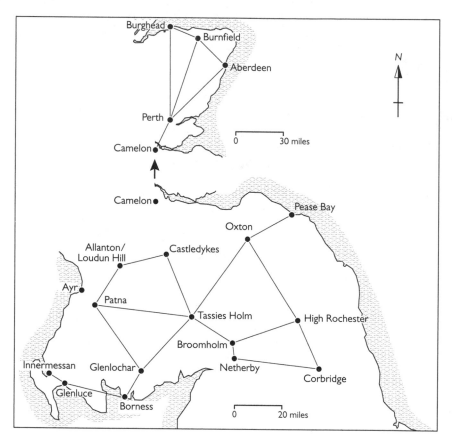

Fig. 12: Ptolemy's map of Caledonia

The lines connecting towns are intended only to facilitate comparison.

Both sections of Ptolemy's map (right) use a 4 by 1 graticule. On a modern scale map, the upper section would be magnified by one-third. It shows forts established only after Agricola's advance into northern Caledonia in c. AD 83 and was probably acquired separately.

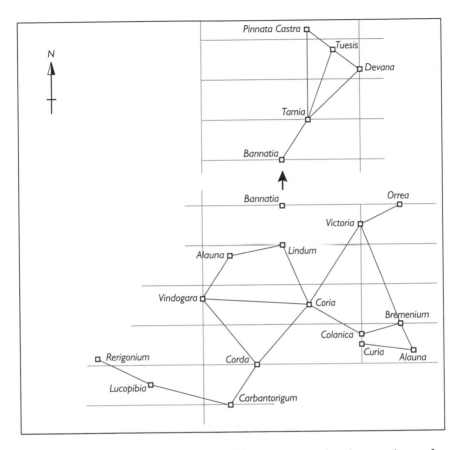

The distension of the map to the south-west suggests that the coordinates for Rerigonium belonged to the less accurate coastal data. Vindogara would be a site near Patna on the supposed Roman road from Ayr if the map is accurate; the bay called Vindogara would suggest Ayr itself.

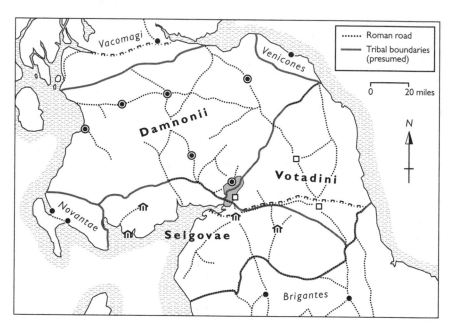

Fig. 13: An Iron Age buffer zone in the region of the
Debatable Land

Three tribal territories met in the area of the Debatable Land. A sixteen-mile stretch of the north-south border route was controlled by three different tribes: Damnonii (Colanica/Broomholm), Votadini (Curia/Netherby) and Selgovae (Uxellum/Stanwix, Carlisle). (See p. 201.)

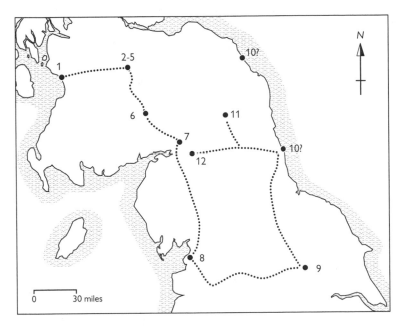

Fig. 14: The Great Caledonian Invasion (1)

The sequence of battles fought by 'British kings' and 'Arthur' according to the
Historia Brittonum, identified with the aid of Ptolemy's restored maps.

More detailed identifications are given on pp. 211–12, 217–23 and 245–7.
1. Mouth of the Glein: Irvine. 2, 3, 4, 5. On the river Dubglas in the Linnuis
region: the river Douglas near Castledykes. 6. On the river Bassas: Tassies Height?
7. Celidon Wood: Liddesdale. 8. Guinnion: Lancaster. 9. City of the Legion: York.
10. The shore of the river called Tribruit: Arbeia/South Shields, or Tweedmouth.
11. Bregion/Bregomion: Bremenium (High Rochester). 12. Camlann: Camboglanna (Castlesteads).

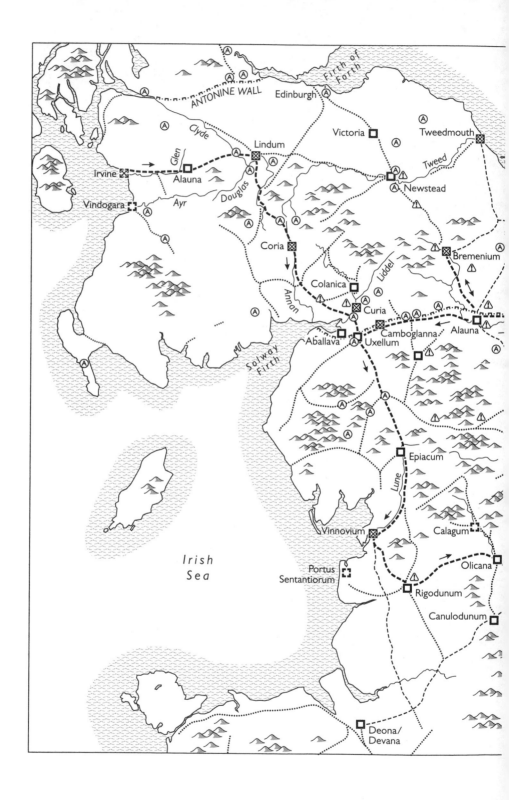

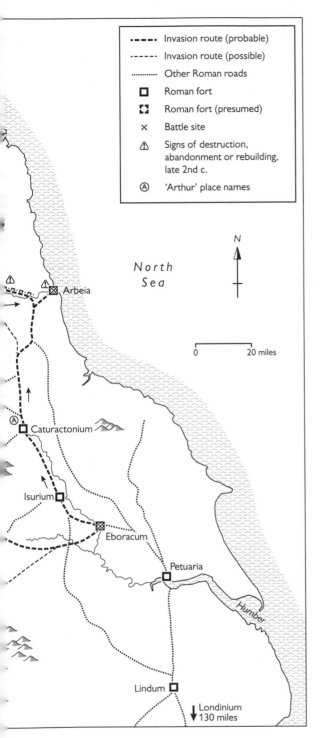

Fig. 15: The Great Caledonian Invasion (2)

The presumed route of the invaders follows the second-century Roman road network, though the prevalence of maritime and inland ports might suggest a coincident series of raids on the western and eastern seaboards.

Legend (from map):

- ▪▪▪▪ Invasion route (probable)
- ----- Invasion route (possible)
- ·········· Other Roman roads
- ▫ Roman fort
- ⸬ Roman fort (presumed)
- × Battle site
- ⚠ Signs of destruction, abandonment or rebuilding, late 2nd c.
- Ⓐ 'Arthur' place names

North Sea

N

0   20 miles

Arbeia

Caturactonium

Isurium

Eboracum

Petuaria

Humber

Lindum

Londinium
130 miles

Chronology

1237   Treaty of York confirms Esk–Solway border.

1245   *October 13* – Scottish and English knights meet at confluence of Reddenburn and Tweed to establish the 'true and ancient marches and divisions between the two kingdoms'.

1295   *October 23* – Franco-Scottish Treaty of Paris ('the Auld Alliance').

1296   *March* – Edward I sacks Berwick. First War of Scottish Independence (to 1306).

1297   *September 11* – William Wallace defeats English at Battle of Stirling Bridge and invades Cumberland and Northumbria.

c. 1300   First English and Scottish Wardens of the Marches.

1307   *July 7* – Death of Edward I.

1314   *June 24* – Battle of Bannockburn: defeat of Edward II by Robert the Bruce.

1315   *July 22–31* – Siege of Carlisle by Robert the Bruce.

1328   *March* – Treaty of Edinburgh–Northampton: confirmation of border.

1332–57   Second War of Scottish Independence: Battle of Annan, 1332; Battle of Dornock, 1333.

1388   *August 5 or 19* – Battle of Otterburn.

1448   *October 23* – Battle of Sark / Lochmaben Stone.

1449–57   Anglo-Scottish treaties confirm ancient neutrality of Debatable Land.

1474   Esk fish garth discussed at Westminster (p. 115).

1482   Berwick captured by English.

1485   *August* – Accession of Henry VII of England.

1488   *June* – Accession of James IV of Scotland.

1494   First survey of Debatable Land boundaries by Scottish and English commissioners.

1502   *January* – Treaty of Perpetual Peace between Scotland and England.

1509   *April* – Accession of Henry VIII.

1510   Second survey of Debatable Land boundaries.

1513   *September 9* – Battle of Flodden Field; death of James IV; accession of James V.

c. 1516   Armstrongs and Grahams settle in the Debatable Land.

1517   First government raids on the Debatable Land.

1525   *October* – 'Monition of Cursing' against the Border reivers by Gavin Dunbar, Archbishop of Glasgow.

1528   *Before April 2* – William Dacre, English warden of the West March, lays waste to Debatable Land and destroys

Armstrong pele tower at Hollows; *December 14* – Treaty of Berwick: reconfirmation of neutrality of Debatable Land, to be inhabited 'neither with stub, stake, nor otherwise, but with bit of mouth for pasturing of cattle between sunrise and sunset'.

1530   *May* – Capture and execution of Johnnie Armstrong by James V.

1534   *November* – Act of Supremacy: Henry VIII 'the only supreme head in earth of the Church of England'.

1537   Legalization of murder, arson, theft, etc. in the Debatable Land. (Proclamation renewed in 1551.)

1542   Survey of Anglo-Scottish border by Robert Bowes (also 1551); *November 24* – Battle of Solway Moss; *December 8* – Birth of Mary Stuart; *December 14* – Death of James V; accession of Mary Stuart; Scottish regency.

1544   Henry VIII orders devastation of the Scottish lowlands (start of 'The Rough Wooing'); *May 3* – Sack and burning of Edinburgh.

1545   *February 27* – Battle of Ancrum Moor.

1547   *January* – Death of Henry VIII; accession of Edward VI.

1548   *August 7* – Mary Stuart sails for France.

1551   *June* – Treaty of Norham: English troops to leave Scotland; Debatable Land to be depopulated.

1552   *Before June* – Map of the Debatable Land by Henry Bullock; *September 24* – Decree of the Border Commissioners: Debatable Land to be divided between England and Scotland.

1553   *After March* – Construction of Scots' Dike / March Bank; *July* – Death of Edward VI; accession of Mary I of England (Mary Tudor).

1558   *April* – Mary Stuart marries the Dauphin, son of Henri II; *November 17* – Death of Mary Tudor; accession of Elizabeth I.

1559   *July* – Mary Stuart Queen consort of France.

1560   *August* – Scottish Reformation Parliament: abrogation of the authority of 'the bishop of Rome called the pope'.

1561   *August* – Mary Stuart returns to Scotland after the death of her husband, François II.

1566   *October 16* – Mary Stuart visits Earl of Bothwell, Keeper of Liddesdale, at Hermitage Castle.

1567   *July 24* – Forced abdication of Mary Stuart; accession of James VI.

1569   *December 24* – Roman Catholic 'Rising of the North'; betrayal of Thomas Percy, Earl of Northumberland, by Hector of Harelaw.

1575   *July 7* – Redeswire Fray: skirmish between English and Scottish wardens of the Middle Marches at Redeswire (Carter Bar).

1579   Lord Herries (John Maxwell, warden of Scottish West March), report on Debatable Land population: 'in the year 1542, they did not exceed the number of 20 or 30 men at most. Now they are grown to three or four hundred'.

1583   Thomas Musgrave, Captain of Bewcastle, report on 'the riders and ill doers both of England and Scotland'.

1587   *February 8* – Execution of Mary Stuart; *July 29* – James VI, Act of Parliament 'for the quieting and keeping in obedience of the disordered subjects, inhabitants of the borders, highlands and islands'.

1593   *December 6* – Battle of Dryfe Sands (Johnstone–Maxwell feud).

1594–97   Poor harvests and famine.

1596   *March 17* – Arrest and imprisonment in Carlisle Castle of Kinmont Willie; *April 13* – Rescue of Kinmont Willie; *early August:* Thomas Scrope, warden of English West March, invades Liddesdale.

1597   *May 5* – Treaty of Carlisle: Anglo-Scottish cooperation in policing of the border.

1598   *Summer* – Plague in Carlisle, Penrith and Kendal.

1600   *June 16* – Murder of Sir John Carmichael, warden of the West March, by Armstrongs and Carlisles; *November 14:* Thomas Armstrong hanged in Edinburgh.

1601   *June – July* – Siege of Tarras Moss and defeat of Armstrongs by Robert Carey.

1603   *March 24* – Death of Elizabeth I; 'Busy Week' (or 'Ill Week'); *July 11* – Union of the Crowns; James VI becomes king of 'Great Britain'; Border counties renamed the Middle Shires; post of warden abolished; Border strongholds to be dismantled; March law replaced by the law of the land.

1604   'Survaie of the Debatable and Border Lands, Belonginge to the Crowne of Englande'; *February 14* – Borderers 'forbidden the use of all manner of armour and weapons, and of horses saving only mean nags for tillage'; offenders to be 'removed to some other place'.

1605   *April – August* – Deportation of Grahams to the Netherlands.

1606   *February* – Hanging of other murderers of warden Carmichael in Edinburgh; *Summer* – Deportation of Grahams to Ireland.

1608   Purge of Borders and Debatable Land by Lord Scott of Buccleuch.

1609 -   Rebuilding of Arthuret Church.

1625   *March* – Accession of Charles I.

1628   Richard Graham (knighted 1629), MP for Carlisle, acquires Netherby estate.

1707   *May 1* – Creation of the United Kingdom (Acts of Union, 1706–7).

1745   Jacobite Rebellion: *November 18* – Charles Edward Stuart ('Bonnie Prince Charlie') enters Carlisle.

1757 -   Development of Netherby, Longtown and Sarkfoot by Rev. Robert Graham.

1771   *November 16–17* – Eruption of Solway Moss.

1792   *Late summer* – Walter Scott enters Liddesdale for the first time.

1793   Newcastleton (Copshawholm) founded by Duke of Buccleuch as a centre for the weaving industry.

Notes

Abbreviations

ALHTS: Dickson et al., eds, *Accounts of the Lord High Treasurer of Scotland.*

APCE: Dasent, ed., *Acts of the Privy Council of England.*

CBP: *Calendar of Border Papers* (i.e. Bain, ed., *The Border Papers*).

CDRS: Bain et al., eds, *Calendar of Documents Relating to Scotland.*

CSPRI: Russell and Prendergast, eds, *Calendar of the State Papers Relating to Ireland.*

CSPRS: Bain et al., eds, *Calendar of the State Papers Relating to Scotland.*

HP: Bain, ed., *The Hamilton Papers.*

LPH8: Brewer, ed., *Letters and Papers, Foreign and Domestic, of the Reign of Henry VIII.*

Muncaster: Royal Commission on Historical Manuscripts, *The Manuscripts of the Earl of Westmorland, Captain Stewart, Lord Stafford, Lord Muncaster, and Others.*

RIB: Collingwood and Wright et al., eds, *The Roman Inscriptions of Britain.*

RPS: Brown et al., eds, *The Records of the Parliaments of Scotland to 1707.*

SPH8: Strahan et al., eds, *State Papers Published Under the Authority of His Majesty's Commission: King Henry the Eighth.*

1. Hidden Places

3 'all Englishmen and Scottishmen. . .': 'A Remembrance of an Order for the Debatable Lannde' (1537): R. B. Armstrong, pt 1, p. xxxvii.

2. Outpost

6 A hundred years ago: Earliest recorded version: 'The Widow in the Train': Wood (attributed to 'Colonel Ewart').

12 'Down a steep bank we slid': Evens, 57.

3. Panic Button

17 'It is hard to be right with the Scots!': Ridley (Baron Ridley of Liddesdale), 125.

4. The True and Ancient Border

23 Hugh de Bolbec: Shirley, I, 186–8 (Latin text); Stones, no. 8 (edition of text). See also Barrow, 36–7. Often misdated 1222 (*CDRS*, I, no. 832) or 1249, which is the date of the subsequent Border treaty (W. Nicolson, 1–7 and Reid, 479–80; T. Thomson et al., I, 413 ff.).

24 the Chevyotte 'mounteyne': Bowes (1550), 203.

25 'ingates and passages forth of Scotland': *LPH8*, XVIII, 2, 285.

5. 'The Sewer of Abandoned Men'

31 'surnames' or 'clans': E.g. Cardew, 83 ff.; Groundwater, 52–5.

31 government officials known as wardens: On March wardens: R. B. Armstrong, pt 1, pp. 2–7; Pease; Rae, 24 and 100; Reid; Godfrey Watson, 37–8.

31 appointed in the early fourteenth century: The title 'Warden of the Marches' dates from October 1309, when Robert Clifford was appointed 'custodem Marchie Scotie in partibus Karlioli contra inimicos et rebelles nostros' (Reid, 482). In 1301, 'keepers of the march': *CDRS*, V, 167.

33 'Nae living man I'll love again': 'The Lament of the Border Widow', vv. 25–8: W. Scott (1803), III, 84.

33 Great Monition of Cursing: R. B. Armstrong, pt 1, pp. 223–5; *SPH8*, IV, 371 and 416–19.

34 'from their cradells bredd': TNA SP 14/6/43: Spence, 'The Graham Clans', 87.

34 'a set of wild men': Carey (1759), xxviii (editor's introduction).
35 'ane spelunc and hurd of thewis': Thomas Scott of Pitgorno to T. Cromwell, in *SPH8*, V, 126.
35 'the sink and receptacle of proscribed wretches': Clarke, x.
35 'a land of contention, rapine, bloodshed': Hutchinson, II, 535–6.
35 a 'degraded piece of land': Hutton, 46.
35 'the sewer of abandoned men': Pease, 62.
35 'a monument to the intractable character of the natives': Hay, 82.
36 'suspicious and taciturn': G. M. Fraser, 2.
36 'racial composition': G. M. Fraser, 2.
36 'Border types': G. M. Fraser, 1.
37 'the people of that countrey': Bowes (1550), 243.

6. Mouldywarp

39 'spies and lookers into the privity [secrets] of the country': Mayor of Berwick on 'the Drie Marches into Northumberland', 1584: *CBP*, I, 142.
39 marks cut in a smooth patch of turf: W. Scott (1803), I, lxxxiii–lxxxiv.
39 a complex communications network: E.g. Godfrey Watson, 132–3.
39 bedsheets spread on hedges and hillsides: Tradition reported to R. B. Armstrong, pt 1, 78 n. 1.
40 'rumours are swift messengers': T. Scrope to R. Cecil, 1598: *CBP*, II, 569.
40 a recent book about the border line: Crofton, 68.
40 the origins of the Armstrongs: R. B. Armstrong, pt 1, pp. 175–7 (the name is recorded in Cumberland from 1235).
41 grew up in Newcastle upon Tyne: Fletcher, 46.

7. Beachcombing

45 'May still thy hospitable swains be blest': J. Armstrong, 66 ('Exercise', vv. 79–85); Mack, 126.

8. Blind Roads

51 'savagely romantic': Lockhart, 114 (letter of 30 September 1792).

51 'These have been all dug up': Lockhart, 113 (letter of 30 September
    1792).

51 'wild and inaccessible district of Liddesdale': Lockhart, 115.

51 'for about 16 miles along the Liddal': Arkle, 73; Chambers, I, 111.

51 'blind roads': W. Scott (1815), 117 (ch. 22).

52 'the people stared with no small wonder': W. Scott, *Guy Mannering*,
    note at end of ch. 38 (omitted from some editions).

52 'England and Scotland is all one': R. Carey to R. Cecil, 1 August
    1600: *CBP*, II, 674.

52 'hideous and unearthly' sounds: Lockhart, 117.

52 'suited himsel' to everybody': Lockhart, 117 (quoting Robert Shortreed).

52 'the bloodiest valley in Britain': G. M. Fraser, 39.

53 'the Edge': E.g. Rutherford, 234–5.

53 'the hardest of all the routes': Foxwell, 563.

53 'leane, hungry, and a wast': Camden (1610), 786.

54 twenty-three-year-old Queen of Scotland: On Mary's official (rather
    than romantic) visit to Hermitage Castle, see especially A. Fraser,
    330–31; Mackie, 322.

54 'the insolence of the rebellious subjectis': 'Instructionis to oure trusty
    Counsallour the Bischope of Dunblane', May 1567 (Keith, I, 594).

54 'the most offensive': E. Aglionby to Burghley, 1592: *CBP*, I, 394.

54 Queen's Mire: E.g. W. Scott (1803), I, xxxvi; Mackie, 138 n.

54 another Queen's Mire: On the Roman road from Raeburnfoot
    (Margary, 463).

55 'Sorbytrees': *The Times*, 25 April 1851, p. 8, and 9 September 1851, p.
    8; *New York Times*, 27 September 1851 (from *The London
    Examiner*). Summary and pictures in Moss.

56 Black Knight of Liddesdale: W. Scott (1812–17), II, 163.

57 types of boulder clay: Davitt and Bonner.

58 a silver spur, several bronze spurs and a gold signet ring: Elder, 70;
    Murray, 32; A. Strickland, V, 19.

58 'supposed to have been deposited': T. Elliot, 92.

58 this 'pass of danger': W. Scott (1803), I, xxxvi.

59 Reivers . . . would 'entice their pursuers': W. Scott (1812–17)
    (English), II, lxiii; see Lesley (1677), 61–2 (Latin) and Lesley (1596),
    I, 99 (Scots).

60 'I ken very weel': Chambers, I, 113.

60 'Every farmer rides well': W. Scott (1815), 141 (ch. 26).

60 'a great disgrace' to go on foot: W. Scott (1812–17), II, lxiii; Lesley
    (1578), I, 62; Lesley (1596), 99.

9. Harrowed

62 'for they have a persuasion': W. Scott (1812–17), II, lxv; Lesley (1578), I, 63; Lesley (1596), 100–101.

62 'a highly successful fashion model': G. M. Fraser, 288.

62 'remained attached to the Roman Catholic faith': W. Scott (1803), I, lxxxv.

63 This 'bauchling': *CBP*, II, 724 ('Manner of holding days of truce', 1600): 'Bawchling is a publicke reprooffe', etc.

63 to 'deal the more deadly or "unhallowed" blows': Elliot-Murray-Kynynmound, 89. Cf. Henderson, 16: 'the reason alleged is . . . that he may gather riches'.

63 '[Bernard] Gilpin did preach': Collingwood, 166.

63 'they're a' buried at that weary Caerl': Whellan, 18. First reported by Bruce (1852), 482.

64 believed to conceal the remains of enemies: Godfrey Watson, 180. 'Deid-stane' is Middle Scots for 'tombstone' (*Scottish National Dictionary*).

10. 'Loveable Custumis'

67 The laws and customs of the borderers: See especially W. Nicolson; also *CBP* (e.g. II, 724), but beware of self-serving misinterpretations by Border officials: e.g. p. 158. Generally: Balfour; Leeson; Neville; Rae; Reid; Tough.

67 'The lawis of marchis': Balfour, 602.

67 the last and still lively remnant: E.g. Neville, 2.

68 'commoun and indifferent to the subjectis of baith the realmis': Balfour, 602.

68 'decentralized system of cross-border criminal law': Leeson, 473 and 499.

70 An entire season's reiving: *CBP*, I, 346 ff.

70 between 1579 and 1587: *CBP*, I, 314–15.

71 One of the largest raids in the winter of 1589–90: *CBP*, I, 348.

72 'They sett him on his bare buttockes': *CBP*, I, 431.

72 'in the dead of winter': In a letter to R. Cecil: *CBP*, II, 629.

72 'never heard of in those parts before': Carey (1759), 114; Carey (1972), 48.

73 'run brandy': Lockhart, 119.

11. Accelerated Transhumance

76 'Liddesdale drow': Jamieson, II, 41; also George Watson, 118.

76 'I set furthe': *CBP*, I, 166.

77 the human population: Spence, 'The Graham Clans', 86; Stedman, 33; Tough, 26–8.

77 'Ride, Rowley, hough's i' th' pot': Sandford, 50. 'Rowley' was a Graham.

77 a dish of spurs: Rev. John Marriott, 'The Feast of Spurs', quoted in W. Scott (1806), III, 452–6; also reported of the Charltons of Hesleyside in Tynedale. The Scott family legend is depicted in a drawing at Abbotsford: 'The Dish of Spurs', by Charles Kirkpatrick Sharpe.

78 'Every now and then, about sundown': McMurtry, 21.

79 'there cannot be a greater mark of disgrace': W. Scott (1812–17), II, lxv; Lesley (1578), I, 63; Lesley (1596), 100–101.

80 'this bribenge they call Blackmeale': *CBP*, II, 164.

81 'such money as he had expended': *CBP*, II, 144.

81 making blackmail a capital offence: T. Scrope to Privy Council, June 1600: *CBP*, II, 665.

12. Skurrlywarble

83 'the sink and receptacle of proscribed wretches': Clarke, x.

83 not to be cultivated, ploughed or 'opened': '*Proviso semper quod nemo utriusque regni edificet, aret, aut colat vel aperiat terram*': Bowes (1550), 177. A similar text in October 1531: *LPH8*, V, 220 ('A proclamation made at Dumfries by the Commissioners of Scotland').

83 'there is no strife for the boundes': T. Dacre to Scots Privy Council, 6 July 1517: R. B. Armstrong, pt 1, p. 209 n.

84 'batable' or 'battable land': 'Batable landez or Threpelandez' in 1449 (*CDRS*, IV, 247; also 251, 256, 261); 'Batabelle Grounde' in 1484 (Cardew, 13; Gairdner, I, 56); 'Super Bundis Terrae Batabilis in Marchiis Scotiae' in 1493 (Rymer, XII, 551); 'Batable Land' in 1510 (Caley, II, 574); 'Bayttable grond' in 1526 (R. B. Armstrong, pt 1, p. 231 n.). Also Wharton to Henry VIII, June 1543 (*LPH8*, XVIII, 1, 444); Bowes (1550), 171–3 and 175; letters to and from Lord Dacre, 7, 21 and 29 August 1550 (Nicolson and Burn, I, lxx–lxxiii); M. d'Oysel to M. de Noailles, 23 August 1555 (Vertot, V, 93–4); T. Scrope to Burgh-ley, April 1597 (*CBP*, II, 301); Camden (1610), 782; Leland, 56.

84 *'terra contentiosa'*: E.g. Nicolson and Burn, II, 516; Rymer, XV, 315.

84 'There is a grounde': Thomas Dacre, warden of the English West March, to the Scottish Privy Council, 6 July 1517.

84n. 'two fertill and plentifull regions': Holinshed, V, 9.

84n. 'land . . . such as is rich and fertile in nutrition': Boucher et al., pt 2 ('Batable').

84 the cantref or hundred of Arwystli: Smith, 191–2 (referring to a paper by A. D. Carr).

84 It was not 'common land': On common land in Northern England and the Scottish Borders: Winchester (2000).

86 'come to take away her grannie's tombstone': Mack, 111.

87 'three parts surrounded by the Debatable ground': 'inveronned of thre partis with the Debatable grounde . . . soo that noo parte therof adjoynethe upon Scotlande, and hathe bene alwayes used as a hous of prayers, and newtre betuixt bothe the realmes': R. B. Armstrong, pt 1, pp. xxxii–xxxiii; also *LPH8*, V, 220. On Canonbie's earlier history: Ratcliff, 151–7. Its status was officially discussed from 1493. Later claims that Canonbie was either English or Scottish are suspect and circumstantial. Its inhabitants paid to use Carlisle markets – a privilege denied to the Scots. See Mackay MacKenzie, 113–15. On the distinction of parish and Debatable Land boundaries, see p. 108.

13. *Exploratores*

89 knowledge of the boundaries: The key documents are Bullock's map of 1552 (TNA MPF 1/257) and the variant copy rediscovered by R. B. Armstrong (pt 2, f. 37). The main texts describing the boundaries are 'The Boundes and Meares of the Batable Land Belonging to England and Scotland' (Bowes (1550), 171–5); 'The partitione of the laite Debatable lande' (1552: *CBP*, II, 821); 'A breviate of the bounder and marches of the West wardenrie betwixt England and Scotland' (1590: *CBP*, II, 821); 'A note of the devision of the bounders of the West Marches betwixt England and Scotland, and a devision of the Batable ground of both the Marches' (T. Scrope to R. Cecil, 1597: *CBP*, II, 301); 'An Abreviate of the survey of . . . the Debateable lands' (Anon. (1604), 12–16); 'Act in favouris of James Maxuell and Robert Douglas' (1605: *RPS*, 1605/6/108); 'Act in favouris of James Maxwell anent the debaitable landis' (1609: *RPS*,

1609/4/40). The translation of *RPS*, 1605 is inaccurate: e.g. Quhitliesyde is Whitlawside, not Watleyhirst. See also Carlyle, 1–2.

89 'wele knowne by the subjects of bothe the realmes': T. Dacre to Scots Privy Council, 6 July 1517: R. B. Armstrong, pt 1, p. 209 n.

89 Surveys were conducted in 1494 and 1510: *CDRS*, IV, 418; *LPH8*, I, 304; Caley, II, 574; Rymer, XIII, 276–7.

89 'wasted and destroyed in our passage': Bowes (1550), 175.

90 'The said bounds and meares': Bowes (1550), 171.

90 'Cocclay rigge': Cf. the otherwise unknown version of Bullock's map in R. B. Armstrong, pt 2, f. 37: 'The great bough called also Cock key rig'.

90 the 'Bateable grounds' in 1597: T. Scrope to R. Cecil, *CBP*, II, 301: 'A note of the devision of the bounders of the West Marches', etc.

90 his 'favourite cow': W. Scott (1803), I, xxxii.

91 a private estate track: Locally known as the Funeral Road – a corpse road probably dating from the seventeenth century.

92 '*in campo inter Lidel et Carwanolow*': Fordun, I, 136.

92 'Arfderydd' is plausibly identified with Arthuret: On the name: A. Breeze (2012).

93 'While her mother did fret': *Marmion* (1808), canto V, 12 ('Lochinvar').

93 the ghosts of two children: Goodman.

94 Lady Graham's prized jewellery: Lady Hermione Graham is referred to locally as 'Lady Graham'.

94 a murderous 'ladder gang': Articles from the *Carlisle Journal* and the *Carlisle Patriot*, 1885–6, in http://www.longtown19.co.uk/the_netherby_hall_burglars.83.html#The Netherby Hall Burglars

94 'strange and great ruins of an ancient Citie': Camden (1610), 781.

94 the West Marches were in an unusually peaceful state: T. Wharton to T. Cromwell, 26 December 1538: *LPH8*, XIII, 2, 476.

94 'Ther hath bene mervelus buyldinges': Leland, 47.

94 Castra Exploratorum: The name is known from the second route of the third-century Antonine Itinerary. On early visitors to Roman Netherby: E. Birley (1953).

94 'Men alyve have sene rynges': Leland, 47.

94 an inland port: On sea levels in the Solway Plain in Roman times (up to 4.8 metres above present levels): G. D. B. Jones, 291–2 n. Modern flood maps give some idea of the river's former domain.

94 'great marks of a ruinous Town': Gordon, 97.

94 '*Scafae exploratoriae*': Vegetius, 4:37; also Emanuele, 28; Shotter (1973).

95 the road from Luguvalium: On possible Roman roads in the area:
    Birley (1953), 28–30; W. Maitland, I, 204; Roy, 105 (IV, 2); Wilson
    (1999), 19 n.; also Richmond (Eskdalemuir).
95 Another road, crossing the Esk: A crossing at Netherby on direct
    roads from Blatobulgium (Birrens) and Luguvalium (Carlisle) is
    implied by the (usually correct) distances of the Antonine Itinerary.
95 Titullinia Pussitta: Collingwood, Wright et al.; *RIB*, 984.
95 'As for the houses of the cottagers': Stukeley, 58.
95 The eruption of Solway Moss: Gilpin, 135–7; Hutchinson, II, 538–41
    (account of J. Farish); Lang, 406–8; Pennant, 75–6.
96 'several foundations of houses': Richard Gough, in Camden (1789),
    III, 201.

14. Windy Edge

97 a temporary marching camp: Pastscape monument no. 1566735:
    photographed from the air by Dave Cowley in July 2010. The Roman
    road once thought to have branched off at Westlinton, where the
    flood defences were mistaken for a vallum, probably ran along the
    line of the Sandysike Industrial Estate road near Longtown towards
    the marching camp.
97 'the greatest factory on Earth': Its story is told in the Devil's Porridge
    Museum at Eastriggs.
98 smuggled across the Solway: McIntire, 168.
98 first recorded in 1398 as the 'Clochmabanestane': Rymer, VIII, 58 (6
    November 1398). Perhaps the 'Locus Maponi' of the Ravenna
    Cosmography (c. AD 700).
98 Maponus, a Celtic god: Inscriptions at Birrens, Brampton, Corbridge,
    Ribchester and Vindolanda: *RIB*, 583, 1120–22, 2063, 2431.2 (in *RIB*
    II), 3482 (in *RIB* III).
100 'Grass decays and man he dies': Engraving in R. B. Armstrong, pt 1,
    facing p. 120.
100 Debatable Land chapels: Generally, Brooke; Winchester (1987), 23–4.
101 'I was on the central boss': John Buchan, *The Thirty-Nine Steps* (1915),
    ch. 5.
101 the 'dry march' of the 'Bateable grounds': T. Scrope to R. Cecil, *CBP*,
    II, 301. Probably the same as 'the marche of Auchinbedrig' (James
    VI, 'Act in favouris of James Maxwell anent the debaitable landis', 12
    April 1609: *RPS*, 1609/4/40). Auchinbetrig is the old name of

Solwaybank (Burton (1849), 168), an Armstrong 'hous of reasonable strenthe' presumed to be in – rather than on the edge of – the Debatable Land in 1596 (*CBP*, II, 181); also D. Scott, 51.

101 an artery of the northern Roman road system: 'Sheppard Frere has drawn my attention to the possibility that the old road from Langholm to Annan might mark a Roman road from Broomholm to Birrens crossing the Esk near the Irvine burn' (Wilson (2003), 115 n. 21). The straight road to Irvine is shown on *Ainslie's Map of the Southern Part of Scotland* (1821) and on later nineteenth-century maps as one of the main roads of the area.

102 'Tarras . . . was of that strength': Carey (1759), 124; Carey (1972), 53.

102 'Was ne'er ane drown'd in Tarras': W. Scott (1803), I, 49.

104 the ruin of a 'chambered cairn': Canmore ID 67899.

15. 'In Tymis Bigane'

106 '*raé*', '*meré*', '*har*': Ragill is now Rae Gill, the hagill is Haw Gill, Meere bourne is Muir Burn, Harla is Harelaw.

106 the old, unimproved fields: Cole.

107 The oldest documents: 'the Batable Landez in the West-marchez' (November 1449: Rymer, XI, 245); 'Batable landez or Threpelandez' (November 1449: *CDRS*, IV, 247); also 251, 256, 261.

107 'in tymis bigane': The Lords of the Council of Scotland, 1526: *SPH8*, IV, 433.

107 in the reign of Edward VI: 'Memoranda on the Borders': *CBP*, I, 32 (in the hand of Walsingham's secretary).

107 'remained undivided': Bowes (1550), 177.

107 dated to the days of Alexander III: Ridpath, 287.

107 'the time of King John and his predecessors': *CDRS*, I, no. 827.

108 obscure Brittonic name: A. Breeze (2008) suggests an origin in Welsh '*serch*' ('love'). On the significance of the Sark boundary: Barrow, 27; Todd.

108 'the bounder of the forest of Nicholl': Anon. (1891), 18.

109 The jug was unearthed at Whitlawside: A bronze tripod ewer (Dumfries Museum): Canmore ID 86394.

109 'between AD 684 and 947': Pastscape monument no. 1358759.

109 A hoard of rings: Canmore ID 67489; Hyslop, 144–5.

110 Brettalach: A. James, 51; Johnson-Ferguson, 148 (Brettalach in 1190; Bretellaugh in 1336); Morgan, 43–4.

110 Wobrethills: A. James, 51; T. Thomson, nos 212 (Wabritshill in 1653) and 242 (Wobrethills in 1661).

110 'Bret' place names: A. James, 51.

111 a small copper terret: Canmore ID 183461, found near Mouldyhills.

16. 'Stob and Staik'

115 the matter was discussed at Westminster: Rymer, XI, 836 (3 December 1474).

115 'fish garth': R. B. Armstrong, pt 1, pp. 171–4 (from 1474) and p. xvi (1494).

115 in 1494 and 1510: CDRS, IV, 418; LPH8, I, 304; Caley, II, 574; Rymer, XIII, 276–7.

116 'the Fisigarthis on the West Marches': Brenan and Statham, 74; Mack, 105–6.

116 the system of partible inheritance: Bowes (1550), 243: 'There doe inhabite in some place three or fower howsholde soe that they cannot uppon so smalle fermes without any other Craftes live truely but either be stealing in England or Scotland' (on Redesdale). The example of the Grahams: Spence, 'The Graham Clans', 84–5.

116 'broken men' or 'clanless loons': Pease, 102.

116 a 'terra inhabitata': Major (1521), I, f. 6 (ch. 5); Major (1892), 19.

117 'peaceful Anglo-Scottish accommodation': King and Penman, 6; Webster, 99.

117 to build a new Hadrian's Wall: Anon. to Elizabeth I, 1587: CBP, I, 300–302.

117 'nor by lande nor by water': CDRS, IV, 247, 251, 256, 261.

118 'stob and staik': E.g. 'A Remembrance of an Order for the Debatable Lannde' (1537): R. B. Armstrong, pt 1, p. xxxvii.

118 '6 miles of the water of Esk': T. Dacre to Privy Council, 17 May 1514: LPH8, I, 1261.

118 'I have four hundred outlaws': T. Dacre to Wolsey, 23 August 1516: original text in Ellis, 132.

119 'now duelland in the Debatable Land': Livingstone, I, 454; Pitcairn, I, 1, 235.

119 'ar in the Debatable landis': R. B. Armstrong, pt 1, p. 211; Hannay, 124.

119 the Storeys, 'Lang Will' and his eight sons: T. Musgrave to Burghley, end 1583: CBP, I, 124–5; Mackay MacKenzie, 117.

119 'Let slip Tynedale and Redesdale': Northumberland to Henry VIII,
     23 August 1532: *LPH8*, V, 541.

120 Hedderskale bog: T. Dacre to R. Maxwell, 24 June 1517: *LPH8*, II,
     1082; R. B. Armstrong, pt 1, p. 209. The name, not otherwise
     recorded, referred to a part of Solway Moss.

120 'Scottish when they will, and English at their pleasure': T. Musgrave
     to Burghley, end 1583: *CBP*, I, 126.

120 'wilde and mysguyded menn': Dr Magnus to Cumberland, 1526: R. B.
     Armstrong, pt 1, p. 231.

120 'That same Debatable grounde': T. Wharton to English Privy Coun-
     cil, 25 September 1541: *HP*, I, 101–2.

121 'to brenne, destroye, waiste': T. Dacre to Scots Privy Council, 6 July
     1517: R. B. Armstrong, pt 1, p. 209 n.

121 an immodest report: T. Dacre to English Privy Council, 17 May
     1514: *LPH8*, I, 1261; Johnstone, 51–2.

121 'only remnants of old houses': T. Dacre to Wolsey, 11 June 1524:
     LPH8, IV, 174; Hyslop, 349.

122 'None of the people of Beaucastell': W. Dacre to Wolsey, 4 August
     1526: *LPH8*, IV, 1060.

122 assembled two thousand soldiers: 'The true Copie of th'Indictment
     of Riche Grahame of Esk': R. B. Armstrong, pt 1, p. xxvi.

122 the new pele tower at Holehouse: Letters of W. Dacre and bills of
     R. Maxwell: R. B. Armstrong, pt 1, pp. xxiv–xxv. On pele towers and
     bastles generally: P. Dixon; Durham; Maxwell-Irving.

122 'Black Jock': R. B. Armstrong, pt 2, f. 8, distinguishing John
     Armestrange alias Black Jock from John of Gilnockie.

122 'a great host': R. B. Armstrong, pt 1, p. 247.

122 'burnt and destroyed': W. Dacre to Wolsey, 2 April 1528: *SPH8*, IV,
     492.

123 a mass attack was launched: *LPH8*, IV, 1935.

123 'a privy postern': W. Dacre to Wolsey, 2 April 1528: *SPH8*, IV, 489.

123 'loveynge bedfello', Elizabeth: E. Dacre to W. Dacre, 2 June 1528:
     LPH8, IV, 1901.

124 'common theft and reset of theft': Pitcairn, I, 1, 152–4 (quoting
     several other accounts).

124 'Farewell! my bonny Gilnock hall': W. Scott (1803), I, 69.

124 'the lordship of Eskdale': Livingstone et al., VIII, 195; Pitcairn, I, 1,
     154 (8 July 1530: 'the Gift of all gudis movabill and unmovabill . . .
     quhilkis pertenit to umquhill Johnne Armstrange').

124 'a parcell of the Debatable grounde': W. Dacre, answer to
     R. Maxwell's bill, 1528: R. B. Armstrong, pt 1, p. xxv.

17. 'Rube, Burne, Spoyll, Slaye, Murder annd Destrewe'

125 proclamations were usually ignored: 'There was ane Act of
Parliament needed in Scotland, a decree to enforce the observance of
the others' (George Buchanan, quoted in Borland, 40).

125 'all Inglichemene annde Scottesmene': 'A Remembrance of an
Order for the Debatable Lannde' (1537): R. B. Armstrong, pt 1, p.
xxxvii.

126 'the West Marches of England': T. Wharton to T. Cromwell, 26
December 1538: *LPH8*, XIII, 2, 476.

127 Battle of Solway Moss: Contemporary reports: W. Musgrave to
Anthony Browne, 24 November 1542 (*HP*, I, 307–8); T. Wharton, 'A
remembrance [of] the overthrow given to the Scots between Heske
and Levyn [Esk and Lyne]', 29 November 1542 (*LPH8*, XVII, 624–5).

127 'sack', 'rase' and 'deface': *HP*, II, 326 (Privy Council, transmitting the
King's orders to the Earl of Hertford).

127 set fire to the woods: *LPH8*, XVIII, 1, 444.

127 'the douncasting of certane houssis': *ALHTS*, IX, 437. On fears of a
Franco-Scottish invasion of the Debatable Land in 1550–51:
Turnbull, ed., 52–3 and 83.

128 'Archebald Armestronge': R. B. Armstrong, pt 1, p. lxi.

129 'by assent and appointment': 'Patten's Account of Somerset's
Expedition': W. Scott (1803), I, lxix; also Anon. (1801), 166–7.

129 without obtaining a licence: Luders et al., III, 751 ('Felonyes uppon
conveying of Horses into Scotland').

129 'the Scotland v. England internationals': G. M. Fraser, 76.

130 'drynkyng hard at Bewcastle house': H. Woodrington to R. Carey, 18
May 1599: *CBP*, II, 605.

130 John Whytfeild: *CBP*, II, 605.

130 the 'wild' women of Kielder: W. Scott (1927), 462 (7 October 1827,
probably referring to the late 1750s).

130 Isabell Rowtledge: *CBP*, I, 69.

131 Margaret Forster: *CBP*, I, 558.

131 'Old Rich of Netherby': *CBP*, I, 125.

131 'Little was her stature': Inscribed on her tombstone on the battlefield.

131 'the riders and ill doers both of England and Scotland': T. Musgrave
to Cecil, end 1583: *CBP*, I, 120–27.

132 'Thus your lordshipe may see': *CBP*, I, 126.

132 'the blessed union or rather reuniting': 'A Proclamation for the union
of the kingdoms of England and Scotland': Nicolson and Burn, I,
cxxii.

132 hanged . . . in the market place at Haltwhistle: Archie Graeme and
     Mary Fenwick: Sitwell, 228.

                        18. The Final Partition

133 'wherein I perceive the Scots take great courage': W. Dacre to
     Privy Council, 17 September 1550: Nicolson and Burn, I, lxxx.
     English fears of French influence can also be seen in a caption on
     the version of Bullock's map rediscovered by R. B. Armstrong (pt 2,
     f. 37): 'Lang holme where the French men have builded a strong fort
     of Earth'.
133 'It is covenanted, concorded and concluded': W. Nicolson, 58.
134 burned and depopulated the Debatable Land: *ALHTS*, X, xvii;
     Boscher, 135–6.
134 partition . . . proposed by the Scots in 1510: Rymer, XIII, 276; R. B.
     Armstrong, pt 1, p. 198.
134 'perusing of olde writinges and examinacion of old men': *APCE*, IV,
     17 (10 April 1552).
134 'the lesse pryvey the Borderers be made': *APCE*, III, 493
     (28 February 1551).
134 at 'muche charge and trouble': *APCE*, III, 493.
135 in the middle of the Solway Firth: Boscher, 138, quoting British
     Library, Mss. Cotton Caligula B, VII, ff. 461–5; Burton and Masson, I,
     124–5.
135 the 'juste and true' map: *APCE*, III, 493 (28 February 1551; Bullock's
     map was completed by May 1552).
135 maps drawn of their estates: Harvey, 38; McRae, 189.
136 'burstit of his ryding': *ALHTS*, X, 82 (May 1552).
136 'a vast extent of view': Pennant, 85; a similar remark in Skene (97–8),
     who saw Liddel Moat in the 1860s.
137 'faithfull subjectes': *APCE*, III, 108.
137n. the commissioners' 'indenture' (24 September 1552): Bain, ed.
     (1898–1969), I, 191.
137 the cost of the 'diche': *APCE*, IV, 241.
137 'groves and holes': 'The partitione of the laite Debatable lande', 1552:
     CBP, II, 821.
138 Blackbank: Boscher, 129–30. Its strategic importance seems to have
     been recognized by the Romans (p. 279). It was also proposed as the
     site of a fort in 'Military Report on the West March and Liddesdale

... prepared ... between the years 1563 and 1566' (R. B. Armstrong, pt 1, p. cxiii).

138   neither side was much concerned: E.g. Salisbury, I, no. 386: 'if [the Commissioners] cannot reduce the Scots to the very direct division, as the Linea Stellata leadeth, they may have authority to relent to the Scots somewhat from the said right line' (21 June 1552); also Haynes, ed., 120–21.

138   'Gallic rigour': Crofton, 44.

138   the border line dipped abruptly: First shown on John Thomson's map of Dumfriesshire (1828), the area was marked 'Disputed' on Thomas Donald's map of Cumberland (1774), but not on Roy's survey of 1752–5.

19. Hector of ye Harlawe

140   'dykes and ditches of the Debatable Land': *ALHTS*, X, 170.

140   'incursions, murders, burnings': Nicolson and Burn, I, lxxxi.

140   'The common thieves of Liddesdale': R. Maitland, 52–5 ('Aganis the Theivis of Liddisdaill').

140   'ane byrnyng irne': *ALHTS*, X, 208.

141   Dacre family had fallen into disfavour: M. James, 99.

141   'idle and unprofitable': Boscher, 203.

141   'narrow and somewhat crooked': Boscher, 202, quoting British Library, Mss. Cotton Caligula B, V, ff. 50–58. This became standard practice in the Borders: e.g. Stevenson, ed., IV, 223 (August 1561).

141   'occupyt and manurit': W. Fraser (1873), I, 219.

141   watches were to be kept: 'The orders of the Watches upon the West Marches made by the lord Wharton', October 1552: Lemon et al., VI, 415; Nicolson and Burn, I, lxxxiv.

142   In 1561, more than one hundred: Spence, 'The Graham Clans', 86 and appendix A.

142   their 'service might be acceptable': Edward Aglionby, 'The devision of the severall charge of the West Borders of England and Scotland', March 1592: *CBP*, I, 393.

142   'shall not suffice to make them good men': Lord Herries (William Maxwell), 23 January 1578: W. Fraser (1873), II, 487.

142   a report to the English Privy Council: *CBP*, I, 120–7.

143   Keepers of Liddesdale: A list of the Keepers in Macpherson, 506.

144   'Little Jock' Elliot: E.g. Birrell, 5–6.

144 'a warre might arise': R. Bowes to Burghley, 8 September 1582: Bowes (1842), 183.

144 'verie ticklie and dangerous': John Forster to Walsingham, 23 April 1584: *CBP*, I, 132.

144 the extraordinary sum of £4,000: G. F. Elliot, 141–2.

145 'the gude auld Lord': 'Jamie Telfer of the Fair Dodhead', v. 93: W. Scott (1803), I, 102.

145 'But since nae war's between the lands': 'Kinmont Willie', vv. 57–60: W. Scott (1803), I, 147.

145 'Sparing neither age nor sex': W. Fraser (1878), I, 58; paraphrased in *CBP*, II, 305.

145 'which is theire chefest profitt': Ralph Eure to Burghley, 29 April 1597: *CBP*, II, 311.

145 'my Lord Buckpleugh did wapp the outlaws': Lowther, 176.

146 A Scottish statute of 1587: Goodare, ch. 8; Groundwater, 9. Act passed on 29 July 1587: 'For the quieting and keping in obedience of the disorderit subjectis, inhabitantis of the bordouris, hielandis and ilis' (*RPS*, 1587/7/70).

146 the Isles of Lewis and Skye: Macpherson, 443.

146 'a set of wild men': Carey (1759), xxviii (editor's introduction).

147 'lurking and hiding themselves': R. Sadler to W. Cecil, 24 December 1569: Sadler, II, 71.

147 'to fly to one of the Armstrongs': Earl of Sussex to Burghley, end 1569: M. Green, ed. (1871), 162.

147 The site of Hector's tower: T. Graham (1914), 137–8: 'Mr. William Armstrong of Calside remembers the site being pointed out to him by the carter who removed the foundation stones.' The 'Site of Harelaw Tower' is marked on the Ordnance Survey six-inch map of 1862 (survey of 1858).

148 'despised and neglected': Watt, 291.

148 'to take Hector's cloak': Percy, I, 279.

148 a member of the Elliot family: Anon. (1833), 154.

148 'a cottage not to be compared to a dog kennel': Earl of Sussex to Burghley, end 1569: M. Green (1871), 162.

148 'his own nearest kinsmen': J. Maxwell, 119.

148 a fantasy of the poem-writing commissioner: R. Maitland, 132 ('Inveccyde Aganis the Delyverance of the Erle of Northumberland', attributed to Maitland by John Pinkerton).

148 'Hector Armestronge of the Harlawe': *CBP*, I, 122 (end 1583).

148 'Hector of the Griefs and Cuts': R. B. Armstrong, pt 2, f. 267; W. Scott (1810), 377.

149 a map of 1590: 'A Platt of the opposete Borders of Scotland to ye
   west marches of England': British Library, Royal MS 18 D.III f. 76.
   Also by Edward Aglionby, a version titled 'A tract of the Bounders of
   the West Marches of England towardes Scotland': TNA MPF 1/285.
   See illustrations.

20. Scrope

150 'Many servants brought in the meat': Johnstone, 91–2.
150 'better to hear the chirp of the bird': B. Dixon, 141.
150 'Yf I were further from the tempestuousnes': Baron Willoughby
   (Peregrine Bertie) to R. Cecil, 12 December 1600: *CBP*, II, 718.
151 'so given over to drunkenness': R. Carey, 'Report on the Middle
   March', September 1595: *CBP*, II, 57.
151 plague, which reached Carlisle: Nicolson and Burn, II, 234; cf.
   Stedman, 36.
151 'The frontier here is very broken': T. Scrope to Burghley, 20 August
   1593: *CBP*, I, 494.
152 a 'mapp or card': T. Scrope to Burghley, 20 April 1597: *CBP*, II,
   301–2.
153 'greate waters and flouds': Lowther to Burghley, 28 September 1592:
   CBP, I, 410.
153 apprentices born beyond Blackford: The 'Dormont Book', in
   Ferguson and Nanson, 66.
153 'newlie comde to the grounde': R. Eure to Burghley, 18 February
   1596: *CBP*, II, 106.
153 'in great ruine and decaye': Anon. (1891), 36. The survey is analysed
   by G. P. Jones.
153 'not worth his pay': R. Musgrave to Burghley, 13 February 1596: *CBP*,
   II, 105–6.
154 'the especial and peculiar property': Walpole, 436.
154 Kinmont Willie: On his arrest and escape: *CBP*, II, 121 ff.; Cameron,
   I, 292–9; Child (ballad and notes); W. Scott (1803), I, 129–43; Spottiswood, 413–15.
154 Day Holm: See fig. 1. Not, as often stated, Tourney Holm, two miles
   downstream at Kershopefoot.
154 'a note of pryde in him selfe': T. Scrope, 'A breviate of part of
   Buccleuch's dealings with me since he became keeper of Liddesdale',
   18 March 1596: *CBP*, II, 114.

155 'her Majesties castle of Carlel': 'The examination of Andrew Grame', 25 April 1597: *CBP*, II, 368.

155 'the two who lay dead at the gate': *CBP*, II, 121; cf. Moysie, 126 (three guards killed).

155 'were gotten under some covert': *CBP*, II, 121.

155 no more than thirty horsemen: *CBP*, II, 476.

155 'With spur on heel, and splent on spauld': 'Kinmont Willie', vv. 67–8: W. Scott (1803), I, 147.

155 reality and border legend: On Scott's sources and 'conjectural emendations' of the ballads: Zug, 237.

157 'a bombastic piece of Scottish propaganda': G. M. Fraser, 330.

157n. 'The same 6 of Apryll 1596': Birrell, 37.

157 'a night laroun': *CSPRS*, XII, 250; Thorpe, II, 714.

157 'by secret passage': *CSPRS*, XII, 217.

157 'I wonder how base mynded': Rymer, XVI, 318.

158 'the breach in the door and wall': *CSPRS*, XII, 287.

158 'growing werie of the towne': J. Carey to R. Cecil, 20 November 1597: *CBP*, II, 456–7.

158 'two and two together on a leash like dogs': Scottish bill against Scrope: *CBP*, II, 259.

158 force should be applied only in extremis: Vice-Chamberlain and R. Cecil to T. Scrope, 29 December 1602: Salisbury, XII, 530–31.

158n. misdefined 'pune' as 'armed justice': *CBP*, II, 260; cf. *CBP*, II, 105, 116, 260, 303 and 668.

158 'as pictures and shadowes to bodies and lyfe': *CBP*, II, 260.

159 'The dishonour to her Majesty': *CBP*, II, 359.

21. Tarras Moss

160 'I made them welcome': Carey (1759), 133–4; Carey (1972), 56–7.

160 'the onelye man that hath runn a dyrect course': *CBP*, II, 631.

160 'and they to be my own servants': Carey (1759), 111; Carey (1972), 47.

161 'inbred thieves': Carey (1759), 129; Carey (1972), 55.

161 Carmichael . . . was shot in the back: *CBP*, II, 743; Pitcairn, II, pt 2, pp. 504–6.

161 prevents the sword from being drawn: Godfrey Watson, 110.

161 'I cannot keep this March': R. Lowther to R. Cecil, 17 June 1600: *CBP*, II, 662.

161 The Bishop of Carlisle was preaching: 26 July 1600: T. Scrope to
     R. Cecil, *CBP*, II, 671. The Bishop of Carlisle was Henry Robinson.
161 'England and Scotland is all one': Carey to R. Cecil, 1 August 1600:
     CBP, II, 674.
162 'He was well pleased I should do my worst': Carey to R. Cecil, 8
     September 1600: *CBP*, II, 685.
162 'caterpillers': Scrope to Privy Council, 31 July, 1596: *CBP*, II, 160.
162 'all fugitives, Scots or English': Carey to R. Cecil, 27 October 1600:
     CBP, II, 700.
162 'I have power enough': Carey to R. Cecil, 13 May 1601: *CBP*, II, 750.
163 'In Tynedale, where I was born': Ridley (Bishop of London), 145
     ('Conferences with Latimer').
163 'before the next winter was ended': Carey (1759), 117; Carey (1972),
     50.
163 'running up and down the streets': Carey (1759), 118; Carey (1972),
     50.
163 within spitting distance of the Spanish Armada: Carey (1759), 18–20;
     Carey (1972), 9–10.
164 '[They] did assure me': Carey (1759), 119–20; Carey (1972), 51. The
     following account of Carey's raid on Tarras Moss is largely based on
     Carey (1759), 121–6, and Carey (1972), 51–3.
165n. 'there are now no trees in Liddesdale': W. Scott (1803), I, 55 n.; also
     Arkle, 67 n. (in 1795); Oram, 28–9.
166 After riding north for twenty miles: According to Carey's original
     account to Robert Cecil (*CBP*, II, 763). His memoirs state thirty miles
     and five rather than three ringleaders caught.
166 a map of 1821: Ainslie's *Map of the Southern Part of Scotland* (1821).
     The Tarras Water Roman road was speculatively described in 1793:
     Roy, 105 (IV, 2). This would have been the first road, coming from the
     south, to head for the fort at Newstead after the crossing of the
     Liddel.
166 'while he was besieging the outlaws': W. Scott (1803), I, 56.
166 The 'uncommodious' house: Carey to Burghley, 15 July 1598: *CBP*, II,
     549.

22. 'A Factious and Naughty People'

168 a guide to Newcastle upon Tyne: Gray, 47.
169 'a little world within itself': 'A Proclamation for the union of the
     kingdoms of England and Scotland': Nicolson and Burn, I, cxxii.

169   a play recently staged in London: Shakespeare, 3–4 (quoting
         P. Hammer and J. Bate).
169   a 'fortress built by nature for herself': Shakespeare, II, 1.
169   'the Navell or Umbilick of both Kingdomes': 'A Speach to Both the
         Houses of Parliament', 31 March 1607: James VI and I, 169.
169   'mean nags' for tilling fields: Muncaster, 229 (14 February 1604).
169   'put away all armour and weapons': Nicolson and Burn, I, cxxviii.
169   Sleuth hounds or 'slough dogs': Nicolson and Burn, I, cxxx.
169n. 'live in sleuth and idleness': Monnipennie, 4 pp. from end
         (unpaginated): 'A Memorial of the Most Rare and Wonderfull Things
         in Scotland'.
169   'Where there was nothing before . . . but bloodshed': James VI and I,
         169.
170   'rebels, thieves, plunderers': 'Grant by Letters Patent of King James I
         to George, Earl of Cumberland', 20 February 1604: Cumbria Archive
         Centre, D GN 4/1.
170   the limits of 'the debatable landis': 'Act in favouris of James Maxuell
         and Robert Douglas' (1605: *RPS*, 1605/6/108).
170   two quite separate commissions: C. Ferguson, 106.
170   'mysguyded menn': Dr Magnus to Cumberland, [1526]: R. B. Arm-
         strong, pt 1, p. 231.
170   'All theeves, murderers, oppressouris and vagabondis': '1604. King's
         Memoriale': Salisbury, XVI, 405.
170   other presumed murderers of Carmichael: W. Scott (1803), I, 122–3.
171   'utterlie frustrated and expyred': C. Ferguson, 105.
171   'Ireland or other far parts': Council of Scotland to Earl of
         Cumberland, Warden of the West March of England, 4 July 1527:
         R. B. Armstrong, pt 1, p. xxiii.
171   'no hope of amendment': Muncaster, 229 ('The King to the
         Commissioners').
171   'banish us (as a tumultuouse Collony)': Spence (1977), 99; also
         Muncaster, 244.
171   Flushing and Brill: Muncaster, 230–35; Spence, 'The Graham Clans',
         93.
171   walking openly in the streets of Edinburgh: Muncaster, 236–9, 248;
         also M. Green (1857–72), I, 237: 'Some loose Grahams have returned'
         (24 October 1605).
171   Sir Ralph Sidley: *CSPRI*, I, 577; Spence (1977), 113. Generally:
         'Transplantation of the Graemes', in *CSPRI*, III, xcv–ciii; J. Graham,
         133 ff.; T. Graham (1930).
172   'their minds are so much at their homes': *CSPRI*, II, 246.

172 A pathetic petition: J. Graham, 194.

172 his 'race' had been blackened: J. Graham, 190.

173 'My thoughts must turn from intercepting of carracks': Williamson, 235.

173 'Even from their cradles': TNA SP 14/6/43: Spence, 'The Graham Clans', 87. See also M. Green (1857–72), I, 73: 'Statement [by the Earl of Cumberland] of the condition of the country since his arrival.'

173 'both the time and anything they had': *CSPRI*, II, 491.

173 'a factious and naughty people': 'Lord Deputy's Advices to Sir Thomas Ridgeway', 1 April 1610: *CSPRI*, III, 421.

173 'so turbulent and busy': *CSPRI*, II, 245–6.

173 'mossy ground' or 'marshland': Hutchinson, II, 530; Nicolson and Burn, II, 465.

173 'known ground': Hutchinson, II, 530; Nicolson and Burn, II, 465.

174n. 'the arable, lay-meadow, pasture': Mordant, I, 420.

174 A list drawn up in 1602: Spence, 'The Graham Clans', 93–100 (from Richard Bell's manuscript 'History of the Borders', ff. 211–15).

174 'the poore are oppressed': T. Musgrave to Burghley, end 1583: *CBP*, I, 126.

174 'the poorer and least dangerous sort': 'The Commissioners of the Middle Shires to the Earl of Salisbury', 13 September 1606: *CSPRI*, I, 578.

175 'loth to take away the lives of his subjects': Lords of Council to Sir Arthur Chichester, 3 June 1607: *CSPRI*, II, 16.

175 they had 'impeded and stayed': Masson and Brown, VIII, 292–3 (26 February 1607).

175 'letter of approval and indemnity': W. Fraser (1878), I, 230–32.

176 'that letter . . . is a very important testimony': W. Fraser (1878), I, 230; also Oliver, 265–6.

176 'the stirring career of the Lord Buccleuch': W. Fraser (1878), I, 233.

176 'the rottin and cankered memberis': Quoted in Meikle, 191.

176 'Do you see that boy?': Carey (1759), 56–7; Carey (1972), 24.

177 'wet moorish mossy ground': Lowther, 174.

177 'The debateable land is three miles long': Lowther, 175.

177 'to inform the lawless people': Carlisle Treaty of 1597: Spence (1977), 84. On the rebuilding of Debatable Land churches: Winkworth.

177 'lewd vices': Sir Richard Graham's petition to the King, 2 June 1631: Spence (1977), 148.

177 'By this church [Arthuret] is the Howe end': Lowther, 174.

177 Sir Richard Graham: See Spence, 'The First Sir Richard'.

178 'having some spark of wit': Sandford, 50 (interpolation in an
      unknown hand).
178 'jested himself into a fair estate': Lysons, 13.
178 'Changes of Times surely cannot be small': A. Armstrong, 6.
178 'By my soul, . . . Had ye but four feet': W. Scott (1803), I, cviii–cix.
179 'From the foot of Sark': R. Ferguson, 297.

24. Graticules

187 Klaudios Ptolemaios: The principal reference is the two-volume
      Greek–German edition: Ptolemy (2006). The variants provide the
      coordinates of Codex Vaticanus Graecus 191 ('X'). Two other Vatican
      mss. give the correct coordinates of Lincoln (Lindum): Ptolemy
      (1508), 46 recto, and Ptolemy (2006), 154 n. 7. For an 'annotated
      translation of the theoretical chapters': Ptolemy (2000). The follow-
      ing notes refer to the traditional divisions of the *Geography*.
187 some 'precise maps': Ptolemy, I, 19.
187 'by using the researches': Ptolemy, I, 19.
187 painted landscapes: Ptolemy, I, 1.
188 in 'a crude manner': Ptolemy, I, 4.
188 people with 'scientific training': Ptolemy, I, 2.
189 '2 by 3' for Gaul, 'approximately 11 by 20' for the British Isles:
      Ptolemy, VIII, 5.1 and VIII, 3.1.
191 Discoveries like this: I realize that this might sound too elementary
      to have been overlooked for seven hundred years. All I can say is
      that complex problems – and there *are* complexities – do not always
      require complex solutions, and, once the principles have been
      deduced, it is a simple matter to put the map to the test. The main
      reasons appear to be an assumption that no barbarian culture could
      have outdone the Graeco-Roman world in cartographic accuracy
      and, conversely, an over-readiness to dwell on Ptolemy's 'gross
      errors'.
         The most detailed attempt to decode Ptolemy's coordinates was
      made by Alastair Strang (1994, 1997 and 1998), who had the merit of
      supposing that they might derive from 'an authoritative map'. The
      extreme complexity of Strang's 'rotational groups' is a result of
      several misconceptions. 1. There was not one but several maps, each
      with its own graticule and orientation. 2. The coastal data was quite
      separate from the 'town' data. 3. Latitude and longitude readings
      were not inherent in the original maps, which were not based on a

'projection': the most accurate ancient maps were based on rhumb lines determined by triangulation rather than by geodetic measurement. (Strang relied on Ordnance Survey maps, which use a complex modern projection.) 4. The 'vital clue' to the lower half of the British map (the alignment of Catterick, Aldborough and York) is in fact its weakest link (p. 256). 5. Decoding of the 'map of Scotland' (which includes three English towns) was based on the a priori misidentification of Trimontium and Colania with Newstead and Camelon. 6. The plotting of the original data was inconsistent or based on an unreliable edition.

192 tin and gold mines: E.g. Dibon-Smith.

194 Its only obviously exotic feature is its orientation: Modern maps are usually oriented with north at the top, though adjustments are often made for the convenience of the user or the map-maker – for example, certain road atlases or the 1552 map of the Debatable Land, which is tilted sixty degrees to the east in order to fit it onto the sheet. The term 'orientation' is a reminder that maps were often designed to be read with east (orient) at the top. The original map of northern England was tilted nineteen degrees west of north and thus aligned with the rising sun of Beltane, the Celtic festival which marked the beginning of summer. Curiously, the map of Ireland – where a tribe called the Brigantes was also present – uses the same orientation (fig. 9). This map is the strongest material evidence for the native rather than Roman military origin of the maps.

194 maps produced by triangulation: Davies.

194–5 fifty-nine Roman miles: Ptolemy, I, 15.6.

195–7 the Roman fort of Whitley Castle: Whitley Castle is unquestionably 'Trimontium' on Ptolemy's map (see fig. 11). On the evidence of a milestone (*RIB*, 2313; G. Maxwell, 379–83), the original location of which is unknown, Trimontium is currently identified with the fort of Newstead (Melrose), under the three Eildon Hills. (The name might mean 'three hills' or simply 'place in the hills'.) Ptolemy attributes the place to the Selgovae, whose territory lies much farther to the south. This would also be more consistent with the address on a Roman letter found under Tullie House Museum in Carlisle: 'To Marcus Julius Martialis, either at Trimontium or Luguvalium' (Carlisle): Frere, Hassall and Tomlin, 496–7.

25. The Kingdom of Selgovia

198 almost one-third were inland ports: See, for example, B. Campbell, 289; Edwards, 366 (medieval water transport); Pedley, 252.

198 Strabo had asserted: Strabo, II, 5, 8.

199 The most likely candidate is Corbridge: Not 'Coria' (like 'Alauna', a common place name). 'Corbridge' is unlikely to derive from 'Coria' or 'Corstopitum'.

199 the 'ancient Citie': Camden (1610), 781.

203 'Dimmisdaill, as the common people say': *'vulgari sermone vocati* Dimmisdaill': Nicolson and Burn, II, 517; Rymer, XV, 315.

203 Three other Dymisdales or 'Doomsdales': Gallows Hill in Inverness; a Doomsdale outside Linlithgow, presumed site of feudal courts of justice; the prison at Launceston.

203 'of doubtful ownership': Tacitus, *Germania*, 29.

204 'English scaremongering': Groundwater, 27.

26. 'Arthur'

205 'plain to be seen' on Canonbie Moor: W. Maitland, I, 204; Roy, 105 (IV, 2).

206 Arthur's Cross: T. Graham (1913), 53–4.

206n. last shown on a map in 1823: Christopher Greenwood, *Map of the County of Cumberland*.

206n. The 'stone which none might lift': T. Graham (1913), 53.

206 he may never have existed: On the problems of a historical Arthur: Halsall; Higham; Padel (1994 and 1995).

207 The 'Arthurs' of the North: On a northern Arthur: A. Breeze (2006, 2012, 2015 and 2016); Bromwich.

207 'from the dayly and daungereous incurtyons': Anon. to Elizabeth I, 1587: *CBP*, I, 301.

208 'bearing torches in a bid to convince Scots': 'Tory's Hadrian's Wall pro-Union torch protest plan', *The Scotsman*, 6 February 2014.

208 '100,000 English people lined up on a wall': S. Campbell.

208 'In divers places of the Borders': Spence (1977), 147.

209 'Na, na, we's all Armstrongs and Elliots': Walter Scott heard a different version, referring to Annandale: 'we are a' Johnstones and Jardines': W. Scott (1815), ch. 26 (omitted from some editions).

209 The list of the twelve battles of Arthur: Nennius, 50.

209 'heaping together all [he] could find': Nennius, 3.

210 the prototype of the [later] Arthur: Principal references to Arthur before Geoffrey of Monmouth: *Y Gododdin*, 99 ('he was no Arthur'); *Marwnad Cynddylan* ('sturdy Arthur's cubs'); *Historia Brittonum*, 56 (Arthur's battles) and 73 (legends of Arthur); *Welsh Annals*, AD 516 (Battle of Badon; also in Gildas, 26.1) and AD 537 (Battle of Camlann).

211 a poet's fabrication: Halsall.

211 if they could be identified: Detailed attempts to identify the battle sites: Alcock, 59–71; A. Breeze (2006, 2012 and 2016); Field (1999 and 2008); T. Green; Jackson (1945, 1949 and 1953–8); Nitze (1943, 1949 and 1950); Padel (1994 and 1995); see also Rivet; Rivet and Jackson.

211 The Scottish Earls of Lindsay: Crawford, I, 3 and 22. On some older maps (e.g. Blaeu), the area is called 'Crawford Lindsey'.

212 'strictly speaking, its parent stream': Clark.

214 first raised in 1924: Malone.

215n. The great 'barbarian conspiracy': Ammianus Marcellinus, XXVII, 8 and XXVIII, 3.

215 'the biggest war' fought anywhere in the Roman Empire: Cassius Dio, LXXIII, 8.

27. The Great Caledonian Invasion

216 'they proceeded to do much mischief': Cassius Dio, LXXIII, 8.

216 signs of destruction or rebuilding: Salway, 223–5; also Burnham and Wacher, 60.

217 began to surround themselves with earthworks: Frere (1984); Salway, 262.

217 The Caledonian warriors were 'very fond of plundering': Cassius Dio, LXXVII, 12.

217 'They plunge into the swamps': Cassius Dio, LXXVII, 12.

218 the river 'Bassas': Practically every place in the British Isles beginning with 'Bas' – from Basingstoke to the Bass Rock – has been suggested. The likeliest pre-Saxon origin is late-Latin *bassus* or Brittonic *bass-*, 'shallow' (e.g. Padel (1985), 18). A stream in Lanarkshire is called Bassy Burn. There are only two occurrences of the name 'Bassy' or 'Bassie' south of the Antonine Wall. The unusual name 'Bassie' may have been assimilated to the more familiar 'Bessie' (which is only occasionally related to a person called Bessie). Three

of the fourteen 'Bessies' in lowland Scotland also occur along the Annan, which is remarkably shallow until it nears Lockerbie.

218 Celidon Wood: The wood where Myrddin took refuge after the Battle of Arfderydd (p. 92), 'apparently thought of as [being] in that neighbourhood' (i.e. by Arthuret and Netherby): Jackson (1945), 48 n. 12.

218n. Celtic '*drumo*' ('ridge') and Greek '*drumos*': A. James, 116. On the fabulous primeval forest: Rackham, 390–93.

218 an inscription of the AD 180s: *RIB*, 946; E. Birley (1986), 27–8; Tomlin and Hassall, 384–6.

219 'Guinnion' . . . 'Vinnovium': On the (contested) etymology of 'Guinnion': Field (2008), 15, Nitze (1949), 592, and references.

220 vestiges of a Roman fort: E.g. Shotter (2004), and generally on Roman and British North-West England.

220 'in the city of the Legion': On 'urbs Legionis' as York: Field (1999). The eighth and ninth battles would thus have been fought in the territory of the Brigantes, who had rebelled against the Romans two decades before. See Speidel, 235.

220 'rearward works establishment': Strickland and Davey.

220 The tenth battle, at 'Tribruit': 'Tribruit' means something like 'blood-spattered'. The Vatican manuscripts of the *Historia Brittonum* call it a '*traeth*', which, in this case, would indicate the strand of a tidal estuary. A battle site with an almost identical name – 'Traethev Trywruid' – is mentioned in an early Welsh poem, 'Pa Gur yv y Porthaur?'. A warrior called Arthur fought at Edinburgh and then 'on the strands of Trywruid'. The two places are paired twice, as though they were adjacent on the army's route. Since the identifiable battles of the *Historia Brittonum* lie within a few days' march of one another, the Traeth Tribruit may have been within striking distance of Breguoin, which is commonly agreed to be Bremenium. Thus: a tidal estuary on the North Sea, no great distance from Edinburgh and High Rochester, with a broad shore on which a battle might have been fought, served by a Roman road and quite possibly a port. It was also a place familiar to British readers several centuries later since the Vatican manuscripts refer to it, in the present tense, as 'the riverbank which we call' Traeth Tribruit.

220 South Shields: The port of Arbeia was served by two Roman roads, and, like many other northern forts, seems to have suffered damage in the 180s. Between the Roman fort and Trow Point, the Herd Sand

has yielded evidence of a Roman shipwreck and finds dating from the late second century.

220 Bregion or Bregomion is the fort of Bremenium: Summary of discussion in Falileyev. Other manuscripts have 'on the [unidentified] hill which is named Agned'. 'Breguoin', 'Bregion' or 'Bregomion' might have suited the rhyme scheme.

221 Three items of cookware: The Amiens Skillet ('MAIS ABALLAVA VXELODVNVM CAMBOGS BANNA ESICA'); the Rudge Cup ('A MAIS ABALLAVA VXELODUM CAMBOGLANS BANNA'); the Staffordshire Patera ('MAIS COGGABATA VXELODVNVM CAMMOGLANNA'). See D. Breeze.

222 'foundations of walls and streets': Camden (1789), III, 201.

222 'fallen in through age': *RIB*, 1988.

222 The blight of landscaping: Bruce (1966), 185.

223 borrowed, corrupted and mislocated: Geoffrey of Monmouth, IX, 1–4.

223 the Insula Avallonis: Geoffrey of Monmouth, XI, 2.

224 'he fought no battle': Cassius Dio, LXXVII, 13.

224 From 'Glan' to 'Camglann': In the emerging Brittonic language, 'Camboglanna' became 'Camglann', and by the time the name was recorded in the *Welsh Annals*, the 'g' had disappeared by the process of 'soft mutation'. 'Camglann' – from '*glan*', 'riverbank' – might have echoed the name of the first battle, at the mouth of the river Glein – from '*glan*', 'clear'.

28. Polling Stations

229 urban and rural voters: S. Thomson, 4–5.

229 'Hands Across the Border' cairn: Stewart.

230 adits were dug into the riverbank: Limeworks day book, 1829–31: Cumbria Archive Service, DCL/P8/24.

230 the vast Canonbie coalfield: E.g. Gibsone, 71–6.

230 the workable seams were exhausted: Canmore ID 92597.

30. The River

237 'a little world within itself': Shakespeare, II, 1.

Works Cited

Alcock, Leslie. *Arthur's Britain: History and Archaeology, A.D. 367–634.* 1971; Harmondsworth: Penguin, 1973.

Ammianus Marcellinus. *Römische Geschichte.* 4 vols. Ed. W. Seyfarth. Berlin: Akademie-Verlag, 1968–71.

Anon. *The Complaynt of Scotland, Written in 1548.* Edinburgh: Constable, 1801.

Anon. *A Diurnal of Remarkable Occurrents That Have Passed within the Country of Scotland Since the Death of King James the Fourth till the year M.D.LXXV [1575].* Ed. T. Thomson. Edinburgh: The Maitland Club, 1833.

Anon. 'A Booke of the Survaie of the Debatable and Border Lands, Belonginge to the Crowne of Englande, Lyinge Betwixt the West and East Seas, and Aboundinge upon the Realm of Scotland . . . Taken in the Yeare of our Lorde God 1604'. Ed. R. P. Sanderson: *Survey of the Debateable and Border Lands Adjoining the Realm of Scotland and Belonging to the Crown of England, Taken A.D. 1604.* Alnwick: n. p., 1891.

Arkle, Rev. James. 'Parish of Castletown'. In *The Statistical Account of Scotland.* Edinburgh: William Creech, 1791–9. Vol. XVI (1795), pp. 60–87.

Armstrong, Archibald. *Archy's Dream, Sometimes Jester to His Maiestue, But Exiled the Court by Canterburies Malice.* 1641. In *The Old Book Collector's Miscellany.* Ed. C. Hindley. Vol. V. London: Reeves and Turner, 1873.

Armstrong, Dr John. *The Art of Preserving Health: A Poem.* London: A. Millar, 1744.

Armstrong, Robert Bruce. *The History of Liddesdale, Eskdale, Ewesdale, Wauchopedale and the Debateable Land.* Part 1. Edinburgh: David Douglas, 1883.

Armstrong, R. B. *The History of Liddesdale, Eskdale, Ewesdale, Wauchopedale and the Debateable Land.* Part 2. (Unpublished manuscript notes and drawings bound in three volumes.) National Library of Scotland. MS.6111–6113.

Bain, Joseph, ed. *The Border Papers. Calendar of Letters and Papers Relating to the Affairs of the Borders of England and Scotland Preserved in Her Majesty's Public Record Office, London.* 2 vols. Edinburgh: H. M. General Register House, 1894–6. (Commonly referred to as the *Calendar of Border Papers.*)

Bain, J., ed. *The Hamilton Papers: Letters and Papers Illustrating the Political Relations of England and Scotland in the XVIth Century, Formerly in the Possession of the Dukes of Hamilton.* 2 vols. Edinburgh: H. M. General Register House, 1890–92.

Bain, J., et al., eds. *Calendar of Documents Relating to Scotland Preserved in Her Majesty's Public Record Office, London.* 5 vols. Edinburgh: H. M. General Register House, 1881–1986.

Bain, J., et al., eds. *Calendar of the State Papers Relating to Scotland and Mary, Queen of Scots, 1547–1603.* 13 vols. Edinburgh: H. M. General Register House, 1898–1969.

Balfour, Sir James, Lord Pettindreich. *Practicks, or A System of the More Ancient Law of Scotland.* Edinburgh: Ruddimans, 1754.

Barrow, G. W. S. 'The Anglo-Scottish Border'. *Northern History*, 1 (1966), pp. 21–42.

Birley, Eric. 'The Roman Fort at Netherby'. *Transactions of the Cumberland and Westmorland Antiquarian and Archaeological Society*, LIII (1953), pp. 6–39.

Birley, E. 'The Deities of Roman Britain'. In *Aufstieg und Niedergang der römischen Welt.* Vol. II. Ed. H. Temporini and W. Haase. *Principat*, XVIII, 1 (1986), pp. 1–111.

Birrell, Robert. *The Diarey of Robert Birrel, Burges of Edinburghe* [1532–1605]. In *Fragments of Scotish* [sic] *History.* Ed. J. G. Dalyell. Edinburgh: Constable, 1798. (Separate pagination.)

Borland, Robert. *Border Raids and Reivers.* Dalbeattie: Thomas Fraser, 1898.

Boscher, Paul Gerard. *Politics, Administration and Diplomacy: The Anglo-Scottish Border, 1550–1560.* Doctoral thesis. Durham University, 1985.

Boucher, Jonathan, et al. *Boucher's Glossary of Archaic and Provincial Words.* Ed. J. Hunter. London: Black, Young & Young, 1832–3.

Bowes, Robert. 'A Book of the State of the Frontiers and Marches Betwixt England and Scotland, Written . . . at the Request of the Lord Marquis Dorsett, the Warden General'. 1550. Pp. 171–248 in J. Hodgson et al., III, 2.

Bowes, R. *The Correspondence of Robert Bowes, of Aske, Esquire, the Ambassador of Queen Elizabeth in the Court of Scotland*. Ed. J. Stevenson. London: J. B. Nichols; Edinburgh: Laing and Forbes, 1842.

Breeze, Andrew. '*Historia Brittonum* and Arthur's Battle of *Tribruit*'. *Transactions of the Dumfriesshire and Galloway Natural History and Antiquarian Society*. 3rd series, LXXX (2006), pp. 53–8.

Breeze, A. 'Brittonic Place-Names from South-West Scotland, 8: Sark'. *Transactions of the Dumfriesshire and Galloway Natural History and Antiquarian Society*. 3rd series, LXXXII (2008), pp. 49–50.

Breeze, A. 'The Name and Battle of Arfderydd, near Carlisle'. *Journal of Literary Onomastics*, II, 1 (2012), pp. 1–9.

Breeze, A. 'The Historical Arthur and Sixth-Century Scotland'. *Northern History*, LII, 2 (2015), pp. 158–81.

Breeze, A. 'Arthur's Battles and the Volcanic Winter of 536–37'. *Northern History*, LIII, 2 (2016), pp. 161–72.

Breeze, David. *The First Souvenirs: Enamelled Vessels from Hadrian's Wall*. Kendal: Cumberland and Westmorland Antiquarian and Archaeological Society, 2012.

Brenan, Gerald and Edward Phillips Statham. *The House of Howard*. Vol. I. London: Hutchinson & Co., 1907.

Brewer, J. S., ed. *Letters and Papers, Foreign and Domestic, of the Reign of Henry VIII Preserved in the Public Record Office, the British Museum, and Elsewhere*. Rev. ed. R. H. Brodie and J. Gairdner. 23 vols. London: Longman, 1862–1932.

Bromwich, Rachel. 'Concepts of Arthur'. *Studia Celtica*, X–XI (1975–6), pp. 163–81.

Brooke, Christopher J. *Safe Sanctuaries: Security and Defence in Anglo-Scottish Border Churches, 1290–1690*. Edinburgh: John Donald, 2000.

Brown, K. M., et al., eds. *The Records of the Parliaments of Scotland to 1707*. University of St Andrews, 2007–15. Online database: http://www.rps.ac.uk/ (accessed 2017).

Bruce, John Collingwood. *Handbook to the Roman Wall*. 12th ed. Ed. Ian Richmond. Newcastle upon Tyne: Harold Hill, 1966.

Bruce, J. C. 'Fresh Observations on the Roman Wall'. *The Gentleman's Magazine*, XXXVII (May 1852), pp. 481–3.

Buchan, John. *The Thirty-Nine Steps.* London: Blackwood and Sons, 1915.

Burnham, Barry C. and John Wacher. *The 'Small Towns' of Roman Britain.* London: Batsford, 1990.

Burton, John Hill. *Letters of Eminent Persons Addressed to David Hume.* Edinburgh: William Blackwood and Sons, 1849.

Burton J. H. and D. Masson, eds. *Register of the Privy Council of Scotland.* 14 vols. Edinburgh: H. M. General Register House 1877.

Calendar of Border Papers. See Bain, Joseph, ed. *The Border Papers.*

Caley, John, et al., eds. *Rotuli scotiae in turri Londinensi et in domo capitulari Westmonasteriensi asservati.* 2 vols. London: Eyre and Strahan. 1814–19.

Camden, William. *Britain, or A Chorographicall Description of the Most Flourishing Kingdomes, England, Scotland, and Ireland, and the Ilands Adioyning, Out of the Depth of Antiquitie.* Tr. Philemon Holland. London: Bishop & Norton, 1610.

Camden, W. *Britannia, or A Chronological Description of the Flourishing Kingdoms of England, Scotland, and Ireland, and the Islands Adjacent, From the Earliest Antiquity.* Tr. Richard Gough. 4 vols. London: John Nichols, 1789.

Cameron, Annie, ed. *The Warrender Papers.* 2 vols. Edinburgh University Press, 1931–2.

Campbell, Brian. *Rivers and the Power of Ancient Rome.* University of North Carolina, 2012.

Campbell, Stuart. '100,000 Green Bottles'. *Wings Over Scotland,* 6 February 2014: http://wingsoverscotland.com/100000-green-bottles/ (accessed 2017).

Cardew, Anne. *A Study of Society in the Anglo-Scottish Borders, 1455–1502.* Doctoral thesis. University of St Andrews, 1974.

Carey, Robert. *Memoirs of the Life of Robert Cary [sic] . . . Written by Himself.* Ed. John Earl of Corke and Orrery. London: R. and J. Dodsley, 1759.

Carey, R. *The Memoirs of Robert Carey.* Ed. F. H. Mares. Oxford University Press, 1972.

Carlyle, T. J. *The Debateable Land.* Dumfries: W. R. McDiarmid, 1868.

Cassius Dio Cocceianus. *Dio's Roman History.* Tr. E. Cary and H. B. Foster. 9 vols. London: Heinemann, 1914–27.

Chambers, Robert. *The Picture of Scotland.* 2nd ed. 2 vols. Edinburgh: William Tait, 1828.

Child, Francis James, ed. *The English and Scottish Popular Ballads.* 1883–98. Vol. III. New York: Dover, 1965.

Clark, Stewart. 'Ayrshire Fishing Guide'. 2011: http://www.ayrshirefishing-guide.co.uk/river-irvine-fishing.php (accessed 2017).

Clarke, James. *A Survey of the Lakes of Cumberland, Westmoreland, and Lancashire.* London: n. p., 1787; 2nd ed., 1789.

Coates, Richard. 'Rethinking Romano-British *Corinium*'. *The Antiquaries Journal*, XCIII (2013), pp. 81–91.

Cole, J. R. *A Survey of the Debatable Land and Glen Tarras, c. 1449–1620.* Master's thesis. University of Manchester, 1982.

Collingwood, Charles Edward Stuart. *Memoirs of Bernard Gilpin, Parson of Houghton-le-Spring and Apostle of the North.* London: Simpkin, Marshall; Sunderland: Hills, 1884.

Collingwood, R. G., R. P. Wright, et al., eds. *The Roman Inscriptions of Britain.* Vol. I. *Inscriptions on Stone.* Rev. ed. by R. S. O. Tomlin. Stroud: Alan Sutton, 1995.

Craigie, William A., et al. *A Dictionary of the Older Scottish Tongue from the Twelfth Century to the End of the Seventeenth.* 12 vols. University of Chicago Press; Oxford University Press, 1937–2002.

Crawford, Alexander Crawford Lindsay, Earl of. *Lives of the Lindsays, or a Memoir of the Houses of Crawford and Balcarres.* 3 vols. London: John Murray, 1849.

Crofton, Ian. *Walking the Border: A Journey Between Scotland and England.* Edinburgh: Birlinn, 2014.

Dasent, John Roche, ed. *Acts of the Privy Council of England.* New Series. 46 vols. London: HMSO, 1890–1964.

Davies, Hugh E. H. 'Designing Roman Roads'. *Britannia*, XXIX (1998), pp. 1–16.

Davitt, S. and G. A. Bonner. *The Construction of Road Embankments with Boulder Clay.* Dublin: An Foras Forbartha, 1977.

Dibon-Smith, Richard. 'Mineral Exploration and Fort Placement in Roman Britain'. *New Ideas About the Past: Seven Essays in Cultural History.* N. d.: n. p. Pp. 65–90. http://www.dibonsmith.com/roman.pdf (accessed 2017).

Dickson, Thomas, et al., eds. *Accounts of the Lord High Treasurer of Scotland. Compota thesaurariorum Regum Scotorum.* 13 vols. Edinburgh: H. M. General Register House, 1877–1978.

Dixon, Bernard Homer. *The Border or Riding Clans, Followed by a History of the Clan Dickson.* Albany, New York: Joel Munsell's Sons, 1889.

Dixon, Philip W. *Fortified Houses on the Anglo-Scottish Border: A Study of the*

Domestic Architecture of the Upland Area in its Social and Economic Context,
  1485–1625. Doctoral thesis. University of Oxford, 1976.
Durham, Keith. *Strongholds of the Border Reivers: Fortifications of the Anglo-Scot-*
  tish Border, 1296–1603. Illust. Graham Turner. Oxford: Osprey
  Publishing, 2008.

Edwards, James Frederick. *The Transport System of Medieval England and*
  Wales: A Geographical Synthesis. Doctoral thesis. University of Salford,
  1987.
Elder, Madge. *Ballad Country: The Scottish Border.* Edinburgh and London:
  Oliver & Boyd, 1963.
Elliot, George Francis. *The Border Elliots and the Family of Minto.*
  Edinburgh: n. p., 1897.
Elliot, Thomas. 'Parish of Cavers'. In *The Statistical Account of Scotland.*
  Edinburgh: William Creech, 1791–9. Vol. XVII (1796), pp. 89–92.
[Elliot-Murray-Kynynmound, Emma, Countess of Minto]. *Border Sketches.*
  N. p.: n. p., 1870.
Ellis, Henry. *Original Letters Illustrative of English History.* Vol. I. London:
  Harding, Triphook & Lepard, 1824.
Emanuele, Paul Daniel. *Vegetius on the Roman Navy: Translation and Commen-*
  tary, Book Four, 31–46. Master's thesis. University of British Columbia,
  1974.
Evens, Eunice. *Through the Years with Romany.* University of London, 1946.

Falileyev, Alexander. 'CT / PT VII, 23–24 *kat yn aber / ioed y dygyfranc adur*
  breuer und die frühwalisische Schlachtenkatalogtradition'. In *Akten des*
  zweiten deutschen Keltologen-Symposiums. Ed. S. Zimmer et al. Tübingen:
  Niemeyer, 1999. Pp. 32–46.
Ferguson, Catherine. *Law and Order on the Anglo-Scottish Border, 1603–1707.*
  Doctoral thesis. University of St Andrews, 1981.
Ferguson, R. S. 'The Registers and Account Books of the Parish of
  Kirkandrews-upon-Esk'. *Transactions of the Cumberland and Westmorland*
  Antiquarian and Archaeological Society, VIII (1885), pp. 280–306.
Ferguson, R. S. and W. Nanson. *Some Municipal Records of the City of Carlisle.*
  Carlisle: Thurnam & Sons; London: George Bell & Sons, 1887.
Field, P. J. C. 'Gildas and the City of the Legions'. *The Heroic Age,* 1 (1999):
  http://www.heroicage.org/issues/1/hagcl.htm (accessed 2017).
Field, P. J. C. 'Arthur's Battles'. *Arthuriana,* XVIII, 4 (2008), pp. 3–32.
Fletcher, Rob. 'The Moleman'. *Scottish Field,* December 2011, pp. 46–7.

Fordun, John. *Joannis de Fordun Scotichronicon, cum supplementis*. Ed. W. Bower. 2 vols. Edinburgh: Robert Fleming, 1759.

Foxwell, E. 'English Express Trains: Their Average Speed, &c., with Notes on Gradients, Long Runs, &c.' *Journal of the Statistical Society of London*, XLVI, 3 (September 1883), pp. 517–74.

Fraser, Antonia. *Mary Queen of Scots*. London: Weidenfeld & Nicolson, 1969; Mandarin, 1989.

Fraser, George MacDonald. *The Steel Bonnets: The Story of the Anglo-Scottish Border Reivers*. London: Barrie & Jenkins, 1971; HarperCollins, 1995.

Fraser, William. *The Book of Carlaverock: Memoirs of the Maxwells, Earls of Nithsdale, Lords Maxwell and Herries*. 2 vols. Edinburgh: n. p., 1873.

Fraser, W. *The Scotts of Buccleuch*. 2 vols. Edinburgh: n. p., 1878.

Frere, Sheppard. 'British Urban Defences in Earthwork'. *Britannia*, XV (1984), pp. 63–74.

Frere, S., M. Hassall and R. Tomlin. 'Roman Britain in 1987'. *Britannia*, XIX (1988), pp. 415–508.

Gairdner, James, ed. *Letters and Papers Illustrative of the Reigns of Richard III and Henry VII*. Vol. I. London: Longman et al., 1861.

Geoffrey of Monmouth. *Historia Regum Britanniae*. Ed. J. Hammer. Cambridge, Mass.: Mediaeval Academy of America, 1951.

Geoffrey of Monmouth. *The History of the Kings of Britain*. Ed. M. D. Reeve and N. Wright. Woodbridge: Boydell, 2007.

Gibsone, Edmund. 'The Coal Formation of Canonbie, &c.' *North of England Institute of Mining Engineers: Transactions*, XI (November 1861), pp. 65–88.

Gildas. *The Ruin of Britain [De Excidio et Conquestu Britanniae], and Other Works*. Ed. M. Winterbottom. London: Phillimore, 1978.

Gilpin, William. *Observations, Relative Chiefly to Picturesque Beauty, Made in the Year 1772*. 3rd ed. Vol. II. London: R. Blamire, 1792.

Goodare, Julian. *State and Society in Early Modern Scotland*. Oxford University Press, 1999.

Goodman, Mike. 'Footprints from Nowhere'. *Carlisle Guide*, September–October 2014, p. 9.

Gordon, Alexander. *Itinerarium Septentrionale, or A Journey Thro' Most of the Counties of Scotland and Those in the North of England*. London: F. Gyles [etc.], 1727.

Graham, John. *Condition of the Border at the Union: Destruction of the Graham Clan*. 2nd ed. London: Routledge, 1907.

Graham, T. H. B. 'Annals of Liddel'. *Transactions of the Cumberland and*

Westmorland Antiquarian and Archaeological Society, XIII (1913), pp. 33–54.

Graham, T. H. B. 'The Debatable Land. Part II'. *Transactions of the Cumberland and Westmorland Antiquarian and Archaeological Society*, XIV (1914), pp. 132–57.

Graham, T. H. B. 'The Grahams of Esk'. *Transactions of the Cumberland and Westmorland Antiquarian and Archaeological Society*, XXX (1930), pp. 224–6.

Grant, William, ed. *The Scottish National Dictionary*. 10 vols. Edinburgh: The Scottish National Dictionary Association, 1931–75.

Gray, William. *Chorographia, or A Survey of Newcastle upon Tine*. Newcastle: S. B. [Stephen Bulkley], 1649.

Green, Mary Anne Everett, ed. *Calendar of State Papers, Domestic Series, of the Reign of Elizabeth, Addenda, 1566–1579*. London: Longman, 1871.

Green, M. A. E., ed. *Calendar of State Papers, Domestic Series, of the Reign of James I, Preserved in the State Paper Department of Her Majesty's Public Record Office*. 5 vols. London: Longman, 1857–72.

Green, Thomas. *Arthuriana: Early Arthurian Tradition and the Origins of the Legend*. Louth: Lindes Press, 2009.

Groundwater, Anna. *The Scottish Middle March, 1573–1625: Power, Kinship, Allegiance*. London: Royal Historical Society, 2010.

Halsall, Guy. *Worlds of Arthur: Facts and Fictions of the Dark Ages*. Oxford University Press, 2013.

Hannay, Robert Kerr, ed. *Acts of the Lords of Council in Public Affairs, 1501–1554: Selections from the Acta dominorum concilii Introductory to the Register of the Privy Council of Scotland*. Edinburgh: H. M. General Register House, 1932.

Harvey, P. D. A. 'Estate Surveyors and the Spread of the Scale-Map in England, 1550–80'. *Landscape History*, XV, 1 (1993), pp. 37–49.

Hay, Denys. 'England, Scotland and Europe: The Problem of the Frontier'. *Transactions of the Royal Historical Society*, 5th series, XXV (1975), pp. 77–91.

Haynes, Samuel, ed. *A Collection of State Papers Relating to Affairs in the Reigns of King Henry VIII, King Edward VI, Queen Mary, and Queen Elizabeth*. London: William Bowyer, 1740.

Henderson, William. *Notes on the Folk-lore of the Northern Counties of England and the Borders*. New ed. London: The Folk-lore Society, 1879.

Higham, N. J. *King Arthur: Myth-Making and History*. London and New York: Routledge, 2002.

Hodgson, John, et al. *A History of Northumberland, in Three Parts*. 7 vols. Newcastle upon Tyne: E. Walker, 1820–58.

Holinshed, Raphael. *Holinshed's Chronicles of England, Scotland, and Ireland*. 6 vols. London, 1807–8. Rpt. Routledge, 1965.

Hutchinson, William. *The History of the County of Cumberland and Some Places Adjacent*. 2 vols. Carlisle: F. Jollie, 1794.

Hutton, William. *The History of the Roman Wall Which Crosses the Island of Britain, from the German Ocean to the Irish Sea*. London: John Nichols & Son, 1802.

Hyslop, John and Robert. *Langholm As It Was: A History of Langholm and Eskdale from the Earliest Times*. Sunderland: Hills & Co., 1912.

Jackson, Kenneth H. 'Once Again Arthur's Battles'. *Modern Philology*, XLIII, 1 (1945), pp. 44–57.

Jackson, K. H. 'Arthur's Battle of Breguoin'. *Antiquity*, XXIII (1949), pp. 48–9.

Jackson, K. H. 'The Site of Mount Badon'. *Journal of Celtic Studies*, II (1953–8), pp. 152–5.

James VI of Scotland and I of England. *Political Writings*. Ed. J. P. Sommerville. Cambridge University Press, 1994.

James, Alan G. 'The Brittonic Language in the Old North: A Guide to the Place-Name Evidence. II. Guide to the Elements'. Scottish Place-Name Society, 2016: http://www.spns.org.uk/wp-content/uploads/2016/09/BLITON2016ii_elements.pdf (accessed 2017).

James, Mervyn. *Change and Continuity in the Tudor North: The Rise of Thomas First Lord Wharton*. York: St. Anthony's Press, 1965.

Jamieson, John. *An Etymological Dictionary of the Scottish Language*. Rev. ed. 4 vols. Paisley: A. Gardner, 1879–82.

Johnson-Ferguson, Edward. 'Place Names: Canonbie, Eskdalemuir, Ewes, Langholm and Westerkirk'. *Proceedings and Transactions of the Dumfriesshire and Galloway Natural Historical and Antiquarian Society*, 3rd series, XVII (1930–31), pp. 135–57.

Johnstone, Catherine Laura. *History of the Johnstones, 1191–1909, with Descriptions of Border Life*. Edinburgh: W. & A. K. Johnston, 1909.

Jones, G. D. B. 'The Solway Frontier: Interim Report, 1976–81'. *Britannia*, XIII (1982), pp. 283–97.

Jones, G. P. 'King James I and the Western Border'. *Transactions of the*

Cumberland and Westmorland Antiquarian and Archaeological Society, LXIX (1969), pp. 130–51.

Keith, Rev. Robert. *History of the Affairs of Church and State in Scotland*. 3 vols. Edinburgh: Spottiswoode Society, 1845.

King, Andy and Michael Penman. *England and Scotland in the Fourteenth Century: New Perspectives*. Woodbridge: Boydell, 2007.

Lang, Andrew and John. *Highways and Byways in The Border*. London: Macmillan, 1913.

Leeson, Peter T. 'The Laws of Lawlessness'. *The Journal of Legal Studies*, XXXVIII, 2 (June 2009), pp. 471–503.

Leland, John. *The Itinerary of John Leland the Antiquary*. Ed. T. Hearne. Vol. VII. Oxford University Press, 1710.

Lemon, Robert, et al., eds. *Calendar of State Papers, Domestic Series, of the Reigns of Edward VI, Mary, Elizabeth, 1547–1580, Preserved in the State Paper Department of Her Majesty's Public Record Office*. 7 vols. London: Longman, 1856–71.

Lesley, John. *De Origine, Moribus & Rebus gestis Scotorum*. 1578. London: Robert Boulter, 1677.

Lesley, J. *The Historie of Scotland*. Tr. J. Dalrymple (1596). Ed. E. G. Cody. 2 vols. Edinburgh and London: Blackwood, 1888–95.

Livingstone, Matthew, et al., eds. *Registrum secreti sigilli regum Scotorum. The Register of the Privy Seal of Scotland*. 8 vols. Edinburgh: H. M. General Register House, 1908–82.

Lockhart, John Gibson. *Memoirs of the Life of Sir Walter Scott, Bart*. Vol. I. Edinburgh: Robert Cadell; London: John Murray and Whittaker, 1837.

Lowther, C., R. Fallow and P. Manson. 'Account of a Journey into Scotland, 1629'. *The Scottish Antiquary or Northern Notes and Queries*, IX, 36 (1895), pp. 174–80.

Luders, Alexander, et al., eds. *The Statutes of the Realm: Printed by Command of His Majesty King George the Third*. 12 vols. London: Eyre and Strahan, 1810–28.

Lysons, Rev. Daniel and Samuel Lysons. *Magna Britannia*. Vol. IV. *Cumberland*. London: Cadell and Davies, 1816.

McIntire, W. T. 'The Fords of the Solway'. *Transactions of the Cumberland and Westmorland Antiquarian and Archaeological Society*, new series, XXXIX (1939), pp. 152–70.

Mack, James Logan. *The Border Line from the Solway Firth to the North Sea, Along the Marches of Scotland and England.* Rev. ed. Edinburgh and London: Oliver & Boyd, 1926.

Mackay MacKenzie, W. 'The Debateable Land'. *Scottish Historical Review,* XXX, 110, 2 (October 1951), pp. 109–25.

Mackie, Charles. *The Castles of Mary, Queen of Scots.* 3rd ed. London: Thomas Tegg & Son; Glasgow: Richard Griffin & Co., 1835.

McMurtry, Larry. *Lonesome Dove.* 1985; London: Pan Books, 2011.

Macpherson, Robin G. *Francis Stewart, 5th Earl Bothwell, c. 1562–1612: Lordship and Politics in Jacobean Scotland.* Doctoral thesis. University of Edinburgh, 1998.

McRae, Andrew. *God Speed the Plough: The Representation of Agrarian England, 1500–1660.* Cambridge University Press, 1996.

Maitland, Richard. *The Poems of Sir Richard Maitland of Lethingtoun, Knight.* Glasgow: The Maitland Club, 1830.

Maitland, William. *The History and Antiquities of Scotland, from the Earliest Account of Time to the Death of James the First.* 2 vols. London: A. Millar, 1757.

Major, John. *Historia maioris Britanniae, tam Angliae quam Scotiae.* Paris: Josse Badius, 1521.

Major, J. *A History of Greater Britain, as well England as Scotland.* Tr. A. Constable. Edinburgh: T. and A. Constable, 1892.

Malone, Kemp. 'The Historicity of Arthur'. *The Journal of English and Germanic Philology,* XXIII, 4 (1924), pp. 463–91.

Margary, Ivan D. *Roman Roads in Britain.* 3rd ed. London: Baker, 1973.

Masson, David and P. Hume Brown, eds. *The Register of the Privy Council of Scotland.* 2nd series. 8 vols. Edinburgh: H. M. General Register House, 1899–1908.

Maxwell, G. S. 'Two Inscribed Roman Stones and Architectural Fragments from Scotland'. *Proceedings of the Society of Antiquaries of Scotland,* CXIII (1983), pp. 379–90.

Maxwell, John, Lord Herries. *Historical Memoirs of the Reign of Mary Queen of Scots.* Ed. R. Pitcairn. Edinburgh: n. p., 1836.

Maxwell-Irving, Alastair. *The Border Towers of Scotland.* 2 vols. Blairlogie: n. p., 2000–2014.

Meikle, Maureen M. *The Scottish People, 1490–1625.* N. p.: Lulu.com, 2013.

Monnipennie, John. *Certaine Matters Composed Together.* Edinburgh: Robert Waldegrave, 1594 (?).

Mordant, John. *The Complete Steward, or The Duty of a Steward to His Lord.* 2 vols. London: Sandby, 1761.

Morgan, Ailig Peadar. *Ethnonyms in the Place-Names of Scotland and the Border Counties of England.* Doctoral thesis. University of St Andrews, 2013.

Moss, Tom. 'Border-Reivers-William-Armstrong-of-Sorbietrees-Liddesdale-An Untimely Death'. https://wwwborderreiverstories-neblessclem.blogspot.co.uk/2013/01/history-of-scotland-william-armstrong.html (2013; accessed 2017).

Moysie, David. *Memoirs of the Affairs of Scotland, MDLXXVII – MDCIII.* Edinburgh: The Maitland Club, 1830.

Murray, J. A. H. 'The History and Antiquities of Hermitage'. *Transactions of the Hawick Archaeological Society,* 1863, pp. 30–33.

Nennius (?). *The Historia Brittonum.* Ed. D. N. Dumville. Cambridge: Brewer, 1985.

Neville, Cynthia. *Violence, Custom and Law: The Anglo-Scottish Border Lands in the Later Middle Ages.* Edinburgh University Press, 1998.

Nicolson, Joseph and Richard Burn. *The History and Antiquities of the Counties of Westmorland and Cumberland.* 2 vols. London: Strahan and Cadell, 1777.

Nicolson, William. *Leges Marchiarum or Border-Laws, Containing several Original Articles and Treaties, Made and agreed upon by the Commissioners of the respective Kings of England and Scotland, for the Better Preservation of Peace and Commerce upon the Marches of both Kingdoms.* 1705; London: Printed for Hamilton and Balfour, Edinburgh, 1747.

Nitze, William A. 'More on the Arthuriana of Nennius'. *Modern Language Notes,* LVIII, 1 (1943), pp. 1–8.

Nitze, W. A. 'Arthurian Names'. *PMLA,* LXIV, 3 (1949), pp. 585–96.

Nitze, W. A. 'Additional Note on Arthurian Names'. *PMLA,* LXV, 6 (1950), pp. 1287–8.

Oliver, J. Rutherford. *Upper Teviotdale and the Scotts of Buccleuch.* Hawick: Kennedy, 1887.

Oram, Richard. 'Hermitage Castle: A Report on its History and Cultural Heritage Significance'. February 2012: http://www.gorrenberry.org.uk/ROfinaldraft.pdf (accessed 2017).

Padel, Oliver James. *Cornish Place-Name Elements.* Nottingham: English Place-Name Society, 1985.

Padel, O. J. 'The Nature of Arthur'. *Cambrian Medieval Celtic Studies,* XXVII (1994), pp. 1–31.

Padel, O. J. 'Recent Work on the Origins of the Arthurian Legend'. *Arthuriana*, V, 3 (1995), pp. 103–14.

Pease, Howard. *The Lord Wardens of the Marches of England and Scotland.* London: Constable, 1912.

Pedley, Robert. *The Brigantes: A Study in the Early History of the North Pennines.* Doctoral thesis. Durham University, 1939.

Pennant, Thomas. *A Tour in Scotland and Voyage to the Hebrides, MDCCLXXII.* Part I. 2nd ed. London: Benjamin White, 1776.

Percy, Thomas. *Reliques of Ancient English Poetry, Consisting of Old Heroic Ballads, Songs, and Other Pieces of Our Earlier Poets.* 3 vols. Ed. H. B. Wheatley. London: Bickers and Son, 1876–7.

Pitcairn, Robert. *Ancient Criminal Trials of Scotland.* 3 vols in 7 parts. Glasgow: The Maitland Club, 1833.

Ptolemy. *In hoc opere haec continentur Geographiae [sic] Cl. Ptolemaei.* Rome: Bernardino dei Vitali, 1508.

Ptolemy. *Ptolemy's Geography: An Annotated Translation of the Theoretical Chapters.* Ed. J. Lennart-Berggren and A. Jones. Princeton University Press, 2000.

Ptolemy. *Klaudios Ptolemaios Handbuch der Geographie: griechisch–deutsch.* 2 vols. Ed. A. Stückelberger and G. Grasshoff. Basel: Schwabe, 2006.

Rackham, Oliver. *Woodlands.* London: Collins, 2006.

Rae, Thomas I. *The Administration of the Scottish Frontier, 1513–1603.* Edinburgh University Press, 1966.

Ratcliff, Garrett B. *Scottish Augustinians: A Study of the Regular Canonical Movement in the Kingdom of Scotland, c. 1120–1215.* Doctoral thesis. University of Edinburgh, 2012.

Reid, R. R. 'The Office of Warden of the Marches: Its Origin and Early History'. *The English Historical Review*, XXXII, 128 (1917), pp. 479–96.

Richmond, Ian A. 'A New Roman Mountain-Road in Dumfriesshire and Roxburghshire'. *Proceedings of the Society of Antiquaries of Scotland*, LXXX (1945–6), pp. 103–17.

Ridley, Nicholas (Bishop of London). *The Works of Nicholas Ridley, D.D.* Ed. H. Christmas. Cambridge University Press, 1841.

Ridley, Nicholas (Baron Ridley of Liddesdale). *'My Style of Government': The Thatcher Years.* London: Hutchinson, 1991.

Ridpath, George. *The Border-History of England & Scotland.* New ed. Berwick: Richardson, 1810.

Rivet, Albert Lionel Frederick and Kenneth Jackson. 'The British Section
    of the Antonine Itinerary'. *Britannia*, I (1970), pp. 34–82.

Rivet, A. L. F. and Colin Smith. *The Place-Names of Roman Britain*. London:
    Batsford, 1979.

Roy, William. *The Military Antiquities of the Romans in North Britain*. London:
    W. Bulmer & Co., 1793. National Library of Scotland facsimile at:
    http://maps.nls.uk/roy/antiquities/contents.html (accessed 2017).

Royal Commission on Historical Manuscripts. *The Manuscripts of the Earl of
    Westmorland, Captain Stewart, Lord Stafford, Lord Muncaster, and Others*.
    London: Eyre and Spottiswoode, 1885.

Russell, Rev. C. W. and J. P. Prendergast, eds. *Calendar of the State Papers
    Relating to Ireland, of the Reign of James I*. 5 vols. London: Longman,
    1872–80.

Rutherford, J. *The Southern Counties' Register and Directory*. Kelso:
    Rutherford, 1866. Rpt. Selkirk: Borders Regional Library, 1990.

Rymer, Thomas, et al., eds. *Foedera: conventiones, literæ, et cujuscunque generis
    acta publica*. 2nd ed. 17 vols. London: J. Tonson, 1726–35.

Sadler, Ralph. *The State Papers and Letters of Sir Ralph Sadler, Knight-
    Banneret*. 2 vols. Ed. A. Clifford. Edinburgh: Constable, 1809.

Salisbury, Robert Cecil, et al., eds. *Calendar of the Manuscripts of the Most
    Hon. the Marquis of Salisbury, K.G. . . . Preserved at Hatfield House,
    Hertfordshire*. 24 vols. London: His Majesty's Stationery Office, 1883–
    1976.

Salway, Peter. *Roman Britain*. Oxford University Press, 1998.

Sandford, Edmund. *A Cursory Relation of All the Antiquities & Familyes in
    Cumberland . . . Circa 1675*. Ed. R. S. Ferguson. Kendal: T. Wilson, 1890.

Scott, Douglas. *A Hawick Word Book*. 2002–16 (version of 17 February
    2017): http://www.astro.ubc.ca/people/scott/book.pdf (accessed
    2017).

Scott, Walter. *Minstrelsy of the Scottish Border: Consisting of Historical and
    Romantic Ballads, Collected in the Southern Counties of Scotland, with a Few
    of Modern Date, Founded upon Local Tradition*. 2nd ed. 3 vols. Edinburgh:
    Ballantyne, 1803.

Scott, W. *Minstrelsy of the Scottish Border* [etc.]. Vols I–III of *The Works of
    Walter Scott*. Edinburgh: Ballantyne, 1806.

Scott, W. *The Border Antiquities of England and Scotland, Comprising
    Specimens of Architecture and Sculpture, and Other Vestiges of Former Ages*. 2
    vols. Edinburgh: Constable; London: Longman, 1812–17.

Scott, W. *Guy Mannering*. Ed. P. D. Garside. London: Penguin, 2003. (First published anonymously in 1815 as *Guy Mannering, or The Astrologer.*)

Scott, W. *The Journal of Sir Walter Scott, 1825–32, from the Original Manuscript at Abbotsford*. Ed. D. Douglas. Edinburgh: Douglas & Foulis, 1927.

Scott, W., ed. *A Collection of Scarce and Valuable Tracts on the Most Interesting and Entertaining Subjects*. 2nd ed. Vol. III. London: Cadell and Davies, 1810.

Shakespeare, William. *Richard II*. Ed. A. B. Dawson and P. Yachnin. Oxford University Press, 2011.

Shirley, Walter Waddington, ed. *Royal and Other Historical Letters Illustrative of the Reign of Henry III, from the Originals in the Public Record Office*. 2 vols. London: Longman, 1862–6.

Shotter, David. '*Numeri Barcariorum*: A Note on *RIB* 601'. *Britannia*, IV (1973), pp. 206–9.

Shotter, D. *Romans and Britons in North-West England*. 3rd ed. Lancaster: Centre for North-West Regional Studies, 2004.

Sitwell, Brig. Gen. William. *The Border From a Soldier's Point of View*. Newcastle: Andrew Reid & Co., 1927.

Skene, William Forbes. 'Notice of the Site of the Battle of Ardderyd or Arderyth'. *Proceedings of the Society of Antiquaries of Scotland*, VI (1868), pp. 91–8.

Smith, J. Beverley. 'England and Wales: The Conflict of Laws'. In M. Prestwich et al., eds. *Thirteenth Century England, VII. Proceedings of the Durham Conference*. Woodbridge: The Boydell Press, 1999. Pp. 189–206.

Speidel, M. P. 'The Chattan War, the Brigantian Revolt and the Loss of the Antonine Wall'. *Britannia*, XVIII (1987), pp. 233–7.

Spence, R. T. 'The Pacification of the Cumberland Borders, 1593–1628'. *Northern History*, XIII, 1 (1977), pp. 59–160.

Spence, R. T. 'The Graham Clans and Lands on the Eve of the Jacobean Pacification'. *Transactions of the Cumberland and Westmorland Antiquarian and Archaeological Society*, LXXX (1980), pp. 79–102.

Spence, R. T. 'The First Sir Richard Graham of Norton Conyers and Netherby, 1583–1653'. *Northern History*, XVI, 1 (1980), pp. 102–29.

Spottiswood, John. *The History of the Church of Scotland*. 3rd ed. London: R. Norton, 1668.

Stedman, John. '*A very indifferent small city*': The Economy of Carlisle, 1550–1700. Doctoral thesis. University of Leicester, 1988.

Stevenson, Joseph, et al., eds. *Calendar of State Papers, Foreign Series, of the Reign of Elizabeth, Preserved in the State Paper Department of Her Majesty's Public Record Office.* 23 vols. London: Longman, 1863–1950.

Stewart, Rory. 'Rory Stewart Responds to Union Cairn Vandals' (24 March 2015): http://www.rorystewart.co.uk/rory-stewart-responds-to-union-cairn-vandals/ (accessed 2017).

Stones, E. L. G. *Anglo-Scottish Relations, 1174–1328: Some Selected Documents.* London: Nelson, 1965.

Strabo. *The Geography of Strabo.* 8 vols. Tr. H. L. Jones and J. R. S. Sterrett. London: Heinemann, 1954–61.

Strahan, Andrew, et al. *State Papers Published Under the Authority of His Majesty's Commission: King Henry the Eighth.* 11 vols. London: John Murray, 1830–52.

Strang, Alastair. *Ptolemy's Geography Reappraised.* Doctoral thesis. University of Nottingham, 1994.

Strang, A. 'Explaining Ptolemy's Roman Britain'. *Britannia,* XXVIII (1997), pp. 1–30.

Strang, A. 'Recreating a Possible Flavian Map of Roman Britain with a Detailed Map for Scotland'. *Proceedings of the Society of Antiquaries of Scotland,* CXXVIII (1998), pp. 425–40.

Strickland, Agnes. *Lives of the Queens of Scotland and English Princesses.* 8 vols. Edinburgh and London: William Blackwood, 1850–59.

Strickland, T. J. and P. J. Davey, eds. *New Evidence for Roman Chester: Material from the Chester Conference of November 1977.* Liverpool: Institute of Extension Studies, 1978.

Stukeley, William. 'Iter Boreale'. In *Itinerarium curiosum, or An Account of the Antiquities and Remarkable Curiosities in Nature or Art Observed in Travels Through Great Britain.* Vol. II. London: Baker and Leigh, 1776.

Tacitus, Cornelius. *Tacitus in Five Volumes.* Vol. I. Ed. M. Hutton et al. Harvard University Press, 1968.

Thomson, Steven. *Referendum 2014: How Rural Scotland Voted.* Rural Policy Centre Research Report, October 2014: www.sruc.ac.uk/info/120485/ thriving_communities_archive/ (accessed 2017).

Thomson, Thomas, ed. *Inquisitionum ad Capellam Domini Regis retornatarum, quae in Publicis Archivis Scotiae.* Vol. I. London: n. p., 1811.

Thomson, T., et al., eds. *The Acts of the Parliament of Scotland.* 12 vols. Edinburgh: n. p., 1814–75.

Thorpe, Markham John, ed. *Calendar of the State Papers Relating to Scotland, Preserved in the State Paper Department of Her Majesty's Public Record Office: The Scottish Series.* 2 vols. London: Longman, 1858.

Todd, John M. 'The West March on the Anglo-Scottish Border in the Twelfth Century, and the Origins of the Western Debatable Land'. *Northern History,* XLIII, 1 (March 2006), pp. 11–19.

Tomlin, R. S. O. and M. W. C. Hassall. 'Roman Britain in 1998. II. Inscriptions'. *Britannia,* XXX (1999), pp. 375–86.

Tough, D. L. W. *The Last Years of a Frontier: A History of the Borders During the Reign of Elizabeth I.* 1928; Alnwick: Sandhill, 1987.

Turnbull, William, ed. *Calendar of State Papers, Foreign Series, of the Reign of Edward VI, 1547–1553, Preserved in the State Paper Department of Her Majesty's Public Record Office.* London: Longman, 1861.

Vegetius. *Epitoma rei militaris.* Ed. M. D. Reeve. Oxford: Clarendon Press, 2004.

Vertot, René-Aubert, abbé de. *Ambassades de Messieurs de Noailles en Angleterre.* 5 vols. Leiden and Paris: Desaint & Saillant, 1763.

Walpole, Hugh. *Rogue Herries: A Novel.* 1930. London: Frances Lincoln, 2008.

Watson, George. *The Roxburghshire Word-Book.* Cambridge University Press, 1923.

Watson, Godfrey. *The Border Reivers.* London: Hale, 1974; Newcastle upon Tyne: Northern Heritage, 2013.

Watt, Francis. 'The Border Law'. *The New Review,* 94 (March 1897), pp. 281–93.

Webster, Bruce. 'Anglo-Scottish Relations, 1296–1389: Some Recent Essays'. *The Scottish Historical Review,* LXXIV, 1 (1995), pp. 99–108.

Whellan, William, ed. *The History and Topography of the Counties of Cumberland and Westmorland.* London: Whittaker and Co.; Manchester: Galt and Co., 1860.

Williamson, George C. *George, Third Earl of Cumberland (1558–1605): His Life and His Voyages.* Cambridge University Press, 1920.

Wilson, Allan. 'Roman Penetration in Eastern Dumfriesshire and Beyond'. *Transactions of the Dumfriesshire and Galloway Natural History and Antiquarian Society.* 3rd series, LXXIII (1999), pp. 17–62.

Wilson, A. 'Roman and Native in Dumfriesshire'. *Transactions of the Dumfriesshire and Galloway Natural History and Antiquarian Society.* 3rd series, LXXVII (2003), pp. 103–60.

Winchester, Angus. *The Harvest of the Hills: Rural Life in Northern England and the Scottish Borders, 1400–1700*. Edinburgh University Press, 2000.

Winchester, A. *Landscape and Society in Medieval Cumbria*. Edinburgh: John Donald, 1987.

Winkworth, Fay V. 'Kirkandrews on Esk: Religious History'. Victoria County History of Cumbria Project. 2013: http://www.cumbri-acounty history.org.uk/sites/default/files/Kirkandrews%20on%20 Esk%20Religious%20History%20%28AW%29%20Feb%2013.pdf (accessed 2017).

Wood, Charles Lindley. *Lord Halifax's Ghost Book*. London: Geoffrey Bles, 1936.

Zug, Charles G. 'The Ballad and History: The Case for Scott'. *Folklore*, LXXXIX, 2 (1978), pp. 229–42.

General Index

Geographical Index

Acknowledgements

It will be obvious how much this book owes to Margaret, but not how much of the Border world was illuminated by her work for North Cumbria Magistrates' Court, Cumbria NHS, the Corporation Board of Carlisle College, the School Admission Appeals Panel, the Society of Friends, the Liddesdale Heritage Centre (Newcastleton) and the rural library Book Drop with its vast and undervalued constituency. Crucially, she was instrumental in saving the cross-border 127A bus service, for which I and many others also have to thank Cllr Val Tarbitt, Rory Stewart MP and the parish councils of Kirkandrews-on-Esk and Nicholforest.

Several people who should have been named on this page would prefer not to be publicly thanked. I kept a list of their names and realized, when I came to write these acknowledgements, that it looked like one of the medieval wardens' lists of reiving families. Each surname is sufficiently well represented in the modern population for the list to be properly impersonal: Calvert, Carlyle, Davidson, Dixon, Dunn, Elliot, Forster, Little, Nichol, Ridley, Robson and Storey.

For documentary help, I am grateful to the British Library, the Bodleian Library, the National Library of Scotland, Historic Environment Scotland, Cumbria Archive Centre, Carlisle Public Library, Tullie House Museum, the Clan Armstrong Trust and, for equally vital assistance, to Bikeseven, Cumbria Woodlands, the Graham Arms, Joan's Cars, Telford's Coaches, and the postmen and postwoman of Longtown.

Alison Robb and Stephen Roberts kindly scrutinized the almost-finished text.

I was privileged to have as my editor Kris Doyle at Picador. I am also grateful to Starling Lawrence, to everyone at W. W. Norton and to Melanie Jackson. I enjoyed the unstinting support of Paul Baggaley, Nicholas Blake, Wilf Dickie, Camilla Elworthy, Gillian Fitzgerald-Kelly and the whole Picador team. On expeditions to that remote capital of the far South, Rogers, Coleridge & White was a home from home.